# Circles and
# Standing Stones

# Circles and Standing Stones

EVAN HADINGHAM

HEINEMANN : LONDON

William Heinemann Ltd
15 Queen Street, Mayfair, London W1X 8BE
LONDON   MELBOURNE   TORONTO
JOHANNESBURG   AUCKLAND


First published 1975
© Evan Hadingham 1975
SBN: 434 431105 7

# Contents

| | | page |
|---|---|---|
| Author's Foreword | | vi |
| A Note on Dates | | vii |
| 1 | A Step Back into the Past | 11 |
| 2 | The First Farmers | 29 |
| 3 | Wooden Cathedrals | 38 |
| 4 | The Great Circles | 50 |
| 5 | Houses and Heroes | 66 |
| 6 | Stonehenge and the Sky | 80 |
| 7 | The Quest for the Calendar | 98 |
| 8 | Megalithic Mathematicians | 116 |
| 9 | The Mystery of the Carvings | 136 |
| 10 | 'That Regiment of Stones . . .' | 152 |
| 11 | Who Were The Druids? | 168 |
| 12 | Christianity: Conflict or Continuity? | 178 |
| 13 | The Druid Revival | 190 |
| 14 | The New Hyperboreans | 204 |
| Appendix One: List of Conventional Radiocarbon Dates | | 211 |
| Appendix Two: Further Reading | | 212 |
| Appendix Three: Exploring Early Britain | | 223 |
| Index | | 235 |

# *Author's Foreword*

There are hundreds of prehistoric monuments throughout the British Isles, and some of the most spectacular are the circles and alignments of standing stones often dramatically situated in remote and barren parts of the country. This book grew out of visits to these sites and out of curiosity that so little was apparently known about their builders. In fact, as more extensive reading soon showed, research in the past decade has told us an immense amount about the society of early Britain and the possible purposes of these strange monuments. However most of this information is to be found in specialized, academic publications and some of it takes the form of complicated mathematical and astronomical theory. An attempt to introduce this recent material to the general public, with all the attendant risks of error and over-simplification, seemed worthwhile.

The book was also written with a conviction that the history of the ideas on early Britain is as interesting as the ideas themselves. The way in which people have imagined their primitive ancestors, during periods such as the 'Druid revival' of the eighteenth century (and here my debt to the work of Professor Stuart Piggott is obvious) or the present theories of astronomer priests and 'ley-men', throws interesting light on the values and outlook of the times.

The specialist in any of the fields covered by this book will find a notable absence of terms conventionally used elsewhere. Simple expressions such as 'azimuth', 'declination' or 'extrapolation' have been avoided because it is felt that they tend to discourage the layman from a basic grasp of the principles involved. Even the widely known word 'henges' has been omitted, because it might introduce a possibly misleading distinction between enclosed and non-enclosed sites. Such simplification may also lead to awkward passages, and in the latter case 'earth circle' is by no means an ideal substitute for 'henge'. But it is hoped that this approach will encourage the ordinary reader to understand the essential arguments and think freshly on the subject.

A full list of acknowledgements can be found at the back of the book, but I must record here my particular gratitude to Richard Turner, without whose constant encouragement and criticisms this book could not have been written, and who spent many hours preparing the text plans. A special word of thanks also to my travelling companions throughout Britain and Brittany, including Ernest Black, Chris Ryder, Clarissa and Dave Keighley, Mrs R. B. Kenward and my parents.

I am grateful to the following experts for their valuable comments on relevant parts of the book: Professor R. J. C. Atkinson, Dr Glyn Daniel, Dr Gerald S.

Hawkins, Dr Douglas C. Heggie, Professor D. G. Kendall, Mrs R. B. Kenward, Dr Euan W. Mackie, and Professor Alexander Thom.

The research facilities granted to me at the Cambridge University Library, the Haddon Library (Cambridge), the British Museum, the London Institute of Archaeology and at the Society of Antiquaries (London) were invaluable.

# A Note on Dates

For reasons that will be apparent to the general reader in Chapter One, the accuracy of radiocarbon dates from the periods discussed in the book is highly controversial. *All* the dates mentioned in the text should be regarded as very rough guides which could be in error by several centuries. Any serious student is urged to refer to the list of conventional radiocarbon dates in Appendix One, although he is reminded that even here there is a 1 in 3 chance of the true date falling outside the stated limits. The dates cited in the text have been calibrated very approximately from the Suess curve published in the *Proceedings of the 12th Nobel Symposium*, New York: John Wiley 1970.

*This book is for my parents*

From Aylett Sammes' *Britannia Antiqua Illustrata*, 1676.

There on the pastoral Downs without a track
To guide me, or along the bare white roads
Lengthening in solitude their dreary line,
While through those vestiges of ancient times
I ranged, and by the solitude o'ercome,
I had a reverie and saw the past,
Saw multitudes of men, and here and there,
A single Briton is his wolf-skin vest
With shield and stone-axe, stride across the Wold;
The voice of spears was heard, the rattling spear
Shaken by arms of mighty bone, in strength
Long moulder'd of barbaric majesty.
I called upon the darkness; and it took,
A midnight darkness seem'd to come and take
All objects from my sight; and lo! again
The desart visible by dismal flames!
It is the sacrificial Altar, fed
With living men, how deep the groans, the voice
Of those in the gigantic wicker thrills
Throughout the region far and near, pervades
The monumental hillocks; and the pomp
Is for both worlds, the living and the dead.

At other moments, for through that wide waste
Three summer days I roam'd, when 'twas my chance
To have before me on the downy Plain
Lines, circles, mounts, a mystery of shapes
Such as in many quarters yet survive,
With intricate profusion figuring o'er
The untill'd ground, the work, as some divine,
Of infant science, imitative forms
By which the Druids covertly express'd
Their knowledge of the heavens, and imaged forth
The constellations, I was gently charm'd,
Albeit with an antiquarian's dream,
I saw the bearded Teachers with white wands
Uplifted, pointing to the starry sky
Alternately, and Plain below, while breath
Of music seem'd to guide them, and the Waste
Was chear'd with stillness and a pleasant sound.
                    —William Wordsworth
                    *The Prelude*, 1805.

From William Blake's *Jerusalem*, 1804–20.

# 1: A Step Back into the Past

In the early years of this century, popular interest in the past was concentrated on a number of civilizations clustered around the eastern Mediterranean. In the 1840s, the royal capital of Assyria had been unearthed at Nimrud by Sir Henry Layard, who brought to the attention of the European scholars and public the remains of a culture known only from the Old Testament, its massive and grim-faced gateway sculptures capturing the popular imagination. Later, in 1871, Heinrich Schliemann revealed an unexpected new centre of pre-classical civilization when he discovered the site of ancient Troy in the mound of Hissarlik in Turkey. A few years afterwards, the tales of Homer seemed to be confirmed when Schliemann recovered the citadel of Mycenae on the Greek mainland, home of Agamemnon himself, with its circle of shaft-graves full of magnificent golden objects. There were the death masks which covered the faces of a royal family, a drinking cup similar to one described by Homer, bronze daggers with boldly embellished hilts, and lively, realistic hunting or religious scenes engraved on the faces of tiny gold seal rings. Centuries before the flowering of ancient Athens, here was a civilization with an equally distinctive, if more heroic, artistic vision. The brilliant centre of this Bronze Age world was identified in the early 1900s when Arthur Evans excavated the ruins of the Palace of Knossos, capital of early Crete, where Minos was once king and where the legendary Minotaur was said to exist in his subterranean labyrinth.

Throughout this fertile period of archaeological discovery, Egypt had always commanded attention with its spectacular pyramids and temples, and with the respect paid to its culture by classical writers such as Herodotus. This attention was redoubled by the sensational discovery of the pharaoh Tutankhamen and the objects which filled his tomb in the Valley of the Kings, by Howard Carter in 1922. Archaeology became headline news, and the emphasis on a group of remarkable Mediterranean civilizations seemed natural.

But while the Achaeans led their expedition against Troy, or the athletes of Knossos challenged the royal bulls in the palace courtyard, what was happening in the rest of Europe? Was the map simply a blank at this time for the adventurer sailing beyond the Straits of Gibraltar? For the turn-of-the-century scholars, accustomed to the classical view of 'barbarian' Europe handed down from Caesar's campaigns, our ancestors in Spain, Germany, France and Britain were simple people, fully occupied with their primitive farming activities, absorbing each new technological or artistic advance as it arrived from the Mediterranean along the trade routes. The innovators of the Aegean and the Near East were responsible for the ideas behind the spread of cereal farming, the keeping of live-

Ideas of hyper-diffusion are popular. Here, 'Merlin, The Egyptian Wizard' beat Amy Johnson to the headlines.

stock, the invention of copper and bronze metalworking, and a major movement of religion and art. Another concept, which seemed to fit the circumstances equally well, was that an actual movement of people brought each new advance to the native population. With the example of so many invasions in our own history—Roman, Saxon, Viking and Norman—the theory of successive waves of prehistoric invasions or migrations seemed highly plausible.

This idea of the spread of civilization from a central source—the 'diffusion' model—fitted in successfully with the growing understanding of the artefacts and associations of civilization itself, and the sequence of their development. In 1836 the Danish scholar Thomsen had suggested the 'three-age' system into which ancient objects and societies could be grouped. First there came the Stone Age, or the Palaeolithic and Neolithic period, when men used flint and other stone tools; then came the discovery of copper and other metals to form the Bronze Age; and finally the Iron Age. Darwin's evolutionary theories reinforced the conviction that a grand process of evolution was also at work in the unfolding of man's cultural history: 'diffusion' helped to fill in the picture.

With this tradition of thought, it was possible for the disciples of a man like Elliot Smith (who in 1911 published *The Ancient Egyptians*) to argue that all civilization came from the seminal influence of the early Egyptians, or the 'Children of the Sun' as W. J. Perry titled his 1923 book. Thor Heyerdahl's recent voyage on his reed boat *Ra* revived the popular currency of this idea, although his success only demonstrated that a journey from Egypt to the Americas *could* have taken place. And from 'hyper-diffusionism' it is a short step to the 'fringe' theories of the world peopled from a lost continent of Mu or Atlantis, theories which are still very much with us today.

What, then, was the correct balance to be struck in considering how Europe came to be civilized? The classic answer came in a book published in 1925, *The Dawn of European Civilization*, written by an Australian who had come to Oxford as a postgraduate student, and had later visited prehistoric sites all over the world. His name was V. Gordon Childe, and he proposed a modified form of diffusionism which became the standard 'model' for most succeeding archaeologists. In Gordon Childe's view, the source for European culture was still the Near East, but it was not confined to any one civilization. At the same time he gave an emphasis to the individual achievement of particular 'cultures', represented by associations of common implements, pottery, ornaments, house forms and religious customs, and this meant, in simple terms, the local modifications of the general stages and trends arriving from the diffusion centres in the Near East. Despite this attention paid to the distinctiveness of local cultures, however, Gordon Childe would probably have agreed with the dictum of his famous Swedish predecessor, Oscar Montelius, who concluded in 1899 that 'At a time when peoples of Europe were, so to speak, without any civilization whatsoever, the Orient and particularly the Euphrates region and the Nile were already in enjoyment of a flourishing culture. The civilization which gradually dawned on our continent was for long only a pale reflection of Oriental culture'.

Up to a few years ago, everything seemed to fit conveniently into this pattern, especially when considering the prehistory of Britain. By the late 1930s plentiful evidence had been assembled that indicated trade contacts with Mycenae, and indirectly with Crete and Egypt. In Cornwall, a magnificent gold cup was found that reminded scholars of those Schliemann had unearthed from Agamemnon's citadel. Beads of a bluish colour, made from a special glasslike material called faience, were found in many parts of Britain; it was thought that they could only have come from Egyptian workshops. Certain pieces of jewellery, such as decorative amber discs bound with gold rims, bore striking similarities to examples from the Aegean. Above all, Stonehenge, that anomalous structure of slabs on Salisbury Plain, could surely have been designed only by a visiting Mycenaean prince. The careful finishing of the stone, and particularly the mortice-and-tenon technique by which the great lintels were fastened to the massive uprights of the temple (exactly paralleled by one of the stone gateways of Mycenae) were much too sophisticated to be the work of barbarian Britons.

To construct a theoretical 'model' of any greater detail—to 'fill in the spaces' between the general concepts of the Neolithic, Bronze and Iron Ages—some means of dating had to be constructed from the finds of excavations. Fortunately a secure chronology was quickly established for ancient Egypt, since its king lists stretched back to the first dynasty, shortly before 3000 BC. A calendar note found on a papyrus scroll mentioned the date when the dog-star, Sirius, appeared to rise in the sun's path above the horizon. Astronomers can independently pin-point this date to 1872 BC. This correlation means that the main historical events, the pottery, ornaments and technology of Egypt can be securely fixed to our own system of conventional dates. Furthermore, since Egypt's trading links were so extensive, this principle could be applied to other cultural centres. For example, objects from Nile workshops have been found on Cretan sites, and Cretan material located in Egyptian tombs. A careful patchwork of comparisons was assembled so that the chronology of Crete and Egypt's near trading partners could be established with almost as much certainty as Egypt's own time scale. We could perhaps say that most of the prehistory of the eastern Mediterranean is now firmly 'anchored' in historical time, all by comparison with those vital king lists.

Outside this area, however, inference and logical reasoning were the only guides. The greatest period of power at the citadel of Mycenae was established as being about 1500 BC. A whole series of deductions followed from this. The spiral patterns discovered on a grave slab from Mycenae, and repeated on many ornamental objects, were echoed on the huge stone temples of Malta: therefore the temples of Malta must have been built no earlier than 1500 BC. Since Stonehenge must have been built by a Mycenaean prince, its construction probably occurred at around the same time. The clear-cut 'model' had emerged from the unwritten past.

One of the most important technical advances in archaeology came in the late 1940s when Professor Willard Libby of Chicago instigated the technique known as radiocarbon dating. Carbon is a fundamental constituent of all animal and plant life. Through the effects of cosmic radiation a very small proportion takes the form of carbon 14, a radioactive substance which decays gradually at a known rate. It takes over 5,000 years for any quantity of radiocarbon to decay to half its original amount; this, in other words, is its radioactive 'half-life'. From a measurement of the quantity of carbon 14 present in any organic materials that may be found on a dig—from charcoal, preserved fragments of trees or grass, bones or antlers—a date to within a certain margin of error can be determined. Even those margins are not a guarantee of accuracy, since the standard limits still present a 1 in 3 chance of the true date falling quite outside them. Nevertheless the 'safe bet' of establishing a date for an excavation, even to within a century or two, was a revolutionary step forward for archaeologists.

When the first radiocarbon dates became known, there was considerable relief, because in general they seemed to confirm the 'model' built up by so many years of patient research. All the same, there was one very odd discrepancy, which the scientists were at a loss to explain. When organic materials from particular Egyptian dynasties were subjected to radiocarbon dating, the results did not match up with the known chronology. In the case of some examples from the third millennium, the samples were 500 years 'too young'. What had happened? Was the radiocarbon technique wrong, or was there some hitherto unnoticed complication in fixing the Egyptian chronology? What was needed was some independent check on the radiocarbon dating method.

This was devised in the 1960s and successfully applied to dates up to about 5100 BC by Professor Hans Suess at a laboratory in La Jolla, California. His procedure was in theory simple: a child knows that by counting the number of rings from the centre of a tree stump outwards, the age of the tree can be discovered. High up in the Californian mountains there grows what is probably the longest-lived tree on earth, the bristlecone pine, which twists its ancient, massive branches into extraordinary shapes. Samples from some of the 5,000-year-old bristlecone pine trunks were taken, so that the age of individual segments of wood could be found simply by counting, then those tiny segments of a particular tree ring were subjected to radiocarbon dating. The discrepancy between the real date, arrived at by counting, and the radiocarbon date, found in the laboratory, could then be compared.

The result of Professor Seuss's investigation was dramatic. Up to approximately 1000 BC the difference between historical and radiocarbon dates was quite small. After that date, however, the discrepancy fluctuated and became progressively larger until some dates in the third millennium were as much as 700 years older than the radiocarbon dates. Immediately the anomalous Egyptian samples moved back in time and fitted more accurately with the king list chronology. The network of

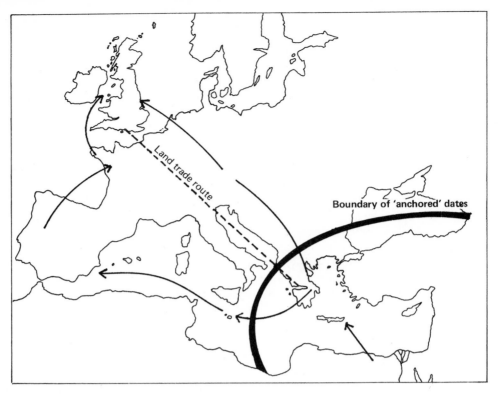

The traditional concept of diffusion. The arrows represent the routes along which prehistoric cultural influences were thought to have spread to north-west Europe. But the boundary line shows the limit to which such influences could be firmly related to objects from the literate Near Eastern 'sources'.

'anchored' dates for Crete and the Near East was unaffected and reinforced by the correction of previously puzzling radiocarbon results. But outside this area—moving into the region of inference and deduction—the implications of the new findings were a shock to archaeologists. Recently obtained dates for the temples of Malta, now corrected, were almost a thousand years older than Mycenae, and Stonehenge suddenly lost its romantic figure of the wandering architect-prince. The mortice-and-tenon joints of Stonehenge preceded the gateways of Mycenae by nearly half a millennium.

As soon as these results were made known, there was another obvious discrepancy to clear up. What about all those appealing links which showed how the European cultures had slowly received ideas from the 'Oriental dawn'? A number of archaeologists, notably Professor Colin Renfrew of Southampton University, began to look again at the traditional links between Europe and the Near East. The peoples of central Europe (especially the so-called Unětice culture) were once seen as playing an important role as 'middlemen' along the land trade route from the East to Britain. The parallels in drinking cups, daggers and other items between the Unětice and Britain remained fairly clear; but the dates for central and northern Europe were all pushed back in time by about five hundred years. This meant that the Unĕtice culture could no longer be regarded as the 'middlemen' for the kingdoms of Stonehenge and Mycenae. The Aegean and Near Eastern link dropped out of the chain, and the relationship of the Mediterranean cultures to Europe has become a difficult and debatable question.

Many other parallels, re-examined in the light of revised carbon dates, seemed to offer alternative explanations never previously considered. The faience beads, for example, were carefully analysed and although their origin was by no means clear, it seemed probable that they were manufactured somewhere in Europe rather than in Egyptian workshops. Microscopic examination of the gold-bound amber discs showed that the rims were decorated in a style which seems to have been a speciality of the Wessex area. The amber may have come from the beaches of East Anglia. Professor Renfrew's complex studies of the origin of metallurgy make it clear that the knowledge of heating ores and casting the molten metal was discovered in several places at different times. For example, the late Boian culture of south-eastern Europe (where Bulgaria and Romania are now situated) was engaged in manufacturing heavy copper axes in open moulds, complete with pre-cast shaft-holes, some time before 4000 BC—two millennia before the ages of copper and bronze were once supposed to have begun. The trading of ideas between cultures still remains a part of our prehistoric outlook, but much more attention is now being given to the inventiveness of individual 'barbarian' communities and the distinctiveness of their cultural achievements.

To sum the situation up in simple terms: ancient Europeans were more clever and more original than archaeologists had ever suspected before. And nowhere is this more apparent than in the case of one of the most important factors of

The rock-cut interior of the Hypogeum of Hal Saflieni, Malta, dating from the third millennium B.C.

European prehistory we have to consider, the growth of religious and funerary ideas. The picture we hold of our ancestors may again be shaken when we see that the origins of an impressive style of tomb-building apparently go back thousands of years to a region as far removed from the Near East as could possibly be imagined.

On a thickly forested hill, not far from the sea at Carnac in Brittany, there rises an impressive grassy mound, with a rough slab of stone placed upright on its summit. A short distance away on the ground is another upright monolith, standing opposite an entrance façade leading into the middle of the mound. At the end of a short, dark passageway is a square chamber built from huge slabs of stone, roofed over by flat blocks supported at about ten feet from the chamber floor. In prehistoric times this structure was probably used as a tomb by successive generations for collective interment, and it has been dated by the radiocarbon method as far back as 5700 BC. It seems to be the earliest European example of constructions using large stones, known as 'megalithic' tombs. What the builders of the Kercado tomb believed in will never be known, but the passage and chamber layout (especially at other sites where the chamber was roofed over by the corbelling technique, creating a kind of dome) has suggested a womb-like place for the rebirth of the dead laid to rest inside. Another possibility is that the stone tombs imitated the forms of wooden houses, so that these constructions were 'houses for the dead'. Why was this idea of the megalithic tomb to have such a strong hold on the minds of simple farmers throughout Brittany?

The megalithic tomb of Kercado, near Carnac, Brittany.

The question poses itself more insistently when we appreciate exactly how elaborate and ambitious some of these monuments were. A little to the east of Kercado, the inland sea of the Gulf of Morbihan flows between dozens of small islands. This area, stretching westwards to the curving promontory of Quiberon with its soaring cliffs, was one of the major centres of prehistoric culture in Europe for many thousands of years. It seems likely that some special sanctity was attached to the region.

In the middle of the Gulf of Morbihan there rises a small island, its south side sloping steeply down to the water, so that from the top of this hill a commanding

A view of the mound of Gavrinis from the Gulf of Morbihan and (*right*) a detail of one of the carved uprights in the passage.

view of the pattern of islands within the circle of distant coastline may be obtained. On this summit stands the burial mound of Gavrinis, a round heap of earth covering a megalithic tomb of major importance. Within the mound twenty-four large uprights support a line of massive roofing slabs, in places over twelve feet across. This forms the passage, leading to the square chamber, which is roofed by huge rocks, one of them over twenty feet long, resting on the upper edges of the six wall stones. The effect is impressive, particularly the smooth workmanship and precision of the joints between the stones, but by no means overwhelming—the visitor has to stoop slightly, even standing in the central chamber.

Shine a torch on the walls of the tomb, however, and Gavrinis is transformed. Every available inch of interior wall is covered with rows of lines carved deeply into the rock. In the torchlight the curves and ripples at first seem random, and then extraordinary patterns begin to take shape. On some stones, tunnel-like concentric arcs mount upward to the ceiling, one on top of another, with fan-like tiers of smaller circles on either side. On other surfaces, such as the two end uprights of the chamber, the lines are much more free, as if following the plan for some elaborate maze. The flow of the curves is often broken by the sharp triangular outlines which probably represent the shape of stone axes. It seems natural that the men whose tools were so important to them would wish to carve their shapes on the tomb, perhaps as a way of thanking or propitiating their deity. But how do we explain the occasional twisting form of what must surely be a serpent, indistinctly carved, but with a small, bulging 'head'? And in the central part of the tomb, what can account for the mysterious feature hewn in the rock on the southern side of the chamber? A deep cylindrical groove is cut horizontally into the stone, with two curving rings of stone left uncarved, so that the visitor can insert an arm behind them into the deep channel. Soot marks blacken the upper surface because countless visitors have rested their lamps and tapers there, but the original purpose of the groove is unknown, and the feature is unique to Gavrinis. Nor is anything known of the burials once placed in the chamber, and there are apparently no local legends to provide any guesses. Furthermore, none of the stones originated from a local source of rock.

Gavrinis, then, confronts us with a people who could not only transport large blocks of stone for distances over land and water, but could also shape them, fit them accurately together and carve intricate patterns on their surfaces. Anyone familiar with classical traditions of representational art could be forgiven for thinking the Gavrinis patterns wild and impersonal. The vision of these people was quite different: it was strangely abstract, expressing itself in contrasting designs rather than in imitations of the human form. Already, by 3500 BC, the Neolithic people of western Europe appear to have established some quite distinctive identity of thought, religion and art.

There are major centres of megalithic tombs in Denmark, Ireland, Spain and Portugal. Before the revision of radiocarbon dating, this pattern of distribution

could be explained by the spread of a 'Mother Goddess' religion from the Near
East, via Crete, Malta, Iberia and the Atlantic seaboard. Now the early dates for
Brittany tombs mean that we must dispense with those all-too-simple maps and
their arrows all stemming from the East. In fact only a handful of useful radiocarbon dates have been obtained for megalithic centres other than Brittany, so that
the relationships between the tomb-building cultures are by no means clear. But
it should be emphasized that the way in which many archaeologists are now
looking at these cultures is not in terms of a simple spread of technology and
religion from this or that centre to the rest of Europe. The assumption that
spiritual ideas were spread in the same pattern as tradeable commodities like tools
or pottery was the questionable basis to major interpretations of the European
past.

Was there, indeed, ever one 'Mother Goddess'? Stylized female carvings are
found in some French tombs, but rarely elsewhere. A suggestion has been made
that the whole decoration on the Gavrinis stones represents a 'degenerate' or
'shorthand' symbol of a feminine deity, but this is surely an over-simplification.
Another 'Mother Goddess' can be found in the small Iberian plaques, made of a
stone called schist, which are usually decorated with simple triangular or lozenge
patterns and with stylized arms and eyes. Although they are often associated with
megalithic tombs generally similar to those in Brittany, the distribution of these
distinctive plaques is restricted to the south-west coasts of Portugal and Spain. If
the megalithic tomb-builders along the Atlantic really were unified by one compelling creed, why have none of these plaques yet been discovered in France?

The traders along the Atlantic seaways must certainly have had sturdy and
competently handled ships, in which all kinds of people could have visited other
centres of population with new ideas. But megalithic tombs remarkably similar to
those in Europe were constructed in Japan, India and elsewhere within historical
times. There is some evidence to believe, then, that megalith building represents a
particular stage of technological and cultural development that many civilizations
pass through quite independent of one another. A particularly interesting example
is Malta, where pottery types generally comparable to early south Italian ware
show that the islands were not altogether isolated from trading influences. Yet
Malta's long and highly individualistic phase of megalithic culture may be interpreted largely as an independent development. One of the world's most unusual
ancient monuments is the Hypogeum of Hal Saflieni, in the suburbs of Valetta.
Here a series of underground catacombs was dug out of the soft limestone over a
long period, linked by stairways and halls, and the stone was carved to imitate the
appearance of megalithic architecture—the doorways were hewn to represent
trilithons. At one stage the Hypogeum probably contained several thousand
bodies, and it is still an eerie experience for the modern visitor. His attention will
also be drawn by the island's magnificent open-air megalithic temples, which do
not seem to have been built for inhumation purposes. The stones are shaped and

in some cases pock-marked with a sharp tool to give a special texture to the surfaces. The relief carvings of the temples have always excited scholar and layman alike. The spiral and circular patterns are so reminiscent of north European megalithic tombs that the visitor may well think that the symbols of Brittany have here been refined and composed into vivid and meticulously executed patterns.

Any such connection must now seem very dubious, however. Evidently these temples were used for a purpose quite different from that of the megalithic tombs. It is possible that part of the function of both the Hypogeum and the temples was to serve an oracular cult, since small compartments suitable for concealing a priest or priestess are found communicating with the main temple enclosures by means of small holes suitable for speaking through. Remarkable sculptures have also been recovered, portraying obese women in various attitudes, including a recumbent figure on a couch, apparently asleep. It seems probable that the ancient Maltese believed in divine revelations through dreams, a belief for which there is no evidence anywhere else in prehistoric Europe at this time. The case of Malta shows the dangers of generalizing about links between cultures and their common beliefs because of superficial resemblances in their art or technology.

In the way that the region around Gavrinis was the focus of intense religious activity for centuries, an area a few miles inland from the mouth of the River Boyne (at the modern Irish town of Drogheda) developed into a major centre for a megalith-building community. The visitor to the great chambered tomb of Newgrange threads his way down a passage sixty-two feet long, leading through the huge covering mound, with ample head room and only a few places where it becomes too narrow to avoid turning sideways in order to pass through. When the central chamber is finally reached, the visitor is at once aware of its spaciousness. The corbelled ceiling, narrowing upwards until the final covering stone is a breathtaking twenty feet above the floor, gives Newgrange the atmosphere of an underground cavern. Three side chambers adjoin the central area, and in each of them is a huge stone basin, smoothly shaped, which probably held the cremated remains of the people for whom the tomb was built. Around the outside edge of the covering mound, along its base at ground level, is set a ring of 'kerb' stones, one of which features the basic design of concentric semi-circles which is a familiar sight at Gavrinis. Other designs, less formally executed and including serpentine lines again reminiscent of Brittany, were actually carved on the backs of these stones, where they could never have been seen. A short distance away from this ring, a great circle of free-standing monoliths surrounds the entire mound, which originally was covered by a layer of quartz stones, so that from a distance, crowning the top of the ridge in the bend of the Boyne, Newgrange would have appeared as a high, dazzling white cone.

The main period of building at Newgrange almost certainly took place within a century of 3300 BC. It was only one of a complete cemetery of chambered tombs and other monuments concentrated in this small area, perhaps covering an

A rubbing of a carved design from an upright in the passage at Newgrange.

extensive period of time. Most of these sites have never been excavated, but recent digging at the huge mound of Knowth revealed carvings in a style suggesting more than superficial links with Brittany. The dominant spiral motif on the main Newgrange stones may in turn have inspired the four small spirals found at Gavrinis. Twenty-five miles from the Boyne, at the Loughcrew site, the designs on the stones share the informal character of some of the minor 'graffiti' work at Newgrange: they seem to have lost much of their regular, perhaps symbolical, element, and instead their patterns are freed into much more playful and obviously artistic arrangements.

Megalithic tombs appear farther northward, with surprisingly thick concentrations on remote islands and Scottish coastal regions separated by difficult and treacherous sailing waters. In the Orkneys, though the central megalithic ideas

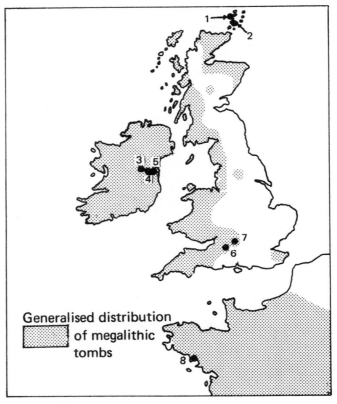

Generalised distribution of megalithic tombs

The distribution of megalithic tombs in north-west Europe, and some important examples: 1—the Rousay group, 2—Maes Howe, 3—Loughcrew, 4—Knowth, 5—New-grange, 6—West Kennet, 7—Wayland's Smithy, 8—Gavrinis.

On the mountain top of Knocknarea, overlooking the town of Sligo, rises this remarkable cairn of stones about 200 feet in diameter and 35 feet high. The cairn is thought to cover one or more chamber-and-passage tombs, but has never been explored. As the legendary grave of Medb of Connacht it featured in the Irish heroic cycles and the early poetry of Yeats.

may have been borrowed from outside, there is an interesting parallel with what happened in Malta. The current emphasis is now on the special environment of these islands and the distinctiveness of their culture, unlike the once common idea that the prehistoric 'missionaries' went as far north as they could go and all ended up concentrated together. Seen in this way, Orkney was not the last outpost of civilization but formed an important and independent centre in its own right.

These islands are treeless and low-lying, so they undoubtedly attracted early settlers with their cattle away from the difficult clearing of thick forests on the mainland. Tombs of the most ambitious construction, which must have taken prehistoric communities many years to build, lie on the most distant of the far-flung islands. A visit to Rousay, a small, hilly strip of land to the north of the mainland, is particularly instructive. Here, on its south coast, lie four major excavated tombs all within about a mile of each other. Within certain similarities of basic layout, the tombs display a remarkable diversity of size and construction. First there is the peculiar 'double-decker' tomb of Taversoe Tuick, two chambers built on top of each other with passages leading in opposite directions. Just a little way farther along the coast is the huge cairn of Midhowe, of an entirely different type compared to the chamber-and-passage plan. It is the grandest of a locally developed variation known as a 'stalled cairn', consisting of a long gallery divided by pairs of upright slabs on either side into 'stalls'; in these compartments, on stone shelves a short distance from the floor, the bodies were laid. There are at least

PAPA WESTRAY

WESTRAY

SANDAY

ROUSAY

Midhowe group

EDAY

STRONSAY

MAINLAND

Maes Howe

HOY

RONALDSAY

● Megalithic tombs
◑ Maes Howe-type tombs
▬ 'Stalled' megalithic tombs

A simplified distribution map of megalithic tombs in the Orkney islands.

seven other stalled cairns on Rousay, with one or two examples on other islands, so that we can guess that the communities here took pride in developing their own special form of megalithic tomb.

Elsewhere, on the Orkney mainland, the stone builders were prepared to expend vast labour on more orthodox styles of monuments. Together with Gavrinis and Newgrange, the cairn of Maes Howe is one of the most impressive relics of European prehistory; like the others, too, it is situated in an area crowded with monuments of many periods, the shores around the picturesque inland loch of Stennes. It differs both from Newgrange and Gavrinis by the nature of the material used in its construction. The long, thin, flat slabs of sandstone rise regularly into a square, geometrically precise, corbelled ceiling. Quite the most impressive feature of the tomb is the fact that the side walls, roof and floor of the passageway consist of four single slabs, each approximately twenty feet long. The transport and erection of such stones would cause problems for the heaviest modern engineering equipment. The precision of Maes Howe, the continuous smooth

The central chamber at Maes Howe, after entry
had been gained through the roof in 1861.

walls of the passage and the rectangular slabs of the chamber, give a startlingly
contemporary look to the tomb, almost as if it were designed by a modern architect. The people of Maes Howe left us no art, although Viking raiders, almost four
thousand years later, broke into the tomb and left a profusion of graffiti, in the
form of runic inscriptions and small carved drawings. Impressive as Maes Howe

The remains of a megalithic tomb at Proleek, County Louth, with a capstone weighing
about forty tons.

is, there is a cairn which must have involved an equal amount of constructional effort—once again, expended on yet another tomb style—on the tiny islet of Papa Westray, forty miles away by sea. Can we conclude otherwise than that a highly organized population, together with some compulsive religious idea which was expressed in many varied forms, was at work on these remote Scottish islands, five thousand years ago?

Gavrinis, Newgrange and Maes Howe are awe-inspiring evidence of a long tradition of religious construction using large stones, many centuries before anyone raised the first megaliths at Stonehenge. They were part of a growth of ideas and art of primary importance in the European past, yet a development so imperfectly understood that the research of recent years has completely over-thrown many years of scholarly conjecture about the origins and influences of its various styles. No longer can we think in terms of the old diffusion model, of the 'Mother Goddess' and her simple path across the Mediterranean and up the Atlantic coasts. Instead, we must recognize at least one strong cultural centre, Brittany, probably linked with Ireland, and accept the individual claims of the independently-minded communities such as Malta, Spain and the Orkneys. The new knowledge that the architectural masterpiece of Newgrange was assembled at about the same time as the pyramids were rising in Egypt should dispense for ever with the notion of 'barbarians' living under the shadow of innovation from the East. Our barbarians had brains, and startlingly original ideas. By about 3500 BC a strong and distinctive culture was flourishing throughout Britain. How did this come about?

# 2: The First Farmers

About eight thousand years ago, the last link between the continent of Europe and the southern coast of Britain was washed away into the newly formed English Channel. For thousands of years before that, men and women had been arriving in England in scattered groups across the Channel and the North Sea land links, entering a thickly forested island which provided ample resources of game and shelter. Generation after generation lived by hunting and fishing, some communities leading a roving life while others built houses and settlements.

The life of one of these settlements has been established in some detail. A small group of families arrived at the edge of a marshy lake in the Vale of Pickering, Yorkshire, soon after 8000 BC. For several winters the site of Star Carr was occupied by these settlers who sheltered on a platform of brushwood laid down close to the edge of the water. From this platform extended two tree-trunks which probably formed rough landing stages. Fishing must have played an important part in their economy, but it is evident from the great number of animal bones discovered, especially those of red deer, that they still relied on a meat diet. Although their existence in the wintertime must have been a continuous struggle against the environment, the settlers were not as savage as might be supposed. These people were probably as skilled in working flint and antler as their Neolithic successors, and at Star Carr they left behind many tools of all kinds. Among these were carefully carved antler spearheads, a mattock made from elk antler (probably used for unearthing roots) and flint knives and blades of every size. A simple kind of glue was extracted from birch bark and used to attach flints to wooden hafts and arrow-shafts. A paddle was found on the site, indicating that the settlers had at least one canoe, while the discovery of tools suitable for dressing skins are evidence that the hunters wore clothing made from animal hides. The most exciting finds at Star Carr were twenty stag frontlets, the antlers still connected to part of the skull, which was lightened and perforated so that it could be worn on the top of the head. Was this mask adopted as a kind of camouflage, as sympathetic magic to attract the deer, or was it used to re-enact the hunt at some form of ritual afterwards? The antler frontlets are the first evidence of beliefs or superstition of any kind yet found in prehistoric Britain.

Farming began in Britain some time after 4000 BC. The earliest types of pottery, generally consisting of plain, round-bottomed bowls, have been found at a number of places mainly concentrated near the coasts of south-west and eastern England. There is a close correspondence between continental pottery from Brittany and Belgium, and vessels discovered at sites such as Hembury in Devon or Broome

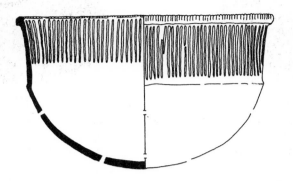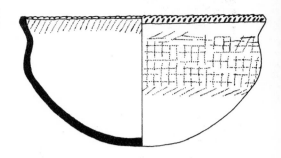

Typical pottery of the Neolithic period, developed from the plain undecorated wares of the first farmers.

Heath, Norfolk. This suggests that farmers were arriving in Britain across the Channel and North Sea during the fourth millennium.

The impressions of cereal grains left in the wet clay of pottery before firing show that wheat and barley were the main crops grown, although cultivation must have been a very wasteful process. A small patch of scrub or woodland would be cleared by felling the trees with stone axes and burning off what was left over. The seeds were planted with the use of some simple kind of mattock or hoe. When the ground was exhausted the farmers moved on and cleared the next patch of woodland. On the verge of these plots grazing animals, such as cattle, sheep and pigs, would inhibit the forest growth by eating seedlings, and eventually permanent pastureland would be created. By about 2500 BC efficient mixed farming must have been practised over much of the coastal and upland regions of Britain.

The economy of the earlier farmers was mainly based on stock rearing; because of the absence of winter fodder, close selection was probably employed. The women perhaps occupied themselves with making leather clothing, since at this period there is no evidence of spinning or weaving. They used flint tools for scraping the skins, and carved bone or antler combs for removing animal hair. Some of these skills could have been absorbed from the hunting and fishing traditions of the earlier inhabitants, but the change from a food gathering to a food producing economy was a vital one. The storage of grain almost certainly led to an increasing population and an eventual surplus of labour. Such conditions eventually encouraged the development of specialist craftsmen in the Neolithic period.

One clear piece of evidence for this is the remarkably widespread trade in the manufacture and exchange of large polished stone axe-heads, essential for efficient forest clearing. Important axe 'factories' were in operation at Great Langdale in Cumberland, Graig Lwyd in Wales and at Tievebulliagh, Northern Ireland. Their products reached many areas of early Britain, including southern England and the Scottish lowlands. Similarly, the demand for smaller tools of good quality led to specialized flint mining, concentrated at well-known sites such as Grimes Graves in Norfolk, where the extent of the mining shafts indicates a full-scale Neolithic industry.

Yet the lives of the early farmers were not limited to these material preoccupa-

tions. As well as the yearly rhythm of harvest and cattle round-up, there was also the disposal and honouring of the dead, a matter of deep concern for many primitive communities. With labour to spare at certain times of the year, people could now join together in creating large-scale communal monuments for the dead. The long barrows which they built were the first prehistoric structures to make a permanent impact on the landscape of the downs, where they can still be seen today in large numbers.

Recent excavations have shown that often these huge mounds of earth covered successive constructions of wood or stone. In many cases, the bodies of the dead (occasionally cremated and quite often dismembered) were collectively laid out inside timber mortuary houses. Eventually these structures were covered over by the burial mound, which was usually heaped up in the outline of a long trapezoid, sometimes preserved by a low retaining wall of wooden stakes or kerb-stones. Part of the material for the mound was dug from long ditches on either side of the barrow, but often, for some curious reason, placed at some distance away from it. The two front edges of the barrow frequently projected forwards in a curve to create a forecourt, reinforced by a semi-circle of posts or stones. In this forecourt the last rites of the dead were presumably carried out.

Most of these features of a typical long barrow can be seen on an impressive scale at the famous site known as Wayland's Smithy, surrounded by a ring of tall trees high up on the crest of the Berkshire ridgeway. This ancient path links Wayland's Smithy with other well-known places such as the Iron Age hill-forts of Uffington and Liddington Castle. For countless generations this trackway served as a major highway through southern Britain, avoiding the marshy impassable valleys below. At Wayland's Smithy the early farmers of this region first constructed a small mortuary building floored with a pavement of stone slabs. The remains of at least fourteen individuals were found lying on this pavement, together with three leaf-shaped flint arrowheads. Over this construction a comparatively small mound, measuring only 54 feet by 27, was heaped up to a height of about three feet above the old land surface.

Probably less than half a century passed before a second barrow was built over the first, in what was then perhaps the 'new style' of megalithic construction. A simple chamber was built, with two 'transepts' adjoining it, and from this inner burial place the entrance broadened out into a prominent façade of upright monoliths, set against the front of the mound. It is these large stones that make the tomb so impressive today. The mound itself was built up from two side ditches, no less than fifteen feet wide and six feet deep, and it was extended to a length of 180 feet, tapering from 48 feet wide at the entrance façade to only twenty feet at its northern end. This trapezoidal outline, which included one near right angle, was carefully marked out with a continuous line of small stone slabs. When the barrow was first excavated in the 1920s the disordered remains of at least eight individuals were discovered inside the stone chamber. This second long barrow was built at

These curious carved stone balls are found mainly in eastern Scotland and are thought to belong to the third millennium.

A long barrow on Thickthorn Down, near Blandford Forum, Dorset.

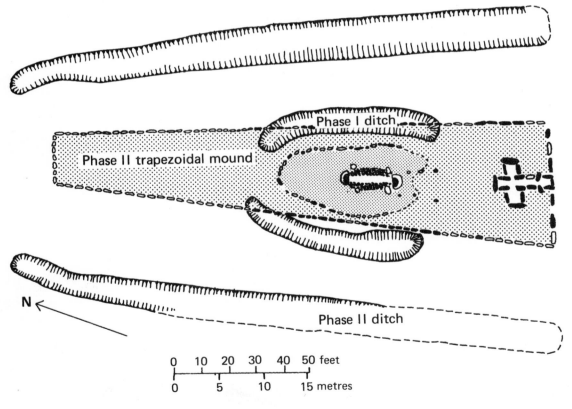

Phase I ditch

Phase II trapezoidal mound

N

Phase II ditch

0 10 20 30 40 50 feet
0 5 10 15 metres

Excavation plan of the long barrow at Wayland's Smithy, Berkshire.

Wayland's Smithy in about 3600 BC and was by no means exceptional of its kind, especially when we compare it with the equally famous example at West Kennet in Wiltshire. Here a mound 330 feet long covered a much more substantial megalithic structure, and it has been established that material for the tomb's drystone walling was brought from the River Frome region, twenty miles to the west. The planning of a long barrow was evidently a carefully considered affair, and perhaps its only parallel in local community effort since prehistoric times has been the building of parish churches. For the first time engineering projects of a high order were being undertaken with the surplus energy left over from the subsistence activities of farming and stock-rearing.

Many questions connected with long barrows remain unanswered. For example, what determined the distinctive trapezoid shape of the mound visible at such monuments throughout the country? In central Europe large wooden houses have been excavated exactly conforming to this shape, and perhaps they remain to be found in Britain. If this is the case, then long barrows might represent 'houses for the dead'. But it is puzzling that so many long mounds and cairns seem to be concentrated in Scotland, especially in the far north. Recent excavation of a number of these Scottish long barrows (such as Mid Gleniron and Camster Long) has shown that they overlie simple round burial cairns, perhaps built many centuries earlier. Archaeologists are beginning to unravel a complex pattern of interaction between the round megalithic tombs—the tradition that was ultimately to inspire Newgrange and Maes Howe—and the long barrows of the western coastal regions. The exact origins of both great styles of tomb construction, and their influence upon one another, is still the subject of intense controversy.

Recent air photography has revealed the extent of another type of monument built on an even more grand and astonishing scale than the long barrows. In 1723 the famous antiquary William Stukeley was exploring Salisbury Plain a few hundred yards north of Stonehenge when he came across a huge earthwork which he called a 'cursus', because to him it seemed to resemble a racecourse. It consisted of

William Stukeley's impression of the western end of the Stonehenge cursus, published in 1740.

parallel twin banks and ditches cut in the chalk, over 300 feet apart, running for a full 1¾ miles across the plain. A long barrow formed the eastern end of the Stonehenge cursus.

Now much less conspicuous because of ploughing damage, these remarkable ritual enclosures must once have been spectacular undertakings for the prehistoric engineers. They have come to light at locations as widespread as Yorkshire and Suffolk, from Bangor in Wales to Twyford in the Thames valley. The cursus monuments often seem to be sited close to rivers and fresh water. One example was found near the River Trent at Aston. Three more were discovered at the village of Rudston, in East Yorkshire, close to a stream that winds through its centre. The monuments vary in size from the shortest example at Northampton—a mere 200 yards long—to the massive Dorset cursus, which runs for no less than six miles across two stretches of downland. The ditches and banks are some 300 feet apart and enclose about 220 acres. The staggering figure of 6½ million cubic feet of chalk must have been excavated from the two parallel ditches and piled alongside to form the banks. Four long barrows were incorporated into the earthworks.

These impressive stones form the façade of the chambered tomb known as Cairnholy I, in Kirkcudbright, and were probably added to an earlier, simple burial compartment located beyond the two tallest uprights. The remains of six hearths, perhaps for ritual purposes, were found in the entrance area, while the façade formed the front edge of a long trapezoidal cairn.

One of these, on Bokerly Down, is among the largest ever recorded (about 490 feet long) while another blocks the path of the cursus exactly at right angles on the crest of Gussage Hill. A third forms the western end of the cursus while a fourth is built into one of the banks. Near by there are at least three other long barrows. A close connection between the communal burial vaults of the first farmers and these cursus monuments is obvious. But what common belief could have inspired such different undertakings? What, indeed, could possibly have inspired the idea of a cursus? The procession that would make its way along six miles of rolling downland between banks of chalk 300 feet apart must have been a very imposing one. Perhaps Stukeley's idea of a racecourse is not so far-fetched —could there have been celebratory games at the time of the harvest, for example?

For further information about the shared interests of the Neolithic farmers, archaeologists have turned to a third type of monument known as the causewayed camp. If current archaeological opinion is confirmed, these circular meeting places may well prove to be the first 'temples' of early Britain, and whatever took place there must have exercised a great influence on succeeding generations.

Men and women were gathering on prominent hilltops in southern England as far back as 4200 BC, the approximate date of Hembury camp, associated with some of the earliest pottery in Britain. The roughly circular enclosures where they met consisted of two or three concentric ditches with frequent gaps and entrances

Plan of the Neolithic causewayed camp, surrounded and partly obliterated by an Iron Age fort, at the Trundle, overlooking Goodwood racecourse in Sussex.

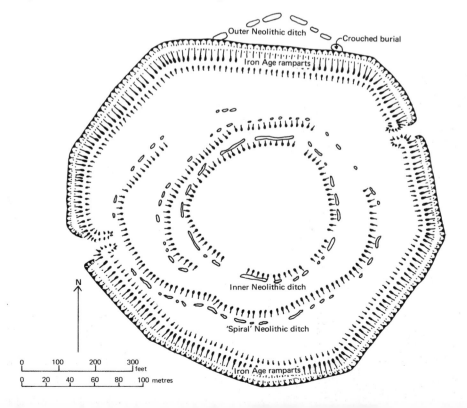

Aerial view of the Windmill Hill site under partial excavation in the 1920s. Note the numerous interruptions in the line of pits in each of the three concentric rings.

interrupting their course. The excavated earth from these ditches was piled up alongside to form banks enclosing the area inside the camp. The classic site, which first identified the early farmers' phase of settlement in England, was at Windmill Hill, not far from the West Kennet long barrow. Here a triple ring of ditches was found, the outer examples being eight feet deep. From these ditches came evidence of short-term occupation in the form of temporary hearths and a large volume of animal bones and refuse. Periodic feasting seems to have taken place at the cause-wayed camps, and to have attracted people from a wide area. For example, analysis of the stone used to temper some of the pottery found at Windmill Hill shows that it must have been brought from the Bath area, about twenty miles to the west. The obvious interpretation is that Neolithic people were meeting together for fairs or festivals at certain times of the year.

There is additional evidence to show that these assemblies were probably not for entirely secular purposes. Indeed, the camps may even have been connected with the beliefs and ceremonies that were associated with the long barrows. In many cases it is clear that the burial chambers of the barrows were successively re-opened and used many times over a long period, and that the skeletons of previous interments were sometimes cleared aside to make room and left in some disorder. Excavations at the West Kennet long barrow showed that a proportion of the skulls and long bones had been deliberately removed, and the scattered finds of bones in the ditches at Windmill Hill and at other camps could originate from previous burials in the barrows. Strange though the idea may seem, the 'bones of the ancestors' may have been periodically taken out from their resting place in the tombs and venerated at the feasts which were celebrated in the ditches of the camps. It has been demonstrated by distinct layers at several sites that the scattered bones and refuse were covered up with care, sometimes with material from the bank.

Excavations in the 1930s at a typical causewayed enclosure known as White-hawk Camp, on the racecourse at Brighton, painted a grim picture of Neolithic life. In the middle of one of the ditches, archaeologists encountered a hearth with a pile of human bones beside it, including fragments from two skulls, and nearby pieces from three more skulls were identified. None of these individuals was over twenty, and the youngest was about six years old. These remains were originally interpreted as part of a cannibal feast, although with more recent evidence for veneration of the dead, perhaps archaeologists may be cautious of such interpretations in the future. But within twenty yards of this discovery, a pathetic scene was revealed: a woman and a new-born child, roughly buried in the ditch, the only possessions beside her being two chalk pendants and a pair of fossil sea-urchins. In the next section of ditch, beyond one of the main causeways, a woman had been thrown into the refuse, one arm twisted behind her back and her knees drawn up under her. Even the simple token burial of the woman and child had not been carried out for her, lying where she fell, the witness to a cruel crime which occurred five thousand years ago. While the collective energy and origin-ality of the first farmers, as displayed in monuments such as the Dorset cursus or the West Kennet long barrow, is impressive and striking, evidently their society was at times a hard and violent one.

# 3: Wooden Cathedrals

The causewayed camps show us that as early as 4000 BC there must have been some unifying social interest which drew people together at certain times of the year. The cursus monuments and many of the larger long barrows imply the efficient organization of manpower and its direction toward a preconceived idea or plan. Who was giving the orders? We can only speculate that local community leaders or the heads of respected families might be in a position to have a monument erected. As the scale of the circular enclosures increases through the third millennium, calling for ever greater resources of labour, we inevitably think in terms of larger communities and a more hierarchical organization of society.

The evidence points to a slow accumulation of traditions rather than any violent breaks with the past. This inference comes from a number of excavated sites with several different phases extending over many centuries. 'Sacred' enclosures, posts or stones were successively added and superimposed over earlier constructions. For example, at Thornborough in Yorkshire and elsewhere, circular earthworks were actually sited on top of long cursus monuments.

The process of development over a long period of time is clearly seen at a site like Barford in Warwickshire, where the first building phase was an interrupted line of pits forming a ring. This monument is reminiscent of the causewayed camps, except for the fact that the material from the pits was piled up to form an outer bank, not an inner one. The excavators discovered a suggestion of a further ring of pits within the enclosure, and a central hole containing a fragment of the typical round-bottomed pottery used by the first farmers. The second phase was marked by the excavation of a larger and continuous ditch surrounding the earlier line of pits, with a single entrance left for access to the monument. In the middle the remains of a large burnt post were located. In the Barford site's final phase—dated to within a range of 3400 to 3000 BC—the earthworks were enlarged for the second time, with a possible entrance in the north-east section indicated by three large post-holes. The remains of a curious flat wooden object, which has been described as a 'tray' or 'platter', were discovered in the ditch.

Enclosures like Barford, with a circular area delimited by a high bank, seem to be the remains of temples, places where meetings or ceremonies of some kind could take place with the exclusion of ordinary people, or at least with their separation from the proceedings if they stood on the high surrounding bank as spectators. A site comparable to Barford, and with a carbon date of 3400 BC, serves to emphasize the odd character of these monuments and their variety of plan. Arminghall in Norfolk consists of two rings of ditches, with a bank heaped

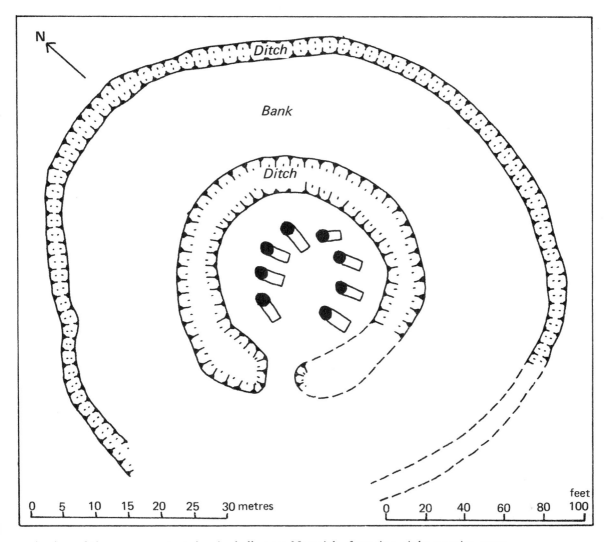

N

Ditch

Bank

Ditch

| 0 | 5 | 10 | 15 | 20 | 25 | 30 metres |

feet

| 0 | 20 | 40 | 60 | 80 | 100 |

A plan of the monument at Arminghall, near Norwich, featuring eight massive post-holes with ramps for easing the timbers into position.

up between them, instead of the single inner ditch found at most other enclosures. Situated inside this precinct was an oval setting of eight massive timber posts, each of them about three feet in diameter. With an average distance of about ten feet between each post it is possible, but unlikely, that the posts could have been linked together or even roofed over. If this possibility is discounted, what was the purpose of this tall ring of timbers? Could they have been brightly painted or carved, like totem poles?

Arminghall and Barford reflect something of the complexity which these earth circles display wherever they are found by archaeologists. There are important groups scattered all over the country, and they probably cover many centuries of prehistoric time. Generally the earlier enclosures have a single entrance and the later examples a double, but any hard-and-fast rule only obscures the many regional and period variations. Sometimes the circles are grouped in centres, such as the six located between the Ure and Swale rivers in the Yorkshire North Riding. Another series was built in the shadow of the great megalithic tombs at Newgrange in Ireland, although the connection between them has not yet been investigated by archaeologists. A link between the Irish circles and the English groups, however, is provided by the site recently excavated at Llandegai near Bangor, on the North Wales coastal plain by the Menai Strait. On this important trade and route centre a cursus and two enclosures were found, the earlier of the two encircling a ring of burial pits, 25 feet across, with a prominent cremation lying outside the surrounding bank and exactly on the axis of the single entrance. Close by was a curious 'model' earthwork, a tiny ditch crossed by two miniature causeways.

Llandegai suggests that some of the circles were built as cemeteries, and concentrations of similar monuments at places such as Dorchester, Oxfordshire, and at Maxey, Northamptonshire, can be interpreted as successive family burial-grounds. The excavations carried out by Professor R. J. C. Atkinson and others at Dorchester showed that three of the monuments there featured rings of pits, with cremations in or near some of the holes. But pits dug in the other circles on the site do not seem to have had any function, and were presumably left open to the sky. One enclosure consisted of three concentric ditches, another was demarcated by a square. All these monuments, on a quite small scale and situated within five

Aerial observation of crop-marks at Dorchester-on-Thames revealed a complex series of monuments, including a cursus, visible as twin parallel lines near the middle of the field.

hundred yards of each other, show a considerable diversity of layout within the basic uniformity of the bank, ditch and pit plan.

The same pattern emerges at Stonehenge—a ring of pits, some with cremations and some not, surrounded by an earthwork—all dating to within a century or two of 2750 BC. This is the stage which archaeologists call Stonehenge I, and which preceded the erection of the famous sarsen stones by over half a millennium. The circular ditch and bank, about 320 feet in diameter, was built with a single entrance facing the north-east. Near this entrance the rough monolith known as the Heel Stone was erected. Within the circle of Stonehenge I a ring of 56 pits was dug into the chalk to depths ranging from two to four feet. These pits, known as the Aubrey Holes after their discoverer, the seventeenth-century antiquary John Aubrey, were filled in with chalk rubble almost immediately after being dug. It has been established clearly by excavation that they never held timber posts or stones. As at Dorchester, cremated bones were associated with many of the holes, but this can hardly be a complete explanation of their function. The holes were set out with such accuracy along the circumference of a circle, 284 feet 6 inches in diameter, that the largest error in their spacing is 21 inches. This is a great deal less than the cumulative error we would expect if the holes had simply been measured off from pair to pair; evidently some other geometrical method must have been used.

If the precision and purpose of the Aubrey Holes should seem baffling, the mystery is deepened by perhaps the most inexplicable of all the earth circles, the monument known as Maumbury Rings situated in the suburbs of Dorchester, Dorset. This high-walled, steep-sided arena was used as an amphitheatre during Roman times, and was later fortified in the Civil War when a gun emplacement was mounted on one of the banks. For many years Maumbury was thought to have been built by the Romans until excavation at the turn of the century revealed the prehistoric origin of the earthworks. Neolithic pottery and antler picks were found, together with crudely carved chalk objects that seemed to link the site with a phallic cult. Near the inside ditch the diggers located a circle of 44 shafts dug in places to the astonishing depth of 35 feet down into the solid chalk. Timber posts can scarcely have been intended to fit holes of this depth, while in many cases nothing at all was found at the bottom of the shafts. Clearly a ring of pits signified something more than a functional means of disposing of the dead.

Maumbury Rings is one of several large circles where a special variety of pottery is found which raises the question of who was responsible for building such ambitious monuments. Until about 2500 BC it is possible to relate most British pottery styles back to the simple round-bottomed bowls made by the first farmers. But the pottery found in considerable quantities at the largest earth circles, known as Grooved Ware, is quite different from the previous ceramic tradition. Many of these vessels are flat-bottomed, and characterized by shallow grooved decoration, or by relief ornament moulded on to the sides in simple patterns. Other than the fact that this pottery appears to imitate the form of

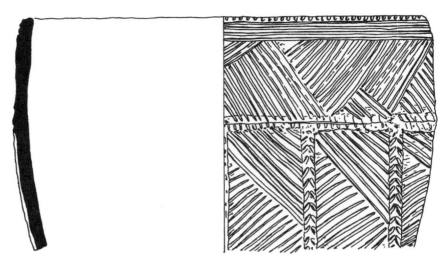

An example of Grooved Ware pottery from Durrington Walls, near Amesbury, Wiltshire.

wickerwork baskets, very little can be said about its origins, except for the interesting possibility of Boyne influences in some of the patterns: there are triangles and lozenges, for example, reminiscent of Newgrange, and at the Durrington Walls site four vessels were found with spiral or circular designs. This does not mean, of course, that the builders of Newgrange were responsible for the erection of the earth circles any more than this special type of pottery necessarily indicates a priestly class or a type of vessel designed for non-secular or ritual use.

Excavations in progress at the northern entrance of the Mount Pleasant enclosure, seen in the background as a wide strip of chalk between sections of the broad and irregularly dug ditch.

But Grooved Ware, and the eight major circle sites on which it has been found in quantity, emphasize how much is still unknown about this extraordinary period of communal activity, and how much intriguing new knowledge has come to light within only the past five or six years of archaeological study.

The late 1960s saw excavations on a grand scale at some of the most important enclosure sites, the work of a team led by Dr Geoffrey Wainwright. Four places in southern Britain have attracted investigation and comparison because of the prodigious size of the earthworks there and the cluster of smaller monuments of all periods around them. The sites at Avebury, Marden, Durrington Walls and Mount Pleasant were obviously centres to which special importance was attached by their builders, and there have been too few excavations at other circles to say whether the pattern of these massive enclosures was followed on a less 'regal' scale elsewhere. The dramatic evidence from Marden, Durrington and Mount Pleasant, all dug by Dr Wainwright, has nevertheless resulted in a major reassessment of these monuments and their original purpose.

To begin with, the dimensions of the sites need to be fully appreciated. At Durrington Walls, only about two miles from Stonehenge, the bank and inner ditch surround thirty acres of an uneven dry valley leading down to the River Avon. The average width of this enclosure is over a quarter of a mile across. The ditch was once fifty feet wide and up to nineteen feet deep, while the bank was piled to an average height of nine feet. In places a level area more than 100 feet across separated the bank from the ditch. Estimations of labour on this scale are extremely difficult, but Wainwright has suggested that 900,000 man-hours was a possible requirement. Marden, Avebury, and Mount Pleasant are all of a comparable size, but the Avebury earthworks must have demanded nearly double the labour expended at Durrington. Engineering of this scope is hard to appreciate on the printed page; and even on the spot, erosion, silting and ploughing damage have reduced most of the mighty earthworks to scarcely visible bumps in the fields. The recent digging operations were almost as ambitious as the monuments themselves, when compared to a conventional excavation. At Durrington, for instance, over 150 volunteers, twelve dumper trucks and three bulldozers were in action. The important point is that at these sites Neolithic men were working at a new level of planning, co-ordination and manpower. If work involved in the earlier megalithic tombs can be compared to parish church building, it may not be too far-fetched to say that at these four sites we have the Neolithic 'cathedrals'.

But at Wainwright's sites prehistoric engineering was not confined to the enclosing earthworks. The excavation of circular patterns of post-holes showed that for perhaps quite a limited period after about 2500 BC, a series of enormous wooden buildings had been erected within the enclosed areas, sometimes (as at Mount Pleasant) long before the main ditch and bank were raised. While there is nothing positive to show that these posts were not left free-standing, as was probably the case at Arminghall, the forest of timber involved (there were nearly

The southern circle of post-holes at Durrington Walls, partially excavated in 1966–7 by Dr Geoffrey Wainwright. Note the earth-moving machines dwarfed by one arm of the massive ditch forming the southern entrance.

180 post-holes at Mount Pleasant) seems naturally to favour the woodenbuilding interpretation. Since the dimensions of the post-holes generally increase towards the centre, the innermost rings of posts were probably the tallest. One may infer, then a huge circular structure, covered with a sloping, conical roof, with a court-yard in the middle left open to the sky. Such patterns of post-holes were in fact

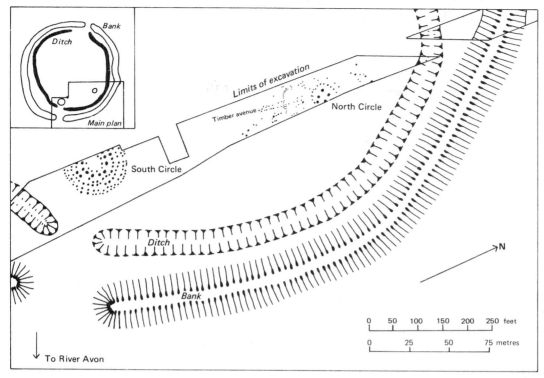

Bank

Ditch

Main plan

Limits of excavation

Timber avenue

North Circle

South Circle

Ditch

Bank

N

| | | | | | |
|---|---|---|---|---|---|
| 0 | 50 | 100 | 150 | 200 | 250 feet |

| | | | |
|---|---|---|---|
| 0 | 25 | 50 | 75 metres |

To River Avon

A plan of the features excavated at Durrington Walls between 1966–7.

known as early as the 1920s and 30s, when two sites were identified, one at Woodhenge, just outside the Durrington bank, and the other at the Sanctuary, not far from Avebury. Yet only after Wainwright's excavations has the idea of a definite phase of circular architecture seemed possible, because of the similarities between the four newly discovered buildings on the various sites.

Once again statistics can scarcely convey how impressive these buildings must have been in their original state. Although removing only a small strip of land across the Durrington enclosure, the diggers nevertheless exposed the remains of two structures, the largest of which had two major building phases and a plan 127 feet in diameter. The post-holes of one of the main inner rings were no less than six feet across and seven feet deep, suggesting that the inner ridge of the conical roof stood nearly thirty feet above the ground. One of the twin entrance posts of this building must have weighed about five tons, so that the manipulation and transport of these huge logs (probably taken from lower-lying forests and floated along the River Avon) must have presented problems similar to the handling of substantial megaliths. Equally large proportions are indicated by the post-holes of the single structure, surrounded by its own individual bank and ditch, on Mount Pleasant. At Marden the exploration of a tiny fraction of the enclosed area resulted in the discovery of a more modest construction, 34 feet across. It completes the impression that these buildings were erected with similar structural plans and purposes in view. And if the reconstructions are correct, how awe-inspiring the

View across the fully excavated area of the Mount Pleasant timber building, 130 feet across, with the post-holes revealed as dark blotches against the chalk. The continuous circular outlines are the foundations of Iron Age huts, built about two thousand years later.

larger buildings must have been: the term 'cathedral' again seems relevant when we try to imagine the high, sloping roof, the maze of supporting posts and the central courtyard illuminating the interior.

Neolithic master carpenters must have been at work here. On the basis of the largest building at Durrington, it has been estimated that this structure would need 3,000 feet of timber in varying thicknesses for the posts. There was also a requirement for some 4,500 running feet of ranges bridging the uprights and forming the rafters. The calculation works out at over 260 tons of wood, necessitating the felling of about nine acres of woodland, in order to construct this one building alone.

The activity that must have surrounded the buildings and their enclosures in late Neolithic times is reflected by the extensive finds from each site. At Durrington, nearly a hundredweight of pottery was eventually assembled from scattered fragments, together with sixty arrowheads and 12,000 struck flints, nearly a third of which had been shaped into implements. The diggers also found the complete or fragmentary remains of 440 antler picks used in the construction of the ditch. To the north of the larger building was a hut with a hearth yielding large amounts of pottery and domestic rubbish. Obviously Durrington Walls had been the focus of intensive activity if not of permanent settlement.

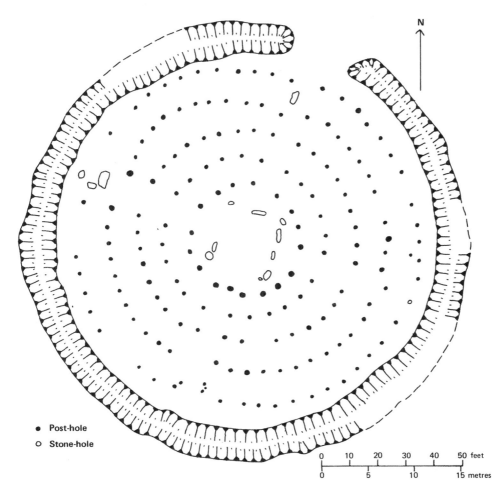

N

● Post-hole
○ Stone-hole

```
0    10    20    30    40   50 feet
|----|----|----|----|----|
0         5         10        15 metres
```

The timber building at Mount Pleasant.

But the evidence showed clearly that the great circular buildings had not been the setting for ordinary domestic activities. Just outside the entrance of the main building a platform of chalk blocks and flint rubble had once stood. Here successive fires had burned and the surface was littered with broken pieces of pot, flints, antler fragments and animal bones. Although large quantities of pottery were found at Durrington, so few of these could be joined together that not even a single complete vessel could be reconstructed from the entire excavation. Fragments from an individual pot were sometimes found widely distributed on the site, which indicates that an activity beyond normal, careless domestic usage was taking place. Indeed, the evidence leads us to imagine 'ritual' feasting and drinking within the structure, accompanied by the partial smashing of the vessels involved. Equally clear signs of this kind of activity were established at Marden. Here, just as at Durrington, the principal entrance causeway had been littered with antler picks and animal bones, presumably deposited by visitors whenever they entered or left the monument.

The great earth circles—and perhaps the dozens of smaller ones too—were not, then, sacred ground for a few, but seem to have been community meeting places, centred in large circular buildings which people did not occupy for any extended time, although their homes may have been only a short distance away. What can the imagination legitimately add to this picture, itself the product of tentative and painstaking archaeological inference?

Dr Wainwright has drawn attention to a parallel social phenomenon among the seventeenth- and eighteenth-century American Indians living in the Cherokee and Creek Confederacy tribal groups. The naturalist William Bartram travelled among these peoples in the 1770s and recorded communal buildings, or 'rotundas' as he called them, remarkably similar to the structures of late Neolithic Britain. The Cherokee 'council or town-house', he wrote,

> . . . is a large rotunda, capable of accommodating several hundred people . . . constructed after the following manner: they first fix in the ground a circular range of posts or trunks of trees, about six feet high, at equal distances, which are notched at top, to receive into them from one another, a range of beams or wall plates; within this is another circular order of very large and strong pillars, about twelve feet high, notched in like manner at top, to receive another range of wall plates; and within this is yet another or third range of stronger and higher pillars, but fewer in number, and standing at a greater distance from each other; and lastly, in the centre stands a very strong pillar, which forms the pinnacle of the building, and to which the rafters centre at top; these rafters . . . sustain the roof or covering, which is a layer of bark neatly placed, and tight enough to exclude the rain . . . There is but one large door, which serves at the same time to admit light from without and the smoak to escape when a fire is kindled . . . All around the inside of the building, betwixt the second range of pillars and the wall, is a range of cabins or sophas, consisting of two or three steps, one above or behind the others, in theatrical order, where the assembly sit or lean down.

Bartram goes on to describe how the Cherokees watched performances of dances 'and other shows at public festivals, which happen almost every night throughout the year', often preceded by a 'spirited, martial speech' from 'an aged chief', recounting the tribe's victories.

The 'rotunda' Bartram encountered at the Indian town of Attaffe, in the Creek Confederacy, was similar in its construction, and there in the evening he visited an assembly of

> . . . the greatest number of ancient venerable chiefs that I had ever beheld: we spent the evening and the greater part of the night together, in drinking Cassine and smoking Tobacco. The great council house or rotunda . . . seems particularly dedicated to political affairs; women and youth are never

admitted; and I suppose it is death for a female to presume to enter the door, or approach within its pale . . . there are people appointed to take care of it, to have it daily swept clean, and to provide canes for fuel, or to give light.

Bartram describes how the sacred black drink of Cassine, extracted from the leaves of a plant, was ceremonially carried inside the building in two conch shells, and passed round from person to person.

The accuracy of Bartram's account was fully confirmed by an excavation that uncovered such a 'rotunda' by the Savannah River, Georgia, and which was dated between AD 1550 and 1600. The diameter of this circular building was more than 110 feet, and it was constructed with a single entrance and a central hearth. Palisade trenches rather than post-holes were dug to support the timber uprights, but a pattern of six concentric rings nevertheless emerged from the excavation work. Outside the building a pit had been dug containing pottery contemporary with the main structure, and it was suggested by the archaeologists that these were drinking vessels—perhaps once filled with the black brew of Cassine—which had been deliberately broken and buried.

There is certainly a close resemblance between the Indians' tribal centres and the structures of early southern England, together with their associated activities. As we have seen already, too much can be made of fortuitous similarities between one culture and another. Yet if the descriptions left by Bartram help us to imagine the people and their activities inside the 'wooden cathedrals', then they are a useful addition to the developing picture of ancient Britain.

# 4: The Great Circles

The village of Avebury in Wiltshire stands at one end of a shallow valley not far from the narrow course of the River Kennet. It is surrounded on three sides by chalk downs, the smooth outline of their crests broken by many small bumps which indicate the remains of burial barrows. The houses, the main street and the fields where sheep and cattle graze are all contained within a vast arena of earth approaching a mile in circumference. From one side of the village the top of Silbury Hill, the largest man-made mound in Europe, appears like a wedge between two folds of the chalk not far away. Partial excavation at Avebury has not yet ruled out the possibility that large wooden buildings were erected on the site, but the main body of evidence relates to the great temple of free-standing megaliths raised here at some period around 2500 BC.

Sarsen stone, a sandstone rock of extreme hardness, can still be found lying naturally in large segmented blocks on the tops of the near-by downs. Huge boulders of this intractable material were selected and moved from the tops of the hills to the site in the valley. Every stone that was moved must have employed at least two teams of workmen, one group to haul the stone forward with thick ropes on wooden rollers, the other to prevent it from sliding away too fast down the slope. The largest of these stones stand by the original entrances to the monument, and the pair close to the southern causeway are both slightly less than twenty-five feet high, and probably weigh up to sixty tons.

The procedure for setting up rocks of such massive proportions has been deduced by modern experiment and excavation. The first step was to dig shallow holes in the chalk to receive the pointed bases of the sarsen boulders. The builders then dragged the stone forward on its rollers to a point just short of the hole, and slowly eased it into an upright position by means of ropes, lever beams and stakes which were hammered against the base. The stones stand today because of the builders' expert judgement of the exact point of balance of the boulders, not through any support from the sides of the holes. Once this delicate adjustment had been achieved, accurately placed lumps of sarsen were piled against the bottom of the stone to secure its positioning. As a final precaution the base was packed with clay before the supports were removed, so that any signs of instability would reveal themselves in cracks or gaps in the clay.

Over sixty of these stones were set up in two circles with almost exactly the same diameters, while another hundred were erected in a very irregular ring just inside the flat ground enclosed by the main ditch. There were other arrangements of stones which may have related to this basic pattern. Two stones in the northern

The south-west sector of Avebury, Wiltshire, seen from the top of the surrounding bank.

During the restoration of the West Kennet Avenue in 1934, one of the fallen stones was raised with wooden wedges and levers, imitating prehistoric techniques.

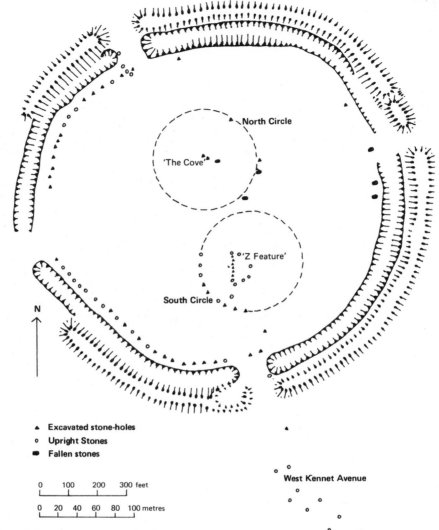

- ▲ **Excavated stone-holes**
- ○ **Upright Stones**
- ◖ **Fallen stones**

0   100    200    300 feet

0   20   40   60   80   100 metres

Plan of the monument at Avebury.

inner circle do not form part of its perimeter but stand in the middle and at right angles to each other, while a third stone, since destroyed, once completed this feature to make a small open-ended stone enclosure, which the antiquary William Stukeley called 'The Cove'. The southern inner circle at Avebury was dominated by a large stone near its centre (which Stukeley named the Obelisk) and an extraordinary jumble of small boulders, placed in long straggling lines and roughly forming the shape of a triangle. Finally, a stone which once had a hole near the top—Stukeley's Ring Stone—stood near by, apparently isolated, between the main circle and the southern inner setting. Only the stump of this has been preserved, and like that of all the other dozens of sarsen stones, its function is unknown.

From the original four entrances in the bank, pathways must have led in every direction over the downs, and from the southern and western causeways massive double avenues of stones stretched away from the great circle. The southern or West Kennet avenue is the only one to have been partially investigated, when the section nearest the village was excavated and restored, like the rest of Avebury, by Alexander Keiller in the 1930s. The re-erected stones present a dramatic introduction to the ring for the visitor who approaches the village along the modern road. Altogether about a hundred pairs of stones marked this processional route. Burials were placed at the bases of four of the megaliths in the section excavated by Keiller. The stones vary considerably in size—some are only four feet high—but the tallest seem to mark changes in the avenue's direction. Although the stones were not artificially shaped in any way, they seem to have been chosen with some care. At several points there are two distinct shapes facing each other on opposite sides of the avenue. One is a tall pillar shape, the other a diamond outline set on its point; many have concluded that this is the expression of a fertility cult.

The avenue once ran from Avebury into the dip of the valley, up the other side and it stopped on the flat top of Overton Hill at the site known as the Sanctuary, over $1\frac{1}{2}$ miles away. Here at least three circular wooden structures had succeeded one another and in turn were replaced by a double ring of megaliths linked to the end of the avenue. The general impression that stone temples superseded the phase of wooden architecture is reinforced by the evidence from Mount Pleasant. On this site a 'cove' of sarsen stones comparable to the one at Avebury was built over the exact centre of the old demolished timber building.

The signs of extensive, if not permanent, occupation at Durrington, Marden and Mount Pleasant conflict with the notable lack of finds within the enclosure at Avebury. During the late Neolithic period there was settlement across the line of the West Kennet avenue, and doubtless at other sites near by, but Avebury ring itself was certainly not littered with material in the same way as Durrington Walls. It may be that the apparent change from wood to stone was accompanied by a more formal and ritualized emphasis in the activities associated with the enclosure.

Indeed, it is easy to stand on the high southern bank at Avebury and, looking towards the centre, imagine a multitude of Druidically-robed priests with arms outstretched, accompanied by blood sacrifices and religious chantings. Turning in the other direction, the line of the avenue disappearing over the slope suggests the solemn pacing of a funeral procession. Less romantic minds may, however, from that same position, notice a number of features which call into question such a simple answer for what went on inside this sanctuary.

For one thing, the southern inner ring appears to have been set out with some care as a perfect circle, while the main outer ring seems quite perversely rough and ready. On the south-west side, the stones appear to stand in an almost direct straight line for a considerable distance. The monument is not focused on the centre point of the great circle, as one might imagine. The two inner rings must have formed separate points of attention, while the middle of the southern circle is cluttered with a confusion of small stones.

Still more unexpected are the deviations of the avenue along its course, which were interpreted by William Stukeley as evidence for a serpent cult. The fact is that the distance between the Sanctuary and Avebury is not covered by the shortest possible route—a straight line—and although the terrain is steep in places, it by no means necessitates the twists in the avenue's path. As the avenue approaches the bank at Avebury, its course deviates sharply away from the monument, and then swerves back again just before entering the ring. Even more notable is the fact that the two huge southern stones, which must surely have marked the entrance, do not stand opposite the original causeway through the bank, let alone line up with the course of the avenue.

Different gangs of workmen, separate building phases, other structures which no longer survive, could account for many of these discrepancies, but the greatest puzzle of all, Silbury Hill, has defied simple interpretations even under the most careful scientific attention. To archaeologists it has often seemed like an outsized round barrow, but it now appears certain that a burial was not located at its centre. Silbury is in fact a huge mound, 130 feet high, founded on a natural chalk spur and built up with nearly nine million cubic feet of rubble. The mound was not crudely heaped up from the centre like a modern industrial tip, but was carefully engineered in a series of stepped horizontal layers created by concentric rings of chalk blocks. Three phases of construction have been identified, when work was twice renewed on a yet-more-ambitious scale. The precise connection with Avebury has not been established, although the carbon date for Silbury's first phase of about 2600 BC may well place it as contemporary with the first construction stages at Avebury, and this possibility is a striking indication of the labour resources available in early southern Britain.

So, too, is the evidence for long-distance transportation of material for stone circles. We know, for instance, that about fifty megaliths were hauled five miles from the Mendips to the Stanton Drew site, just south of Bristol, for the arrangement of a cove, two avenues and three circles. A more impressive case is the

Silbury Hill. The ditch visible today (*right*) provided six million cubic feet of chalk for the final stage of the mound. It is here seen under excavation in 1969.

rebuilding of Stonehenge which took place some time before 2000 BC. At least 82 'bluestones', each weighing over four tons, were brought from Mount Prescelly in south-west Wales to the old enclosure, probably following a land-and-water route of some 240 miles. Recently traces of a glacier flowing eastwards have been located in the Bristol area, and this has raised the possibility that these stones were moved at least part of the way in very ancient times by entirely natural means. On the other hand, until actual glacial 'erratics' of the required bluestone rock are found near by, it seems more likely that the materials for Stonehenge II were brought to the site by man-power alone. We can only guess at the motives for such an exploit. Axes and other implements fashioned from bluestone rock were traded widely, and fragments of Prescelly stone found at one end of the Stonehenge cursus and a boulder discovered in a long barrow about twelve miles from Stonehenge suggest that special or sacred value was attached to the material some centuries before the erection of Stonehenge II.

It was probably during this phase that a two-mile avenue of parallel banks and ditches was dug leading from the River Avon to the circle. The usual assumption is that the bluestones were hauled along this avenue on the final overland stretch of their journey. They were erected in a double ring within the old enclosure, but for some reason one quadrant of the circle was never completed. Perhaps the builders' ideas were so ambitious that the bluestone circle and all the labour expended on it was abandoned in favour of the equally arduous task of assembling the final, great circle of sarsen uprights and lintels so familiar to Stonehenge visitors today. If the distant origin of the bluestones is correct, it implies not only remarkable resources of man-power, but to some extent a sharing of common values over a wide area of southern Britain.

In fact the map can be extended much further. On a small strip of land dividing the fresh-water lochs of Stennes and Harray on the Orkney mainland, there stands an imposing megalithic circle repeating some of the essential features of Avebury, over 900 miles to the south. The builders of the Ring of Brogar chose a dramatic site, with magnificent views of land and water in every direction. All around the shores of the lochs are the cairns of the tomb builders, and the great mound of Maes Howe is visible a short distance away. As we have seen, the Orkney islanders evolved their own styles of megalithic tombs substantially different from, say, the southern Scottish groups. But the Ring of Brogar suggests close contact with the ideas of stone circle builders in the rest of Britain. It is hard to believe that the builders of Brogar independently arrived at the concept of a temple of stones enclosed by a bank and inner ditch, broken by two entrances, similar to the layout of so many sites throughout Britain. Probably about sixty megaliths originally stood here, and the 27 that remain indicate that the stones were set out in a precise circle. The diameter of this circle was virtually identical with the southern inner ring at Avebury: this of course may be pure coincidence. In fact there were no internal stone features at Brogar, although until excavations are carried out the

The Ring of Brogar, Orkney, seen from the air.

The Ring of Brogar seen from its encircling ditch.

possibility of wooden structures cannot be discounted.

So much attention has been paid to Stonehenge and Avebury that we are accustomed to think of the idea of stone circles spreading from these great 'capitals' to the rest of Britain. Yet the size and scale of the Ring of Brogar challenges the assumption that it was necessarily an inferior, provincial copy of Avebury. The great Wessex monuments could indeed be imagined as the climactic expression of stone circle ideas, originating in Ireland or the north of Scotland some centuries before.

A surprising factor, perhaps, is the great period of time involved in the spread and continuation of this tradition, recently indicated by radiocarbon dates for a few stone circles. If the ring of free-standing megaliths which surrounds the tomb of Newgrange was set out before the mound, as seems likely, then they both probably have the same rough date of 3300 BC. In contrast, a stone circle at Scone in Perthshire presents a date of about 1500 BC. So these two monuments give us a possible time range for the building of stone circles of well over a thousand years. This long period suggests that it may be mistaken to seek for a single origin or social impulse behind their construction, despite the intriguing similarities between so many widely-spread sites.

Archaeological excavation is often limited in the light which it can throw upon the problem, because most stone circles are notoriously 'clean' for archaeologists searching for dating clues. The monuments are sometimes associated with attractive pottery cups known as beakers, found side by side with Grooved Ware and other ceramic types. The origins of the beakers have been carefully studied in recent years and are known in some detail. The evidence points to an expansion of population in the delta and middle regions of the Rhine, followed by actual emigrations of settlers from these areas in two waves around 2500 and 2200 BC. They seem to have come to Britain looking for fresh farming land or else as traders

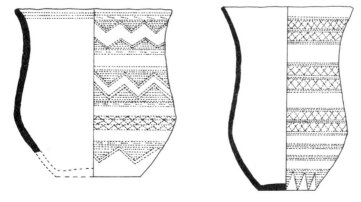

Typical examples of Beaker pottery from Garton Slack, East Yorkshire, and (*right*) Boyton, Wiltshire.

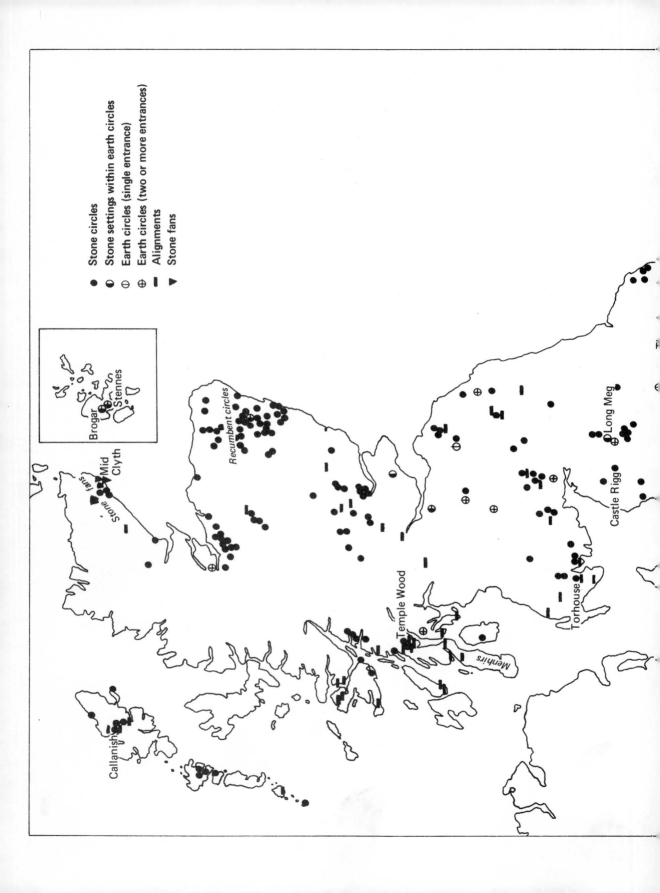

Stone circles •
Stone settings within earth circles ◑
Earth circles (single entrance) ⊖
Earth circles (two or more entrances) ⊕
Alignments ▮
Stone fans ▶

Brogar
Stennes

Recumbent circles

Mid Clyth

Stone fans

Callanish

Temple Wood

Menhirs

Torhouse

Long Meg

Castle Rigg

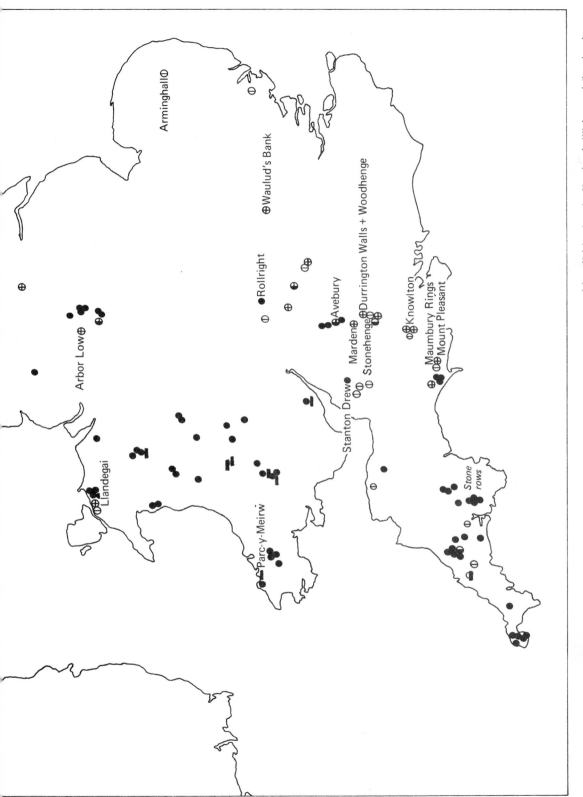

Arminghall⊕

⊖Waulud's Bank

⊕Waulud's Bank

⊕ ●Rollright

Arbor Low⊕

⊖ ⊕

●Avebury
⊕Avebury

Marden⊖
Durrington Walls + Woodhenge
Stonehenge⊕ ⊕

⊕Knowlton

Maumbury Rings
⊕Mount Pleasant

Stanton Drew●
⊖ ⊖

Llandegai
⊕Llandegai

Parc-y-Meirw

Stone
rows

Megalithic sites in England, Wales and Scotland.

in copper ores. Before they arrived, metal objects had probably circulated in Britain from the early gold and copper industries in Ireland. The Beaker prospectors may have re-used the metal from such objects, or exploited local ores, to manufacture their distinctive short dagger blades and axes. As well as these indications of material prosperity, the Beaker people also brought with them one special religious practice: the burial of single bodies under round mounds of earth —the barrows which must once have been the principal landmarks of the prehistoric horizons.

Wherever they spread, through Britain or on the continent, the Beaker people seem to have readily adopted native customs and house types. Perhaps the only real evidence for any kind of clash with the existing social order is provided by the deliberate filling in of the West Kennet long barrow by Beaker people, after something like 800 years of use. Was this a deliberate act of policy, discouraging old religious beliefs?

The thought of 'invaders' usually brings to mind aggressive figures who overturned old religions and substituted their own new order. The arrival of the Beaker people provides a convenient explanation for the undertaking of concerted building programmes such as Avebury or Stonehenge II, and for the apparently widespread and stable social order implied by closely comparable monuments such as the Ring of Brogar. But the Beaker settlers were probably quickly absorbed into the native population, and the continuity over the centuries between causewayed camp, earth circle and stone ring seems a fairly safe assumption. The scale and apparent uniformity of the megalithic monuments built after about 2500 BC may be nothing more than a reflection of developing prosperity and wide-ranging trade contacts. The unique evolution of stone circles in Britain—there are no monuments with the same circular layout or density of distribution anywhere else in Europe—argues for a persistent and vigorous tradition of native ideas.

It would be surprising if certain local communities had not developed their own particular traditions of megalithic temple-building. Some of the monuments fall into distinct geographical types, such as the 'recumbent' circles found in Aberdeen-

An unusual megalithic site known as Phobull Fhinn (Finn's People) near the desolate shores of Loch Langass in North Uist. This seems to comprise an auxiliary circle and one or more stone avenues, as well as the main ring. It also seems to have been built on an artificial platform above the loch (*right*).

The 'recumbent' stone circle at Balquhain, Aberdeenshire.

shire and also in south-west Ireland, which feature a large stone lying flat on its side (generally in the south-west quadrant of the circle) framed by two uprights at either end. In the Irish recumbent rings, the two uprights form an entrance to the circle and are positioned diametrically opposite the flat stone. The general similarity between the two styles of monument could be coincidental, but is perhaps more likely to reflect an interesting pattern of trade and exchange between Scotland and Ireland.

A specific western Irish centre, which may have been as important as Avebury was for southern England, can be identified around the shores of Lough Gur in County Limerick. A large number of sites from many periods can be visited, including several stone circles, megalithic tombs and Neolithic house foundations. A few of these have been excavated, including the main surviving stone circle, 150 feet in diameter, which is remarkable for the absence of any kind of enclosing ditch. Instead the stones are placed edge to edge in a continuous ring, with an earth bank rising to support their outside faces. The largest of these stones is in the shape of a massive rectangle, four feet thick by seven feet wide, with fourteen feet

The massive stone, nearly nine feet tall, which stands in the main circle at Lough Gur, County Limerick.

The Timoney Hills stones,
County Tipperary.

above the ground and five more sunk below the surface. To hide the rocks which supported the bases of the stones, clay was packed down to a depth of over two feet across the entire area of the enclosure. So the entrance passageway, lined with upright stones, rises impressively from normal ground level to the elevated surface inside the circle. Unlike many stone circles, the main Lough Gur ring was littered with Beaker pottery, especially near the stones. The excavators had little doubt that the pottery fragments found close to the stones indicated deliberate smashing in some dedicatory rite.

Similar regional concentrations are known in many parts of Ireland, and are not confined to circular arrangements. Perhaps the most intriguing of all is the site near Roscrea, County Tipperary. Apparently in the 1930s about three hundred small upright stones could still be counted in several large fields which cover the ridge of the Timoney Hills. The site has been raided for road-making material, and it is doubtful if more than a few dozen stones can be seen today. Even so, their arrangement calls into question most of the explanations usually supplied for megalithic monuments. Apart from a few very broad and ill-defined arcs, the stones form no sensible plan at all. Alignments of two or three megaliths start and finish abruptly on uneven ground, while a number are spread over a wide area and so much at random that it would be difficult to relate them to each other in any significant way. Certainly it is hard to conceive of ceremonial or community gatherings at such a broadly scattered and apparently chaotic site.

An impressive alignment at Eightercua, County Kerry.

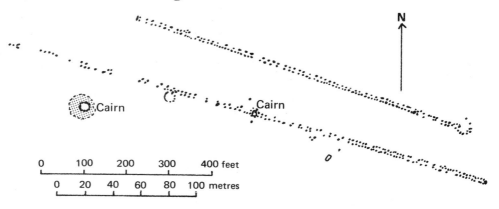

Two of the Merrivale stone rows on Dartmoor, based on a rough survey of 1860.

Other non-circular monuments can be found elsewhere in Britain. The walker on Exmoor is likely to come across triangles and quadrilaterals set out with very small stones. On the bleak heights of Dartmoor, among several fine megalithic rings, there are over sixty straight or gently curving stone rows. In general, the direction taken by the rows seems to be influenced by topographical factors, and the longest of all, the Stall Moor row, meanders for over two miles through a thirty-degree range of compass bearings. In most cases barrows are placed at the ends of the rows or are closely associated. This characteristic is shared by perhaps the most unusual type of all the monuments, found in the far north of Scotland, near the coast of Caithness. About half-a-dozen fan-shaped settings of stone, in almost every case close to one or more burial cairns, are known in this area. The best of these sites is situated not far from the town of Wick, where in boggy moorland more than two hundred small stones are aligned in a radiating fan-like pattern. Mid Clyth, like some abandoned, weathered graveyard, defies explanation.

If there are many bizarre exceptions to the general rule of megaliths arranged in circles and sometimes within a bank and inner ditch, it is only one more indication of the surprising extent and vitality of early Bronze Age culture in Britain, and of the risks of generalizing about it. The building activity was widespread, involving a definite circular tradition with details of basic layout repeated at seemingly isolated sites, but the regional variations must guard us against any simple solutions. Moreover, the special problems of stone circles frequently seem more complicated after first-hand impressions gained by visits to the sites. At some of the most important megalithic centres, the climate and local environment have changed dramatically since prehistoric times, and the strangeness of the monuments is often emphasized by rocky moors or stark heathland. It is hard to imagine the thriving centres of population that must once have been concentrated at places as deserted today as Brogar or Collanish. It is also difficult to think in terms of individuals and of everyday life when most of the remains that have survived seem to refer to expressions of their corporate and religious ideas. Why are there so many circles, and so little evidence of the settlements and the lives of the people?

# 5: Houses and Heroes

The western coast of the Orkney mainland is exposed to the full force of the Atlantic seas and winds, from the rocky cliffs of Yesnaby towards the south, up to the low-lying dunes of Birsay in the north. Midway between these contrasting regions the coastline is indented by the sweeping outline of the sandy Bay of Skaill. In 1850 a severe storm blew away the dune on a part of the inlet known as Skara Brae and revealed the stone walls of an ancient village, complete with a main 'street' linking roughly circular huts which may have been roofed over with timber and hides. Within the huts were found many details of domestic life, such as the stone beds on which the farmers and fishermen of the settlement slept, no doubt cushioned by mattresses of heather. The furniture in the houses includes what can only be described as stone 'dressers', with cupboards and compartments suggesting the storage of food, clothes or utensils. Stone hearths, together with small watertight basins in the floor, possibly for keeping shellfish or fresh water, are to be seen in most of the rooms. The builders of Skara Brae evidently took few pains over sanitation, since they piled their rubbish against the outside walls of each hut until the village was almost buried in its own refuse. Doubtless there was a practical reason for this untidiness, since the mound of rubbish afforded additional protection against the cold winds and furious winter gales that blew in off the Atlantic.

It was one such storm and a shifting sand dune that obliterated the village after an unknown period of occupation. As was the case at Pompeii, the inhabitants seem to have been taken by surprise and fled in haste, for many of their prized possessions, such as necklaces made from animal teeth and bone, or pins of walrus ivory, were left behind. The remains of choice meat joints were discovered in some of the beds, presumably forming part of the villagers' last supper. One woman was in such haste that her necklace broke as she squeezed through the narrow doorway of her home, scattering a stream of beads along the passage-way outside as she fled the encroaching sand. Such was the end of the self-sufficient community of Skara Brae. The apparent absence of goods traded from elsewhere may reflect something of the independent spirit of the tomb-building communities, to which the people of Skara Brae were probably related. Yet it is surprising that the fairly coarse pottery used by the villagers is similar to the Grooved Ware of the great enclosures of southern England. The significance of this style of vessel is still not entirely understood.

The intimate story told by these ruins has no parallel at any domestic site south of the Orkneys. There are no villages like Skara Brae because of the readily

The winding 'street' at Skara Brae linked a number of houses with stone furnishings (*below*). Here is a typical interior with a 'dresser', small watertight compartment on the floor, and, in the foreground, a hearth.

available timber from which such settlements were probably made elsewhere. Only in these treeless islands was Neolithic man forced to build his houses out of stone, and only for that reason was the life of Skara Brae preserved in such detail.

Even so, it is remarkable that the Grooved Ware users of southern Britain were capable of building such substantial wooden buildings as once stood at Durrington Walls or Mount Pleasant, and yet appear to have lived in nothing grander than small huts or tents, the traces of which are presumed to have been eroded away. In view of the large amounts of pottery found outside and close by the great buildings, it is probably safe to think of houses clustered around them either close by or within the main enclosure ditch, just as the Indian villages of the Creek Confederacy were grouped around their 'rotundas'.

The evidence for houses or settlements of the Beaker people is even more slender. There are fewer than a dozen sites where remains can definitely be interpreted as Beaker houses. Perhaps these people were wandering nomads, who never stayed in one place long enough to warrant more than the pitching of light tents. On the other hand the chance impressions of barley and wheat grains on pottery before firing, together with the discovery of grain storage pits, proves that for at least part of the year Beaker communities led a settled farming existence. Autumn and spring sown crops were probably cultivated at the Belle Tout site, now perched on the cliffs at Beachy Head, and here, as in many other cases, the Beaker houses seem to be defined by very nebulous patterns of post-holes. An explanation for the uncertainty in the plans of these structures may reside in the theory of 'settlement drift'. This idea proposes the slow, successive shifting of a house site as wooden posts and foundations rotted and storage pits became contaminated.

There are simpler solutions to account for the disappearance of settlements in

The typical remains of a Beaker house as excavated at Gwithian, close to the north Cornish coast, and (*right*) the stone foundations of a rectangular Neolithic house on Knockadoon, Lough Gur, County Limerick.

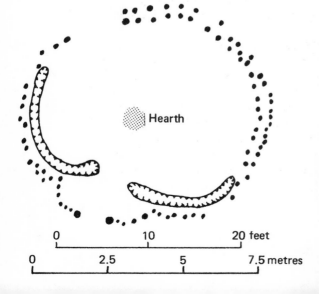

the south. Houses could have been raised on turf or clay foundations, which would leave no trace. Soil erosion has removed nearly two feet of ground surface from many chalk and limestone areas, so that only the heaviest post-holes would still remain preserved. A significant point may also be that settlements are not to be found where we might expect them, high up on the crests of the downs close to the barrows. The majority of Wessex barrows are in fact sited so that they appear to lie on the summit of the nearest ridge when viewed from the bottom of the valleys. The visitor is often quite disappointed to find that the barrow he has reached is not, after all, situated on the very top of the downs. The 'false cresting' of many barrows, which was noted as early as the eighteenth century by William Stukeley, implies that the builders intended their monuments to be most impressive when seen from below. Many of the earth and stone circles, which perhaps had more functional links with the community, are located in valleys and if their builders lived anywhere near the slopes, then domestic evidence might well be preserved under many layers of subsidence and hillwash.

In any case the distinction between 'ritual' circles and everyday dwelling places may be a false one. At Lough Gur, for example, apart from the main stone circle (unusual for the large amount of pottery found there) several sites exist formerly thought to be temples, which on investigation have proved to be enclosed habitation sites and, in one case, a Bronze Age cemetery. Similar instances of the interrelationship between house, temple and tomb are known from several parts of the country, notably the 'Benie Hoose' site in the Shetlands, where a stone house not unlike those at Skara Brae was actually converted into a temple or tomb by the addition of a forecourt.

Generally speaking, the evidence from the few unambiguous Beaker house sites indicates that the structures were built for small family groups and that they conformed to roughly circular or oval shapes. So far these houses have only been found together in small numbers, rarely exceeding half-a-dozen structures, and we have seen the archaeological difficulties, such as settlement drift, that may account for the scarcity of remains. Indeed, if we are to imagine settlements on the scale that would have been fitting for a local ruler or king at Stonehenge or Callanish, then our only guide must be exciting evidence from one familiar site, brought to light in 1970.

After the great wooden building at Mount Pleasant had fallen into disrepair, Beaker settlers cleared the inner enclosure around it on the top of the hill. The ditch surrounding the building was filled up with an ashy layer containing many sarsen chips, Beaker pottery fragments, flints, bones and several stone mauls. This activity can be dated to about 2100 BC. The material discovered in this layer suggests the burning of the remaining parts of the earlier timber building, and the preparation of the megaliths which took its place. Where the open courtyard of the building had once been, four pits were dug at the corners of an exact square with sides a little over twenty feet long. On three sides of this square was erected

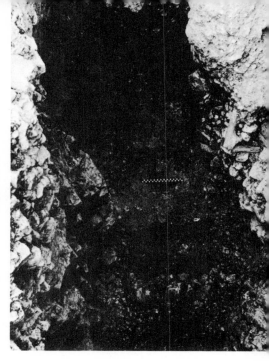

An excavated part of the palisade trench at Mount Pleasant, about three metres deep. The impressions left by the great oak posts are visible at the bottom of the trench, while the section (top of picture) is darkened by burning. Note fragmentary antler picks still in place.

a 'cove' arrangement of sarsen stones facing south, with northern, western and eastern outliers situated approximately where the corridors of the old building had met the line of the outermost circle of posts. We have seen that several of these 'cove' patterns are to be found on principal megalithic sites such as those at Avebury and Stanton Drew. The activity that took place around this central construction work, however, is so far unique in British archaeological records.

Just inside the ditch and bank of the main enclosure, and roughly following their line around the hillside, a continuous trench was excavated into the chalk, averaging about three feet across and no less than nine feet deep. Into this vertical trench were set huge oak posts, probably about one and a half feet thick and stand-

Dr Geoffrey Wainwright looks on as the BBC 'reconstruct' the Mount Pleasant palisade by sliding Post Office telephone poles into part of the original trench. The poles give some impression of the height of the palisade, but the posts would have been about twice as thick, standing cheek-by-jowl around the hilltop.

ing a clear eighteen feet above the land surface, erected cheek by jowl around the entire circumference of the hill, with two narrow entrances in the east and north opposite original causeways across the enclosure. At the east entrance comparatively low gateposts were installed, although they were a massive three feet in diameter, with a narrow gap of only about four feet between them. This enormous palisade must have required the clearance of nearly ninety acres of forest from the River Frome valley below. From the large quantity of Beaker pottery found in the palisade trench it is natural to interpret the great wall as a defensive protection for a very large settlement, with the stone cove functioning as a ritual centre for the community. No inner post-holes were located to indicate the presence of a rampart around the top of the wall, but with oak timbers of these dimensions it is quite possible that a series of upper look-out platforms was arranged by bracket-like supports and reached by ladders from the ground. At some period the palisade was systematically destroyed by a fierce fire at regular intervals along its length, and by the deliberate removal of some of its posts.

The Mount Pleasant palisade is the only structure that might even remotely be termed defensive ever to be associated with a megalithic site. The *inner* ditch at the majority of enclosed circles would make the earthworks useless as defensible places of refuge. Yet despite the large area enclosed by the palisade, the size of the wooden wall itself and the probability that it formed the most important centre of activity and power in the Dorchester region, it is hard to believe that it was a unique structure. There is a good chance that at other megalithic centres large enclosing stockades remain to be discovered by chance and extensive surveying, in the same way as the Mount Pleasant example was located.

Why was there a need for at least one defensive structure of this type? The

Three elaborately finished battle-axes from Wiltshire burials, now in Salisbury Museum.

excavation of round barrows indicates that warriors if not actual warfare existed in Bronze Age Britain. Stone battle-axes and hammers, together with metal daggers and rapiers, are frequently found with barrow burials. They were probably marks of prestige or rank and were useful in hunting, while they support the possibility of civil or tribal conflict. It is easiest to imagine small-scale slave or cattle raids in the tradition of the Irish heroic cycles, led by warriors and princes attempting to assert their authority, which was perhaps symbolized by great constructions like that at Mount Pleasant.

Some of these men undoubtedly commanded respect in their time. The old man who was laid to rest in a round barrow at Kellythorpe, near Scarborough, Yorkshire, once stood five feet ten inches tall, and the 1851 excavators thought that they had located the severed head of a hawk just above his knees—a fearsome symbol of authority, perhaps. He was laid on his side in a long shroud made from nettle stems soaked in water and woven into cloth. This was fastened at the neck by three conical amber buttons, probably made specially for the occasion as ornament. With his body were placed a bronze knife and the wrist guard, made of polished stone and fastened with golden rivets, which had once protected his forearm from the rebound of a bow string. At his feet was positioned a beaker, perhaps the cup from which he used to drink barley beer, and around his body was placed a ring of sea urchins. Heavy stones were fetched from eighteen miles away and a massive stone coffin was built for him. Over the top of this coffin earth was heaped up to form a mound also covering the secondary burials of two small children. There can scarcely be any doubt of the reverence paid to the old man at Kellythorpe, but how does he fit into a wider social scale? What of the many barrows containing skeletons lying on their sides, like the old man, but only scraps of beakers found with them? And what happened to the hundreds who worked at the task of creating great banks of earth and shifting the huge stones; surely they were not given the privilege of a single mound which would stand out on the horizon as a landmark? They, perhaps, were unceremoniously buried where they fell, or found their way into the chambers of the long barrows, among the bones of generations of downland farmers.

Round barrows were built in a remarkable variety of size and form. The basic 'bowl' shape, consisting of a mound heaped up from a carefully dug circular ditch, could be anything from 15 to 100 feet in diameter, and was sometimes varied by the building of double or even triple barrows within the same ditch. Rarer forms, such as the embanked 'pond' barrows with a sunken central area, are found side by side with conventional types. Women were usually buried in flat 'disc' barrows surrounded by a ditch, scarcely less impressive than the male graves, against which they are often closely sited. The female burials are identifiable partly by anatomical examination of the bones and partly because of the small tools, necklaces, beads and trinkets associated with them. The rich funerary objects accompanying some female graves in Wessex do not suggest a necessarily inferior status

Air view of the cemetery known as Lambourn Seven Barrows, Berkshire, including bowl, double-bowl and disc types.

for women in early British society, although the occasional presence of male and female skeletons close together under the same barrow mound could indicate the dispatch of a wife or lover on the occasion of the man's death.

However much archaeologists continue to fill in the details of customs associated with the barrows, they will probably never be able to tell us of their religious connotations and of their real meaning in Bronze Age eyes. Most inhumed bodies were deposited in a crouched position on their left-hand side, suggesting the attitude of sleep, and the provision of grave goods may be taken as evidence for belief in an after-life. Additionally, there might have been some concept of an underworld, in view of the human remains and Beaker pottery found deep in dangerous natural rock fissures at the Windypits site in the Ryedale valley, North Riding. Discoveries of this kind may bring us close to the tradition of ideas that could have prompted the rings of pits at Maumbury, Stonehenge and elsewhere.

An equally close connection with the influence of circular temples is shown by the rings of stakes or light posts which are found underneath many barrows. It has been plausibly suggested that these represent the actual remains of the dead man's house, or else of a mortuary construction, yet in most of the cases where these rings have appeared, the stakes have not exceeded three inches in diameter and sometimes were actually removed with some care before the barrow was raised over the holes. The discovery of a number of barrows with up to three concentric circles of posts may, perhaps misleadingly, remind us of the plans for the great wooden buildings. If these timbers were too light to support a roof, it may be that the act of setting out a circular shape with a ring of posts had some special religious significance, perhaps in the same way as the Christian cross can influence the shape of a gravestone or the plan of a church.

Although probably much visited, barrow groups are not necessarily reliable guides to population centres. There seems to be no reason why they could not have been sacred areas, set apart from normal land use, and occupied at certain times of the year for the disposal of the dead. Cremated remains, buried in urns which were often deliberately turned upside down, were possibly the remains of those who had died too far away or at the wrong time of the year to be interred at the traditional places or periods of burial.

Large barrow groups often seem to lie along what must have been 'highways' through ancient Britain, and they perhaps guided travellers along important routes such as the Dorchester ridgeway, where some 180 mounds have been counted in modern times, with hundreds more lying on near-by slopes. Major clusters of barrows, often roughly aligned in straight rows, help to define regions that were of particular importance to Bronze Age people, and not surprisingly these occur close to the biggest earth and stone monuments. Some of the best-preserved of these concentrations can be seen today at Normanton Down, close to Stonehenge, on Oakley Down in Dorset, near the Knowlton circles, and at Lambourn not far from the Berkshire ridgeway and Wayland's Smithy. The different sizes and configurations of round barrows in these groups are very striking indeed, and if they represent clan or tribal cemeteries, it is tempting to imagine that once they could be 'read' and reflect the history of generations in the way that family vaults have functioned in more recent times.

At several barrow groups archaeologists have managed to piece some of the story together from internal evidence. One case is the impressive series of cairns and monuments situated on one of the largest and most fertile low-lying areas in western Scotland, the Kilmartin valley in mid-Argyll. The first stone cairn built here covered a chamber and a number of bodies associated with round-bottomed bowls. It is in fact a typical example of a megalithic tomb, belonging to the so-called Clyde-Solway group, and probably dates to about 3500 BC. About a thousand years later, the cairn was still in use or had retained its sanctity, because a Beaker burial had been inserted in the chamber. By that time, too, a great linear

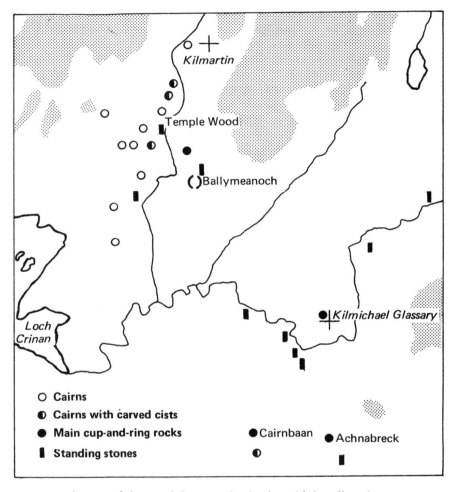

A map of the surviving remains in the mid-Argyll region.

cemetery of cairns had grown up stretching to north and south of the original
cairn, and all containing stone cists for the burial of individuals. It is likely that
these cairns represent the successive burials of a ruling dynasty, built one by one
alongside some important trackway leading down to Loch Crinan. Slight variations in the building and decoration of each cist suggest that the cairns cover well
over a thousand years of late Neolithic and Bronze Age times. Clearly, despite
technical innovations, new settlers and changes in funerary ritual, the mid-Argyll
region seems to have enjoyed an immensely long period of social stability.

    In addition a number of cists have been found near-by, not covered by cairns and not placed in line with the main cemetery, which probably continue the history of the area into later Bronze Age times, to about 1700 or 1600 BC. Two of these cists contained the crouched bodies of women, buried with striking crescent-shaped necklaces of jet beads. The occurrence of these rich female burials else-where in south-west Scotland has led archaeologists to suggest that by about 1700 BC power could have passed into the hands of a matriarchy.

Alongside the 'royal' cairns the prehistoric inhabitants left some remarkable monuments in stone. Some of the most elaborate 'cup-and-ring' carvings in Britain were inscribed on large natural rock outcrops in the valley. The significance of these carvings is discussed in a separate chapter, but it is interesting that simple cup-marks also occur on the cist covers of the cairn cemetery. These mysterious symbols appear, too, on the surfaces of large standing stones set in linear formations at Ballymeanoch and Temple Wood. The double line of mega-liths at Ballymeanoch runs close to a double-entrance earth circle about 130 feet across, in which at least one burial of the Beaker period was deposited. It is obvious that this small area of the Kilmartin valley had a regional importance relative to similar ceremonial centres at Lough Gur, Brogar or Stonehenge.

This growth must have come about because of the favourable position of the Kilmartin area as a route centre for travellers passing along the Scottish coastlands from the north, south or from Ireland. Evidence of commodities that might have been traded as a result of such contacts has been found in the cairns. For example, carvings of axe-heads are scattered over several cist-covers and their shape is similar to the outline of an Irish style of bronze axe. Other carvings, notably a multiple lozenge design found on a cist-slab ploughed up by the Crinan, may conceivably link the area with the rich warrior burials of Wessex.

The finding of two lozenge-shaped gold plates in a Wessex barrow was con-

Digging in progress at the Shapwick round barrow, Dorset, in 1838, subject of *The Barrow Diggers: A Dialogue in imitation of the Grave Diggers in Hamlet*, by Charles Woolls.

nected with an 'excavation' that first began to draw real attention to these burials. The prominent mound known as Bush Barrow is situated within sight of Stonehenge. Sir Richard Colt-Hoare's diggers set to work here in September 1808, and uncovered the skeleton of a tall, sturdy man, lying on his back in a north-south direction. Just above the skull Colt-Hoare unearthed what he thought was the remains of a shield, composed of scraps of wood and bronze rivets. By the shoulder lay a flanged axe, and below it a pair of large bronze daggers. Beside these daggers Colt-Hoare found 'a curious article of gold', which was a magnificently wrought belt-hook, probably once fixed to one of the wooden or leather dagger cases. Colt-Hoare was more impressed, however, by the wooden pommel of the smaller dagger, decorated in a zig-zag pattern by thousands of minute gold pins. His account of their discovery presents a chilling picture of archaeological methods at the time:

> So very minute indeed were these pins that our labourers had thrown out thousands of them with their shovels, and scattered them in every direction, before, by the necessary aid of a magnifying glass, we could discover what

A high level of craftsmanship in the working of sheet gold is evident in this detail of a typical 'lunula' now in the National Museum of Ireland. The manufacture of these crescent-shaped neck ornaments was concentrated in the north and west of Ireland, and the decoration seems to be influenced by the symmetrical designs of Beaker pottery.

they were, but fortunately enough remained attached to the wood to develop the pattern. Beneath the fingers of the right hand lay a lance head of brass, but so much corroded that it broke to pieces on moving . . .

On the breast of the skeleton lay a large lozenge-shaped gold plate, covered with an intricate design of parallel lines and zigzags. Colt-Hoare's final discoveries included the smaller decorated lozenge of gold, and a 'very curious perforated stone', the head of a ceremonial sceptre which had once been decorated by bone mounts encircling the haft.

Ever since the digging up of 'golden' barrows, mainly in the last century, such as those at Upton Lovell, Wiltshire, Clandon in Dorset and Manton, near Avebury, controversy has surrounded the significance and trade contacts indicated by the finds. The natural assumption was that such burials reflected the height of power in southern England associated with the builders of the final great sarsen temple at Stonehenge in about 1900 BC. This aristocracy no doubt gained its wealth through the handling of trade between the gold and copper resources of Ireland and the metal-using cultures of central and western Europe. Even if the far Aegean contacts were discounted, as represented by precious objects like the amber discs and the faience beads, seemingly upset by the revision of radiocarbon dates, Wessex must have played an important rôle in European trade.

But the radiocarbon chronology had one more trick to play on archaeologists. No dates had been available for the important Bronze Age barrows, and when excavations at a typical site such as Earls Barton in Northamptonshire finally produced samples for analysis, the results were surprising. The few dates so far obtained indicate dates several centuries more recent than was expected. The peak of power in Wessex, as represented by the wealthy barrows, seems to have begun in about 1700 BC, and the date for Earls Barton, perhaps belonging towards the end of this period of prosperity, is around 1400 BC. This result apparently demonstrates that the instigating of great communal or religious undertakings like the sarsen temple at Stonehenge was not necessarily linked with obvious material or economic prestige. Re-arrangements of the bluestone structure were probably made when the Wessex aristocracy was at its height, but for the originator of the temple plan, it seems that we must look beyond Mycenaean princes and such obvious figures as the Bush Barrow 'king'. Another very important result of the new barrow dates is that the old Aegean and Egyptian trade connections, chiefly represented by the faience beads, can once again be revived, and may yet prove to be a convincing explanation for these exotic objects. Within two or three years, from a superficial point of view, the interpretation of this material has come full circle.

One recent piece of research has contributed significantly to our view of the 'golden' burials, however. Minute examination of the decorated goldwork from Clandon, Manton, Bush Barrow and Upton Lovell has suggested that in all probability the most impressive pieces were never worn, but instead were specially made for the funeral rites of the dead. Furthermore, the microscope revealed that one single tool had been used to execute all these magnificently precise and bold designs. It is possible, then, that the epoch of prehistoric Britain's greatest economic power could have been less than a generation long, and that one master craftsman, a Wessex Daedalus, has emerged from the shadows of Stonehenge.

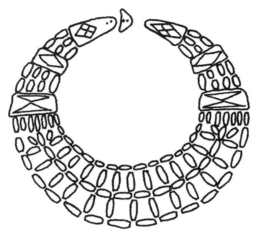

A jet necklace from Poltalloch, Argyll.

# 6: Stonehenge and the Sky

The average visitor to Stonehenge who arrives at the centre of the ruin may well feel confused. If he has emerged from the car park tunnel and made his way along the well-trodden path, he may perhaps fail to notice the fact that he has crossed the line of a bank, a ditch and a ring of white concrete markers. A jumble of fallen stones lies at his feet, while others stand soaring above his head. Turning for some source of comfort in the midst of his uncertainties, he will probably seize on the one familiar view that awaits him—the sight of the Heel Stone to the north-east, so symmetrically framed by three huge sarsen archways. Here, surely, is what Stonehenge was all about, this impressive alignment to the midsummer rising sun, a place for dawn ceremony and sacrifice to some unknown god. If our visitor manages to exclude the Druids from his thoughts, the associations of this famous view will probably be the chief impression he will carry away with him.

Interest in the Heel Stone's positioning does indeed go back to the beginnings of serious study of the monument. In William Stukeley's celebrated work published in 1740, *Stonehenge, A Temple Restored to the British Druids,* he notes that the principal line of Stonehenge points to the north-east, 'whereabouts the Sun rises, when the days are longest'. Perhaps he was repeating some piece of traditional knowledge; on the other hand his own powers of observation were quite capable of noting some of the special skills incorporated in the monument. After commenting on the architectural refinements of the sarsen stones, including the downward taper of the lintels on the trilithons to compensate for the effect of perspective, Stukeley was ready to assert that 'we see here plain, natural, early geometry, what we may call the first rudiment of art, deduced from reason'. In his opinion a unit of length which he termed the Druid's Cubit, $20\frac{4}{5}$ inches long, had been used in setting out the proportions of the stones and their positions around the circle. The builders probably had the use of a magnetic compass, he thought, and so he ingeniously attempted to calculate the date of Stonehenge from the rate of change of the earth's magnetic variation. His Druidic speculations were conveniently reinforced by the date he arrived at, 460 BC. It is an interesting point that amid the wildest conjectures about the religious practices at Stonehenge, Stukeley was concerned with investigating the level of practical skills displayed by its builders.

Stukeley's interpretation was so influential that it was only on minor points that an antiquary such as Dr John Smith disagreed. For example, Smith denied Stukeley's contention that the popularly nicknamed Altar Stone was actually used for human sacrifice, since he had tried heating a fragment of it in a crucible and

Stonehenge from the air.

successfully reduced it to powder—'very unfit surely for burnt offerings!' he remarked. But Smith has a greater claim to originality because he was the first to propose a systematic astronomical explanation for the layout of Stonehenge. Born in Glasgow, Smith became one of the doctors practising early smallpox inoculation, and his activities in the Wiltshire village of Boscombe evidently caused such a stir that he was forced to divert himself from these 'noysey wretches' by frequent visits to Stonehenge, about six miles away, from which 'I conceived it to be an Astronomical Temple'. Smith published his theory in a book printed in 1771 and entitled *Choir Gaur, The Grand Orrery of the Ancient Druids* (an orrery being the old name for a mechanical model made to represent planetary motions).

He amplified Stukeley's mention of the midsummer alignment by explaining that with 'The Arch-Druid standing against his stall, and looking down the right line of the temple, his eye is bounded by Durrington Field, (a charming horizon, about two miles distant) he there sees the sun rise from behind that hill . . .' The number of stones incorporated in the various rings were once part of an elaborate calendar system, designed to match the lunar months with the solar year, while the inner trilithons represented a zodiac of the sun, moon, stars and five planets. Like Stukeley, he had observed that these inner trilithons stood on the line of an

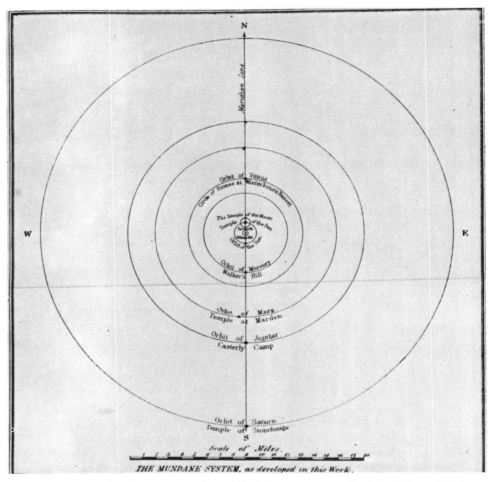

The astronomical scheme imposed on Wiltshire monuments by Rev. Edward Duke.

ellipse, its north-eastern end supplied by what was in fact a sector of the surrounding ruined bluestone circle. This ellipse was a symbolic shape, 'to give a phase of the moon when she was six days old, and an egg-like form to the earth . . . The Druids in the creation of the world, conceived all nature to spring from this egg of the earth, which mystery they concealed from the world in other works, besides this of Stonehenge.'

The explanation of Stonehenge as a lunar temple was repeated by many subsequent writers, if sometimes not expressed in quite such an esoteric form. Interest in the astronomical approach was quickened in the nineteenth century by increasingly precise knowledge about the movements of the heavenly bodies. A frequently proposed theory was that the layout of monuments around Stonehenge, including the barrow groups on the near-by downs, represented a vast planet-arium. The Reverend Edward Duke, writing in the *Salisbury Journal* of the 1840s, considered that most of Wiltshire once consisted of a huge model of the solar system based around a meridian line 32 miles long, 'pivoted on Silbury Hill, 16 miles distant from Stonehenge'.

Apart from these more grandiose theories, astronomical attention was still centred around the Heel Stone when viewed through the sarsen archway, and the possibility of dating the monument by the change in the sun's apparent yearly path around the earth (which astronomers know as the ecliptic). This imaginary path traced out by the sun is inclined to the earth's axis at an angle which is increasing very slowly at a known rate, so slowly indeed that at the latitude of Stonehenge the difference in the sun's position on the horizon at midsummer over a thousand years is less than half of its own diameter. By comparing the present rising point of the midsummer sun with the axis of Stonehenge, it was theoretically possible to arrive at a construction date. Considering the slow rate of change in the angle (or 'obliquity') of the ecliptic, it is not surprising that Dr Eddowes' calculations for the British Association in 1899 were hardly more impressive than Stukeley's magnetic method and resulted in a date of AD 476.

A rather more careful approach to the same problem was tried in 1901 by Sir Norman Lockyer, who must have appreciated the basic difficulty that a line drawn from the centre of the sarsen circle through the Heel Stone has *never* coincided with the midsummer sunrise. Today the first flash of sun appears just to the left, or north, of the Heel Stone, but the further back in time the calculations are taken, the more the extreme point of sunrise moves to the north. In 2000 BC, by the time the sun had risen high enough in the east to appear to be shining directly over the tip of the Heel Stone, it would have already cleared the horizon by a distance of more than one of its own diameters. Therefore the Heel Stone has to be discounted as in any sense an *accurate* marker of the midsummer sunrise.

Fortunately for Lockyer, another line was available, apparently in the required place, more than one degree to the north of the tip of the Heel Stone. This was the axis line of the sarsen temple and with his attempts to define this line Lockyer's troubles began. The drawing of an axis requires at least two points to be known along its length, and while one of these points could easily be determined (the mid-point of the sarsen archway, stones 30 to 1) the observing spot near the centre of the circle could not be verified. Lockyer's idea was that someone standing behind the great trilithon, looking through the narrow gap between the two stones like a marksman aiming through the backsight of his rifle, would see the sun rise between the 'foresight', the sarsen archway. But stone 55 of the great trilithon fell over many centuries ago, and when Lockyer made his observations stone 56 was still leaning appreciably towards the centre. So the backsight of the megalithic 'rifle' could only be established by an arbitrary estimate of where and how wide

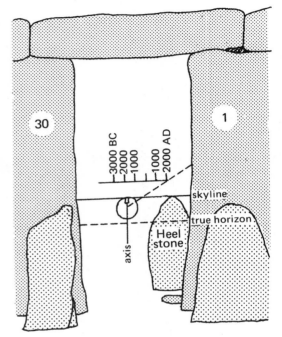

The view from Lockyer's observation point behind the great trilithon, showing the axis he determined by measurement of the Avenue. The scale demonstrates the inaccuracy of the dating technique involving the rate of change in the obliquity of the ecliptic.

the gap between stones 55 and 56 had once been.

To help overcome these difficulties, Lockyer assumed that the axis, if projected beyond the sarsen circle, formed the middle line of the avenue leading away from the circular bank and ditch. Modern excavation has established that the avenue is in fact earlier than the sarsen ring and was probably built during the period known as Stonehenge II. If we overlook this fact, which Lockyer could not have known, the attempt to find the central line between a pair of banks and ditches was in itself a most difficult undertaking. Luckily, the direction of six pegs positioned by Lockyer at various intervals along what he judged to be the half-way point of the avenue only varied by six minutes of arc (or 1/10 of a degree) and this satisfied Lockyer. From the axis measured between the stones of the archway 30 to 1 and this middle line of the avenue, Lockyer calculated his date. It was 1680 BC, which, in view of more accurate knowledge of the rate of change of the obliquity, can be corrected to 1840 BC. That this date is anywhere near the truth is all the more remarkable for the fact that if the observer at the centre used his left eye rather than his right, or the other way round, there would be a difference of *five hundred years* in the calculated date.

Lockyer's activities would be of no great concern to us if they did not illustrate some of the essential difficulties met by any astronomer interested in Stonehenge. After half a century of excavations, notably the meticulous work by Professor

The eastern edge of the outer sarsen circle; with prehistoric axe carvings visible on stone 4 (near centre of picture).

Atkinson and others between 1950 and 1958 which established five different phases of building and modification, these difficulties have multiplied even more.

A bold attempt to re-examine Stonehenge in the face of this complex body of evidence was made by Dr Gerald S. Hawkins, an English-born astronomer from Boston University. In his widely publicized book, *Stonehenge Decoded*, he describes how a visit to Stonehenge in 1961 to film the midsummer sunrise convinced him that *all* the principal sight-lines incorporated in the monument should be investigated for astronomical possibilities. Only a computer could deal with all the calculations for the extreme sun and moon positions that occurred four thousand years ago and relate them to the alignments, which were measured from a Ministry of Works plan. No fewer than 120 pairs of alignments were examined in this way, a job which took the computer less than a minute. Dr Hawkins has vividly described how '12 of the significant Stonehenge alignments' were discovered to indicate extreme positions of the sun, and 12 more were directed towards extreme positions of the moon.

When Dr Hawkins published the first of his papers in 1963, the popular response

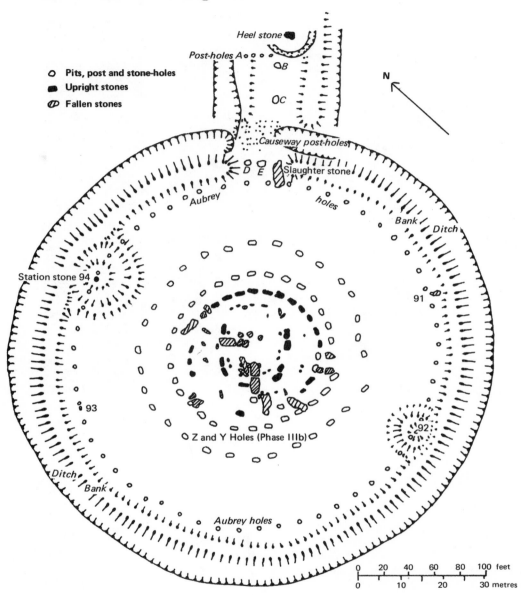

Plan of Stonehenge.

was nothing short of sensational, and in one of the chapters of *Stonehenge Decoded* he has fully described the intense interest aroused. In academic circles most of Dr Hawkins' theories met with general acceptance. Professor Atkinson wrote a number of criticisms for the periodical *Antiquity*, in which he thoroughly investigated the strengths and weaknesses of Dr Hawkins' argument. These included questions related to the accuracy of the alignments, the use of separate features possibly displaced or of different date, and to archaeological errors that appeared in the first edition of the book. Professor Atkinson nevertheless tentatively accepted 'that the positions at least of the Heel Stone and the Station Stones, and, indeed, the latitude of Stonehenge itself, are astronomically determined . . .' Dr Hawkins' work led to important contributions from Professor Fred Hoyle and other astronomers. If we examine, one after another, the various stages of Stonehenge established by excavation, we can set some of the recent theories of these experts in their historical context, and judge for ourselves how and during what periods Stonehenge may have been operated as an astronomical observatory.

Stonehenge I is dated by a piece of antler associated with the original ditch construction, yielding a rough date of 2750 BC. The spoil from this ditch was heaped up in a bank that was probably something like six feet in height. For at least part of its circumference it may therefore have created an artificial horizon for the observer of average height at the centre, perhaps levelling out the irregularities in the Stonehenge skyline. Excavations have so far not been carried out in the central area of Stonehenge, but on the basis of the other comparable earth circles at this time, it is quite possible that a small round building occupied the key observing position.

This position was presumably the centre from which the circle of Aubrey Holes was set out at some time (perhaps as much as several centuries) after the original ditch and bank construction. The exact spot cannot be determined with any accuracy today, but the indications are that it was about three feet to the southwest of the centre for *all subsequent structures at Stonehenge*. So the approximate axis, running from this point to the middle of the early entrance, was about five degrees to the west of the phase II and III axis. This consideration is of fundamental importance to all speculations about Stonehenge. Perhaps from the old centre the Heel Stone was fractionally more accurate as an indicator of the midsummer sun; at any rate it was not the centre of attention for an observer looking towards the entrance. The Heel Stone was probably seen close to the right-hand side of this entrance, although of course it stood some distance beyond it. The centre line of Stonehenge I was probably 'framed' between the middle pair of four large postholes (marked A on the plan) which Professor Atkinson has suggested might, if linked together, have formed some kind of wooden prototype for the later trilithon architecture. It was also 'framed' by two large stones which may have stood as a gateway, occupying holes D and E. The focus of attention for anyone at the centre of Stonehenge I would therefore have been an axis line and not the

Heel Stone. What can have been the possible significance of this general orientation of the monument towards the north-east? Both Dr Hawkins and C. A. Newham have shown convincingly that this direction would have been of great importance to the builders if they were interested in recording the behaviour of the moon over long periods of time.

The movements of the moon seen from the earth are quite different from the apparent path of the sun across the sky. The sun rises every day at a slightly different point along the horizon, and it takes six months to complete a swing

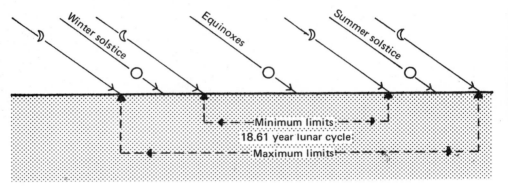

Diagram of the western sky showing extreme positions of the sun and moon.

between its maximum northerly position (the midsummer solstice) and its maximum southerly position (the midwinter solstice). The moon, however, takes *two weeks* to cover the distance between the extreme positions of its orbit, and to a casual observer the moon's place in the night sky is far less predictable from day to day than the direction of sunrise or sunset.

But there is a further complication of the moon's motion. It *is* possible to set up a fixed marker like the Heel Stone to show very roughly the furthest point of the solar swing each year, but it is *not* possible to set up such an indicator for the position of the moon every month. If such a stone were set up, the observer would find it useless after several months, because the extreme positions themselves alter slowly over a cycle of 18·61 years. What this means in practice is that any marker set up to observe one of the far positions of the moon would only do so *exactly* once every 18·61 years.

If we imagine that our Neolithic observer wanted to record this lunar cycle, then one method would have been to observe the full moon nearest the winter solstice each year from the centre of the enclosure, and to mark its rising point by a stake or a post some distance away, perhaps in the area of the entrance causeway of the circle. When the observer came to set up his annual marker, he would find that its position was slightly to the left or right of last year's marker, because of

Stonehenge from the west.

the slow shift of the limits of the moon's orbit over the 18·61 cycle. At the end of several of these cycles, the entrance to the enclosure would consist of a maze of posts corresponding to the movement of the moon each year.

This is exactly what excavations of the Stonehenge entrance revealed—a regular pattern of some forty post-holes, which coincide in a remarkable way with the calculated positions for midwinter moonrise. No one has yet suggested how these posts could have served any more functional purpose, such as supporting a gateway or porch, and indeed this possibility seems remote. Mr Newham calculates that since roughly six rows of posts are present, this represents observation of six lunar cycles, or well over a century of systematic astronomical work. These post-holes only correspond to the northern half of the moon's nineteen-year cycle, however, and we must assume that there were regular intervals of nearly a decade during which observation by this technique was apparently not carried out. One explanation is that the builders were only interested in finding the extreme northern limit of the moon.

The builders of Stonehenge would not, of course, have thought in terms of a figure like 18·61 years, especially if they were observing at regular annual times in a solar calendar. But if they had thought in terms of repeating periods of exactly nineteen years, their observations would have become unpredictable after as little a time as two cycles, and if an eighteen-year period had been selected, the error would have been apparent even more rapidly. Dr Hawkins proposed that three consecutive cycles, perhaps two periods of nineteen years and one of eighteen, would have approximately matched up the lunar cycle with a total of 56 solar years, without the possibility of serious discrepancies developing for a considerable length of time.

In other words, the most significant celestial rhythm for the Neolithic observers outside the solar year and the lunar month could have been, according to Dr Hawkins, a period of 56 years determined by extreme positions of the moon. The detection and continued observation of so long a cycle might seem quite impractical without some counting or recording device. This is exactly the function proposed for the Aubrey Holes. That mysterious ring of pits, exactly 56 of them, spaced so regularly just inside the edge of the bank, could surely have been a Neolithic 'computer'. By placing markers of some kind around this circle (one stone moved three holes each year seems to be the most practical suggestion) the lunar cycle and the pattern of celestial phenomena associated with it could be carefully recorded and predicted.

Those phenomena were the eclipses of the sun and moon which must have been of special interest to the observers. The capability to predict that either the sun or moon was to be imminently obscured would presumably have been a subject of great concern and perhaps a source of power for the astronomer priests. A lunar eclipse is caused when the moon moves into the earth's shadow created by the sun. If the moon rises directly opposite the setting sun, then an eclipse of the moon is possible, and there will be a further 'danger' period fifteen days or half a month later when the moon will have moved round in line with the sun and may pass in front of it, causing an eclipse of the sun. Dr Hawkins' demonstration that the Neolithic observers may have been fully aware of these possible events is connected with the (approximate) axis of Stonehenge. At midwinter the sun sets at a point on the horizon very roughly opposite the midsummer sunrise. During the period of Stonehenge I, if we accept the evidence of the causeway post-holes, the nearest full moon to the time of the winter solstice was being carefully observed, and if this moon was seen to rise over the Heel Stone—and so in line with the earth and sun—then an eclipse of the sun or moon would follow, although only about half of these would actually be visible from the latitude of Stonehenge. Dr Hawkins has therefore suggested that as well as indicating midsummer sunrise, the Heel Stone was used as an eclipse predictor, with the help of the Aubrey Holes as a way of keeping track of the significant moonrises.

Elaborations of this basic idea have been suggested by Professor Fred Hoyle, C. A. Newham and others. Mr Newham, for example, had an ingenious theory that the Aubrey Holes were in fact dug to support a ring of posts, in order to predict the *summer* solstice moon limits on the basis of the winter observations carried out at the entrance. The two phenomena are however not related in the symmetrical way which the builders might have expected, and so they abandoned the project without erecting the posts. This depends on the unlikely chance that the problem of relating summer and winter moon positions had not been noticed by some form of direct observation at midsummer. In view of the numerous post-holes found in the south-eastern sector during excavations in the 1920s, it is quite possible that alignment posts similar to those at the entrance causeway were once set up for exactly this purpose. Dr Hawkins' idea of the Aubrey Holes as a counting or recording device deserves more careful consideration. Moving some fairly substantial boulder (or burying a marker) around a ring of filled-in pits may seem an improbable undertaking, but the number and even spacing of the Aubrey Holes surely demand some kind of explanation.

The answer may come from the discovery of other comparable archaeological sites in the future. Although most of the cremations in the Aubrey Holes appear to have been secondary, intrusive burials, some of them occur in the primary filling, and this recalls the pits found within earth circles at Maxey and at Dorchester, Oxfordshire. Unless someone is prepared to show that the 44 shafts dug deep into the chalk at Maumbury Rings had some practical astronomical use, it can be argued that the digging of an apparently non-functional pit, sometimes associated with the rite of cremation, had some powerful intrinsic meaning in terms of religion or ritual. The relevance of 56 to the pattern of eclipses has been the subject of considerable controversy. The number certainly could have been useful simply to follow the cyclical movements of the moon. Even if the Aubrey Holes were not operated as a 'machine', could they be a monument built partly to record a valuable and perhaps sacred lunar number?

Whatever we may think of these theories of eclipse prediction during the period of Stonehenge I, the cornerstone of the astronomical argument rests on the much more straightforward explanation of the four 'Station Stone' positions near the bank, which form an imaginary rectangle enclosing the central area. The evidence

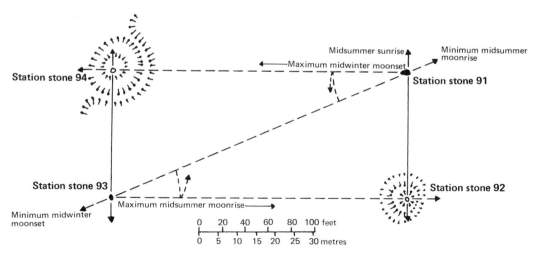

The rectangle formed by the positions of the Station Stones.

for their place in the Stonehenge sequence needs to be most carefully considered. Dr Hawkins finds significant alignments from the Station Stones to features of Stonehenge I. This is possibly supported by the fact that the Heel Stone of Stonehenge I, together with Station Stones 92 and 94, are each surrounded by a shallow circular ditch. The apparent intention of the builders in drawing attention to these three stones is in itself highly interesting, since on Dr Hawkins' plan they all serve as important lunar foresights. So the astronomers would probably like to see the Station Stones claimed for Stonehenge I.

The archaeological clues, however, suggest that the Station Stone positions are not likely to be earlier than period II. The intersection point of diagonal lines drawn across the rectangle lies close to the centres of Stonehenge II and III. The shallow ditches dug around Stones 92 and 94 are flattened on the outside to avoid cutting into the Stonehenge I bank, while one of them cuts through an Aubrey Hole. The filling of the Heel Stone ditch contained a fragment of bluestone, again suggesting that the ditch belonged to period II, although we may recall evidence that bluestones were brought into Wessex long before that time. On one of the two surviving stones (93) the 'tooling', which shows that the stone was shaped in just the same way as the main sarsens of period III, extends well below ground level, so the actual stones marking the rectangle are likely to be contemporary with the great sarsen temple. But it is quite possible to argue that they replaced earlier markers belonging to Stonehenge II or even Stonehenge I.

This concern for the precise age of the Station Stone layout might seem pedantic, if it were not for the great importance of these positions in the astronomical theory. The combinations of critical sight-lines indicated by the sides of the rectangle can hardly be the result of chance. Since the short sides of this rectangle are roughly parallel with the Heel Stone, they duplicate the midsummer sunrise alignment, while the long sides of the rectangle both indicate extreme positions of the moon. Stone 92, seen from 93, shows the furthest southerly point reached by the rising full moon at midsummer, and stone 94, seen from 91, points to the furthest northern limit of the setting full moon at midwinter. In the light of this interpretation the Station Stones represent a most ingenious astronomical conception. The short sides of the rectangle point to the extreme solar positions, while the long sides point to two maximum positions reached by the moon at midsummer and midwinter over its swing of 18·61 years. Furthermore, a diagonal line drawn from stone 93 to 91 shows *the other two* extreme (minimum) lunar positions at midsummer and midwinter. What seems to make the achievement of the Station Stones even more remarkable is the fact that this particular set of astronomical relationships could only be observed at the latitude of Stonehenge. As Dr Hawkins pointed out, the same figure could not have been set out any further north than Oxford without the sides of the rectangle becoming noticeably distorted. At Stonehenge then, it seems that the movements of the sun and moon were linked together in a harmonious geometrical relationship that could not be achieved elsewhere.

One further point of astronomical interest and of uncertain date came to light quite recently. During 1966 the car park to the north-west of the monument was extended, and during building operations three large post-holes were uncovered, each about two and a half feet in diameter. This places them in the class of the Durrington Walls post-holes, and it is likely that the timbers positioned in the holes stood as high as thirty feet. Yet these posts evidently did not support any kind of structure, since they are thirty to forty feet apart from one another, and there is every reason to suppose that they once stood as distant alignment posts for the key observing positions at Stonehenge, in fact providing more accurate markers than any of the remains in the immediate vicinity of the enclosure. Their locations do not correspond to any important sight-lines from the centre of Stonehenge, but Mr Newham found a series of alignments from the Station Stones and the Heel Stone. These proposed alignments include a number of 'near misses' of the sun and moon, as well as different observation requirements (full orb, last light and so on) but once again it is hard to ascribe this combination of critical directions to chance alone.

Stonehenge II, the first bluestone circle erected on the site, has been approximately dated to the start of the second millennium. The avenue linking Stonehenge with the River Avon was probably dug at this time, and it is tempting to imagine that it marked the last stretch of the epic journey of the bluestones from Mount Prescelly. They were set up in the unusual arrangement of a double circle, and as we have seen the centre of this monument was slightly different from that of Stonehenge I. The change in orientation seems to be indicated by the widening of the entrance causeway to accommodate the starting point of the avenue, since the eastern end of the old ditch was filled in, when already partially silted, to clear the gap.

The double bluestone circle was the first structure at Stonehenge to indicate the sunrise line unambiguously, since its axis was 'framed' by four pairs of stones at the entrance to the circle, and probably coincided with another two stones, B and C, set on the approximate middle line of the avenue. If this monument had survived Lockyer's task would have been much easier, but in fact a large sector of the western side of the circle was never completed.

Stonehenge IIIa is the name given to the most radical transformation of Stonehenge, the erection of the sarsen uprights and lintels at the end of their twenty-mile haul from the downs near Avebury, in about 1900 BC. The bluestones of period II were removed from their sockets, which were packed down with chalk to make way for building operations. The elaborate task of shaping and dressing the sarsen began by pounding the stones with heavy mauls. Professor Atkinson has compared the various techniques available for erecting the stones, and has shown how a combination of levers and ropes, including a 'crib' or lattice of logs for slowly raising the lintels up to the required level, could all have been involved

The fallen sarsen stone 59, showing the ridges left by unfinished tooling operations. The next stage would have been to bash out the longitudinal ridges with heavy stone mauls, followed by further refinements of shaping and polishing.

in the project. Anyone who has visited Stonehenge with an observant eye will be familiar with the refinements, such as the accurate spacing and curve of the outer lintels, or the mortice-and-tenon joints connecting them to the uprights. Until recently it was the unique quality of the Stonehenge III architecture that made the conclusion of close Mycenaean contacts or even domination over the Wessex aristocracy in the early stages of the Bronze Age almost inescapable. Now it seems possible that many of these features could have originated in the techniques developed to build complex wooden structures such as the buildings at Durrington Walls or Mount Pleasant.

At the same time as the Station Stones were erected—perhaps replacing earlier posts—it is logical to assume that other outlying features of period IIIa were raised as well. Just as a pair of stones at the entrance had formed a kind of gateway during the period of Stonehenge I, so the 'Slaughter Stone' and another upright at stone-hole E were probably erected on either side of the axis, and it is quite possible that they blocked the view of the Heel Stone from the centre.

The final set of astronomical theories concern the sarsen stones, and have been proposed by Dr Hawkins in *Stonehenge Decoded*. The same principal alignments to

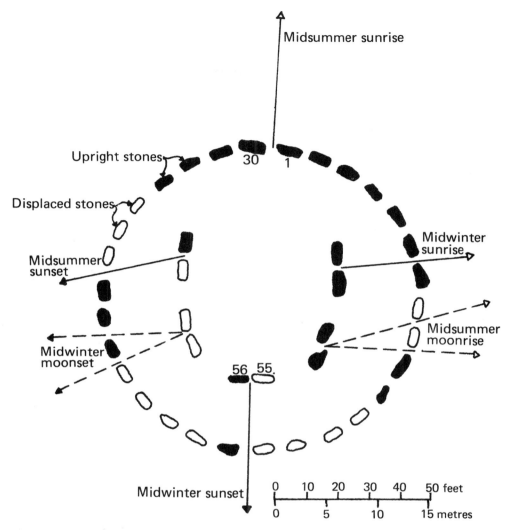

Midsummer sunrise

Upright stones

30    1

Displaced stones

Midwinter
sunrise

Midsummer
sunset

Midsummer
moonrise

Midwinter
moonset

56  55

Midwinter sunset

| 0 | 10 | 20 | 30 | 40 | 50 feet |

| 0 | | 5 | | 10 | | 15 metres |

Dr Hawkins' alignments for Stonehenge III, preserving those apparent in the Station Stone rectangle. But note how many involve the positions of stones now displaced or fallen.

extreme sun and moon positions are involved, but instead of being indicated by 'distant' stones (remembering that the diagonals of the Station Stone rectangle are only some 280 feet long, for example) they are 'framed' between the sarsen archways, while the narrow trilithon gaps serve as the backsights. The most controversial point here, and indeed in most of Dr Hawkins' theories, is the accuracy of the proposed alignments. At the preliminary stages of his work, any sightline within a ±2 degree margin of error was counted as significant, a limit that is generally considered to be far too great. Errors of the order of a degree or, say, thirty minutes of arc seem fairly negligible on paper, but when such deviations are actually measured on the Stonehenge skyline they mean that the average Stonehenge foresight could be moved several feet away from its present position and still be considered as indicating a 'significant' alignment. Professor Atkinson calculates that with a pair of sticks lined up against the sun or moon it is possible to measure in terms of five minutes (or 1/12 of a degree). Where Stonehenge III is concerned, the problem is much more critical, since any visitor can appreciate that the sarsen archways, viewed through the narrow gaps of the trilithons, enclose a wide area of skyline. In any case we cannot be certain that the various bluestone arrangements of period III did not block these viewpoints. All but one of the trilithon alignments depend on the estimated positions of stones now displaced or fallen.

In 1965 Dr Hawkins attempted to secure greater accuracy by supervising a very precise aerial survey of Stonehenge, carried out by the technique known as photogrammetry. Stereoscopic photographs taken of the monument from an aircraft were automatically transformed into plans by a special mapping machine. The result was that the errors for the sightlines were reduced to an average value of ± 1 degree. Professor Hoyle suggested one explanation for the discrepancies by pointing out that it would be much better to 'aim' for an observation just before or after the extreme position of the sun and moon. Nevertheless the trilithon alignments of Stonehenge III still 'miss' the theoretical angles by a very wide margin—by nearly four degrees in one case. 'The angular errors at this phase of

Dr Gerald S. Hawkins and a recent survey team working on the desert markings at Nazca in Peru. He has shown these are *not* primarily astronomical in significance.

Stonehenge' Dr Hawkins explained in an interview in 1971,

> . . . may be slightly greater but if anything the builders' precision has increased as the scale of the structure has become smaller. The error in the positioning is in terms of inches where it was in feet before. So far as the builders were concerned, Stonehenge III was more precise than Stonehenge I. I believe it was a spectacular climax in building, and it is mainly an architectural question as to why they chose the lintel form. But the trilithons are an odd, asymmetrical arrangement, and they do work astronomically—the only gaps you can see through are the ones that work.

A numerical consideration of the various bluestone and sarsen arrangements, which will remain uncertain until further excavation, *may* indicate an attempt to record important astronomical cycles and *may* make the case for the Aubrey Holes as a calculator slightly more convincing. By this kind of interpretation, the thirty pillars of the outer sarsen circle are seen as representing the lunar month; the inner bluestone horseshoe (probably nineteen carefully dressed blocks) the rough solar equivalent of the 18·61 year lunar cycle, and so on. There does seem to be a large number of such numerical coincidences at Stonehenge, although their interpretation will always be open to argument. What is surely important is that though the final temple at Stonehenge may well have symbolized a high level of astronomical proficiency, it was not in any sense an accurate observing instrument, and the demonstration of this proficiency from the ruins actually on the site today is full of difficulties. Perhaps further excavation will one day change the picture dramatically.

If the great sarsen temple really did sum up centuries of meticulous observation by an astronomer priesthood, we should not lose sight of the fact that at the peak of the Wessex aristocracy it must have stood for much more—as a trade centre or even as a royal palace, perhaps. The overwhelming impression that the trilithon architecture still makes on visitors today is a reminder that power and prestige may have played as leading a part in its design as any astronomical considerations. So many assumptions and problems of method are involved when interpreting Stonehenge as an observatory that such an inquiry might seem less productive than asking where and how the observing knowledge could actually have originated. At the time when *Stonehenge Decoded* was published in 1965, there was little evidence that any prehistoric European culture had ever been interested in the sky, no reference point for the historical imagination to grasp and compare with what may have been happening at Stonehenge.

Did a fully fledged system of observation and theory just spring out of nowhere at Stonehenge, or did it develop slowly elsewhere? Few people could have guessed that in 1967 an extraordinary new body of evidence would help to answer many of these questions.

# 7: The Quest for the Calendar

Sir Norman Lockyer had attempted to place his work on Stonehenge in the wider context of other megalithic monuments. After interesting himself in the astronomical orientation of Egyptian temples in the 1890s, he turned his attention to Britain and examined a wide variety of alignments from stone circles, rows, avenues and megalithic tombs throughout the country. As at Stonehenge, his inquiries were centred on the possibility of dating sites by the slow change in the apparent movement of the sun's extreme positions, but he also deduced that some alignments were used for the operation of a calendar dividing the year into eight parts. This calendar was based on the solstices, the equinoxes and on May Day and November dates for which he found plentiful evidence in Celtic folklore, and which were marked by the major positions of the sun or by 'warning' stars which rose just prior to the critical calendar time. In addition, Lockyer considered that many lines indicating stars were used as 'clocks' to help tell the time at night.

We have seen that Lockyer's work was seriously hampered by the lack of specific archaeological evidence on the dating of stone circles. For any one alignment he was often presented with as many as three or four stars as possible candidates, ranging over a period of about two thousand years before the Romans. The list of probable star 'targets' was as low as that only because the very brightest, or first magnitude, stars can be observed rising or setting close to the horizon. Atmospheric haze effectively 'blacks out' the background of less brilliant stars at low altitudes. Towards the end of his work, Lockyer thought that the bulk of his evidence indicated a comparatively late average date for many monuments of about 1400 BC.

The lack of a real archaeological background against which to set his conclusions affected Lockyer in rather more serious ways than simple matters of chronology, however. With remarkable self-confidence, he constructed the theory of a unified system of astronomy throughout the country, his May Day alignments (apparently centred around a date of 2000 BC) indicating a 'May Worship' cult, superseded by an invasion from Egypt or Greece of solstitial worshippers in about 1600 BC. A typical expression of his developing ideas occurs in a letter written to a friend after visiting the Aberdeenshire 'recumbent' stone circles—

> The circle results are splendid, but they want a lot of working up. I found all the Cornish astronomy, with a quite different style of circle. The mean date of building was 1600 BC or 600 BC, the question is indeterminate as data are wanting about the star used—Arcturus or Capella. I am inclined to the latter, and an incursion of true Celts, and skulls and race may help the inquiry

Sir Norman Lockyer, 1836–1920.

eventually. Every circle (I saw 28), is perfectly clear in its meaning. The only puzzle is that the May year stones have generally been displaced—a religious row I suppose with the (later) Solstitialists . . .

Lockyer was editor of the distinguished scientific periodical *Nature* for some years, and he published most of his findings in its pages. Among these contributions was a summary called 'Some Questions for Archaeologists' in which his speculations on megalithic astronomy were transformed into wild assertions. According to Lockyer, megalithic tombs were built primarily as observatories or even as houses for astronomer priests, and burials were later inserted by new immigrants 'who imitated them, and built round barrows without living chambers for the dead'. The rowan and thorn were worshipped by the May cult, and the mistletoe by the later sun watchers.

. . . The wells, rivers, and lakes used by the priests were, as holy places, invested with curative properties, and offerings of garments (skins?), and pins to fasten them on, were made at them to the priests, as well as bread and wine and cheese . . .

One man who adapted Lockyer's approach while managing to preserve a cool head in the face of astronomical evidence was Rear Admiral Boyle T. Somerville, whose naval duties in 1908 took him close to the Donegal coastline at Lough Swilly. Here he surveyed a group of megalithic monuments which seemed to confirm Lockyer's calendar system, and he extended his researches to other Irish sites. A stroke of good fortune occurred during the next year when storms off the Outer Hebrides prevented his hydrographic work and led him to visit a megalithic

Somerville's work in Ireland included two important sites at Lough Gur, County Limerick, both involving winter calendar dates. At the main stone circle a convincing alignment is defined by the entrance passageway and the 'notch' formed by two stones on the opposite side of the circle, although the horizon is obscured by a building. On Knockadoon (*below*) the small stone at the edge of a burial ring (Windle's site J) was related to a distant horizon feature. This illustrates the variety of indicators selected for possible alignments, which is one of the chief problems of megalithic astronomy.

The Callanish ring from the east, facing the entrance to the chambered cairn with the Great Menhir behind it.

monument of immense significance for archaeological and astronomical investigation.

The circle and alignments of Callanish are situated on a low promontory of land at the head of Loch Roag, a long inlet sheltered from the furious seas that break along the Atlantic coastline of the island of Lewis. From a distance, the dense group of tall stones stands out like a strange, unnatural forest against the sky. A huge menhir, a single pillar nearly sixteen feet high, rises from the approximate centre of a non-circular ring of stones, about forty feet across, also surrounding a small burial cairn and chamber on the eastern side of the ring, next to the central stone. From the four points of the compass alignments run away from the main circle, including a long avenue of nineteen megaliths in the northern direction.

Looking from the southern edge of the ring down the line of the Callanish avenue.

The two stones at the end of this avenue are turned at right angles to its course, as if they were meant to indicate a terminal point. Three stones stand just outside the ring, but form no part of the overall symmetry of the monument. Callanish is dominated by a large outcrop of natural boulders, towards which the south avenue runs. Near by, to the south-west, another chambered cairn lies exposed as a result of peat clearing, and there must surely be many more in the vicinity waiting to be uncovered. Within two miles of the main circle are four or more major megalithic sites, two of which evidently surrounded some kind of cist-and-cairn arrangement. At Callanish, then, whatever was symbolized by these impressive stone settings was very closely linked with burial customs and the rites of the dead.

Somerville approached these circles, however, not as an archaeologist or anthropologist, but as a skilled surveyor, and his large-scale plan of the main monument at once revealed some remarkable geometrical features. For one thing, the west and east alignments, together with the central line of the avenue, all met at one point near the cairn edge in the south-east part of the ring, and this seemed to define an obvious position for an observer. This idea was further supported by

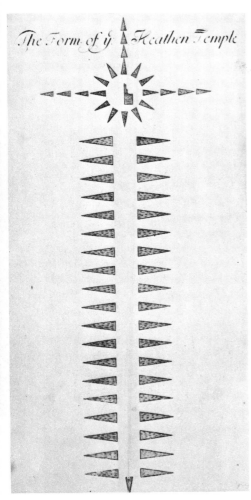

The earliest plan of Callanish, from Martin's *Description of the Western Islands of Scotland, 1716*.

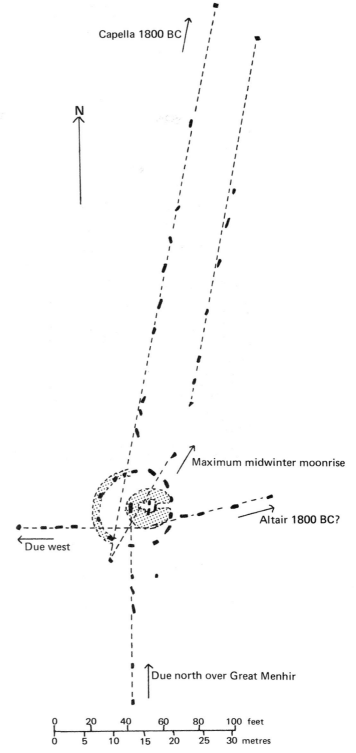

A plan of Callanish, based on Somerville's 1912 survey.

the fact that the end stones of the west and east lines stood at exactly equal distances from this point. The central avenue line precisely coincided with the two central upright slabs of the small chamber in the burial cairn, so that this construction was evidently contemporary with the setting out of the alignments. The south row of stones defined a line which passed exactly through the large central menhir, and the view over the tops of these stones from the near-by boulders seemed another likely position for an observer. What could this elaborate geometrical layout, surely not coincidental, possibly mean?

Somerville's paper concluding that Callanish was an astronomical observatory was published in 1912. It was read by a young man called Alexander Thom, who then was at the beginning of a distinguished career in engineering science. Thom was impressed by Somerville's paper, but had no opportunity to pursue his interest until quite by chance Callanish was forced on his attention once again. One night in 1934, he was sailing off the west coast of Lewis when bad weather forced him to take shelter in the quiet waters of Loch Roag. He dropped anchor, and noticed that the moon had just risen. Against its disc was silhouetted the cluster of standing stones, and it was only then that he realized that he was close to the monument he had read of so many years before.

'We had a meal', Professor Thom told the author, 'and then we went ashore to visit the stones. I stood on the rock outcrop to the south and looked along the

Callanish at evening.

line of stones over the top of the great menhir. The pole star was shining directly over this line, and so Somerville was right that this line accurately defined a meridian or north line—in fact to within ·1 of a degree. This was an extraordinary thing, because I knew that four thousand years ago there was no Pole Star there to help them set out this line. How did they do it? They had no compasses, and the 'Boy Scout' method of finding the shortest shadow cast by a stick requires a level surface, and anyway would not give the accuracy we find at Callanish. I can only think that they may have used plumb-lines to sight with and observe the stars slowly revolving around the pole.'

The work of Somerville, Hawkins and Thom at Callanish established other remarkable astronomical facts about the monument, and the apparent completeness of the remains there dispenses with many of the problems of method encountered at Stonehenge. Just as the southern row and the central stone define an accurate north line, so there are four stones showing a precise alignment to the west and therefore indicating sunset at the equinoxes. The avenue and the other, roughly eastern, line of stones do not direct an observer to the other cardinal points, however. Somerville showed that the two rows of the avenue both indicated the rising of the bright star Capella in 1800 BC, and that the line to the east was directed towards the rising of the fainter constellation of the Pleiades in 1750. Professor Thom thinks that this line may instead have shown the rising of the first magnitude star Altair in 1800. While the choices available for these star alignments may continue to make them controversial, there was one prominent alignment at Callanish that Somerville could not link to any major star. This is the line between two of the outlying, non-symmetrically placed stones across the central circle. The 'foresight', or farthest stone away from the observer, is a slab positioned noticeably out of line with one of the arms of the avenue, and it is angled in a quite different direction. Somerville finally concluded that this direction marked the northerly limit of the 18·61 lunar cycle, and so he provided the very first evidence that prehistoric observers were interested in the movements of the moon.

Dr Hawkins proposed other lunar alignments for the Callanish stones, but it is important to realize that practically none of the suggested astronomical uses of the monument involves stones farther apart than 100 feet. This is a crucial point at Callanish as at Stonehenge, since it affects the accuracy with which observations could be made. To take the case of the Heel Stone seen from somewhere near the centre of Stonehenge, for instance. As the sun appears to move north toward its extreme position at midsummer, the daily change in the location of its rising point progressively diminishes until for several days around the time of the summer solstice the sun seems to rise at roughly the same point on the horizon every morning. After the extreme position is reached, the distance between rising points progressively increases as the sun 'travels' back southwards once again. The vital question for anyone interested in the astronomical alignments of the megalith builders therefore concerns precision. Were they trying to discover the *exact* day of the solstice, in order to maintain an accurate calendar? Or were they simply directing attention in a general way to movements of the sun and moon which were important to them, mainly for symbolic or religious reasons?

The change in the sun's position a day after or before the solstice is so very minute that it would present problems to an observer if accuracy was the aim. The surviving stones at Callanish and Stonehenge could not be used for precise astronomical work. If a midsummer observer at Stonehenge tried to line up the rising point of the sun against the tip of the Heel Stone each day close to the solstice, the actual shift in his observing position at the centre of Stonehenge would be about half an inch. The situation is even worse at Callanish, where the ring of stones is much more closely grouped than at Stonehenge. Let us take Somerville's alignment to the extreme rising moon at midwinter, seen along the line of the two 'outlying' stones. Dr Hawkins confirms that this line, measured accurately through the centre of the stones on his aerial survey and against the horizon plotted from the Ordnance Survey map, does indeed indicate this astronomical phenomenon with less than half a degree of error. This is certainly remarkable, but the fact is that for practical purposes the pair of stones would be useless for accurate lunar observations. Stand at the backsight and shake your head from side to side, and you will see the stone only some seventy feet in front of you 'move' significantly in relation to the horizon.

In other words, the remains at Callanish and Stonehenge suggest that the purpose of their builders was to erect an imposing monument, which clearly indicated many significant astronomical directions, but could not be used as an accurate observatory.

Another convincing case of a 'symbolic' astronomical alignment has emerged from new work under Professor O'Kelly at the tomb of Newgrange. For many

The façade at Newgrange under reconstruction in 1969. In the foreground is the decorated entrance stone with flanking line of kerbstones. Above the entrance is the roof-box structure probably designed for ritualistic, astronomical purposes.

years archaeologists had been puzzled by an architecturally redundant slit or 'roof-box' over the entrance to the tomb. It was recently discovered that for a few minutes shortly after dawn on midwinter day, the sun shines through the roof-box and light penetrates all the way down the passage, a distance of 62 feet, illuminating the central chamber. This confirms a local tradition, disregarded until now, that at a certain time of the year the triple spiral carving at the end of the chamber was lit up by the sun. The Newgrange evidence surely presents us with a deliberate and symbolic astronomical alignment. Even supposing that the tomb had been re-opened each winter for people to watch the sun (or for the insertion of new burials) the alignment could not have been used for precise calendar observations. Yet no one has suggested any non-astronomical function for the roof-box, and the whole structure of Newgrange seems to have been orientated towards midwinter, perhaps a time of rebirth and renewal.

At the site of Ballochroy, on the west coast of Kintyre, Professor Thom drew attention to a setting of stones that seems to reflect similar intentions on the part of its builders. Ballochroy consists of a large megalithic cist, which archaeologists interpret as a structure that might originally have been covered over by cairn material and built for collective burial, perhaps well before 3000 BC. Just over a hundred feet away are three large stones standing in a line, with the flat faces of the stones set roughly parallel to one another. If a visitor stands anywhere near the main stones, he will see that they are clearly aligned with the cist, and that the whole arrangement obviously points to the distant outline of Cara Island, a few miles out to sea in the south-west direction. From the Ballochroy stones the mid-winter setting sun in megalithic times would appear to set just behind the far end

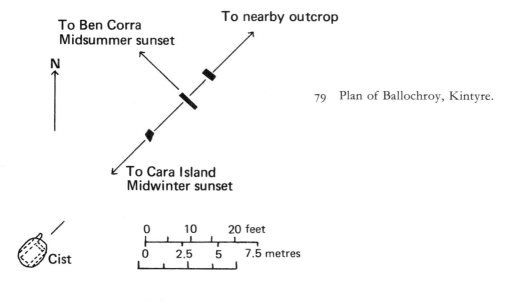

79  Plan of Ballochroy, Kintyre.

A sketch of the Ballochroy stones and the alignment to Cara Island, carefully traced from a photograph. The approximate path of the midwinter setting sun is indicated by the arrow.

of Cara Island. Here again we have an unambiguous alignment involving a burial monument and directed towards the sun at midwinter.

But there is one substantial difference between Ballochroy and the other sites discussed so far. Here the sun did not disappear behind a near-by stone, but behind the distant outline of Cara Island. If an observer had attempted to line up the end of the island with the last flash of the sun each evening, in order to find the exact day of midwinter, he could have succeeded where a midsummer observer using the Heel Stone at Stonehenge would have failed. Because of the greater distance between the observer and his foresight, the change in his successive observing positions on the site would be in terms of feet and not inches. Using a marker each evening, he could properly record the tiny apparent shift in the sun's path across the horizon. In other words, Ballochroy could have been used as an accurate solar observatory.

Professor Thom was also concerned with the series of directions indicated by the flat faces of the stones, and the central one in particular. Nineteen miles away to the north-west the visitor sees the spectacular outline of the Paps of Jura, a series of high, rounded peaks with steep valleys dividing them. The positioning of the centre stone is precise enough, and the curve of the distant mountains sufficiently exaggerated, to direct the visitor's eye clearly towards the slope of Ben Corra, the most northerly of the Paps. Thom has shown how the midsummer sun seen from Ballochroy would set behind Ben Corra, sinking in a direction almost parallel to its slopes. The edge of the sun's disc would momentarily reappear on the right-hand side of the mountain, and continue to graze the lower slopes until it had finally set in the valley. On successive evenings the observer would watch as the sun disappeared behind the peak, and when it began to emerge again he would move rapidly along the line of the stones, keeping the tiny flash of light just 'twinkling' along the slope down to its final vanishing point. He would mark the position he had reached every evening, and this would correspond to the daily change in the sun's position. Thom has emphasized how accurate the observations made by this technique could have been by calculating that one minute of arc, a tiny fraction of a degree, would produce a change in the observer's position of some thirty feet. This means that not only could the day of the solstice be discovered by direct observations, but that changes in temperature or pressure over the sea might appear to create irregularities in the sun's movement each evening. So as well as being a site where an accurate calendar could be regularly checked, Ballochroy may also have been set up as an observatory to investigate apparent anomalies in the sun's positions that we now know would have been the result of changes in atmospheric refraction.

Ballochroy is a very convincing astronomical site, especially in the way in which the stones simultaneously indicate clear alignments for both midsummer and midwinter—the key points in any solar calendar. But the stones themselves cannot tell us that any of this precise, regular observation was ever carried out. It remains an assumption, though a likely one, that megalithic observers were attempting to establish a calendar accurate to within a day, requiring such a detailed interest in the sun's motions.

If there was only one arrangement of megaliths that exhibits such features, Professor Thom's case for a precise calendar would be much less compelling than it is. In fact, Thom built up a careful analysis of other alignments indicated at megalithic sites throughout Britain, selected according to his own judgement of how unambiguously the chosen natural foresights were indicated by the stones. The result of his analysis was the conclusion that the stone circle builders were using a calendar divided into sixteen parts, which essentially represents a more precise, subdivided version of the eight-part calendar detected by Sir Norman Lockyer half a century before. Thom found that the best solution to the sun's positions indicated by the various sites involved a calendar comprising four 'months' of 22 days, eleven 'months' of 23, and one with 24. This arrangement would allow any one alignment showing a date in the spring half of the year to be used again to show a corresponding date in the autumn.

One site in particular has drawn attention as another place where the accuracy of such a calendar could possibly have been checked each year. Kintraw is a small level area of land, some thirty-five miles north of Ballochroy, where the coast road winds down through steep hills to the head of Loch Craignish. If an ancient

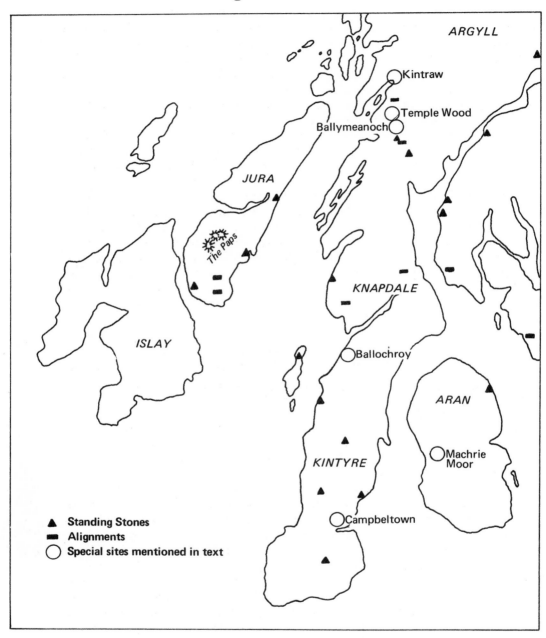

Sites on the Kintyre peninsula and on the islands nearby.

visitor had come to this spot from Ballochroy, he would perhaps have journeyed up from Kintyre along this road, travelling close to the great line of cairns and standing stones in the Kilmartin valley, or, more probably, he would have sailed up the Sound of Jura, leaving the Paps behind him to the south-west. As he pulled along Loch Craignish, these distinctive peaks would still be visible, 'framed' on the horizon by hills and islands on either side. In particular a steep 'notch' formed by two of the Paps, Ben Shiantaidh and Ben à Chaolais, is immediately noticeable on the horizon from the vicinity of Kintraw, though not from the small level plateau of the site itself. A ridge of land, now covered over with trees, projects forward into the loch, obscuring the view to the Paps by a matter of a few feet. If any astronomical work was carried out at midwinter using the prominent 'notch', twenty-seven miles away, the observer's position must certainly have been at a higher level. Any observations at this site would also require a considerable amount of sideways movement, because a change in the midwinter sun's position as tiny as that measured a day after the solstice (about one 300th of a degree) would make a difference of nineteen feet in the observer's position. In other words, the sight-line at Kintraw offered remarkable possibilities for highly accurate solar observations, but where was the observing to be done in the restricted space available?

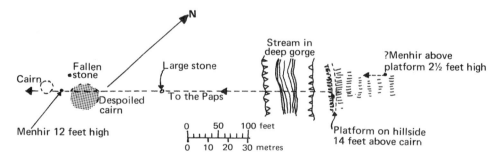

Plan of the remains at Kintraw, Argyll.

The principal remains to be seen today on the plateau are a standing stone, twelve feet high, and the remains of a cairn which once might have provided the extra height necessary for someone to see the Paps. When this cairn was excavated in 1959 and 1960, a small stone cist enclosing a cremation was found, and also traces of a post about five inches in diameter, which had once stood on the original ground surface. It is possible that the correct or final observing position was marked by the five-inch post, and the cairn built up around it partly to allow annual calendar checks to be made from the top of the cairn. The large standing stone could have been a general indicator of the required observing direction.

But how did the original builders know where to place their post or cairn? To

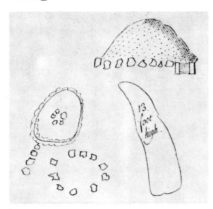

The earliest known drawing of Kintraw, copied from a sketch made by the antiquary Edward Lhwyd or his assistants on their tour of Britain between 1697 and 1701. Lhwyd's original drawings were destroyed in a fire. Although the sketch is not very clear, it seems to indicate stones now absent from the site.

find the solstice line, they needed an elevated position, and one with ample room for sideways movement. The matter puzzled Thom for some time before he investigated the precipitous hillside to the north of the plateau, separated from it by a deep and impassable gorge. There he found a narrow terrace, rising slightly as it wound round the hillside, with rather confined space for observing the 'notch', now just visible over the tree-covered ridge. On the hillside terrace was a boulder close to the line between the cairn and the notch, and Thom suggested that this was a fallen menhir. He also proposed that megalithic observers had once used this platform, perhaps even with a fence set round it to protect themselves from the steep hillside during their observations. Was the platform itself a natural or man-made feature?

In a unique collaboration of skills, the archaeologist Dr Euan MacKie set out to test the hypothesis devised by Professor Thom. In a week of excavations in August 1970 MacKie examined the boulder and the area of the platform on either side. He soon established that there were *two* large stones, not one, and that they were positioned so that the space between them formed a kind of wedge shape, more or less marking the spot where the winter solstice observation would have been made. Although the boulders were shown not to be fallen menhirs, it is difficult to see how two rocks could have rolled down the hillside and come to rest in such an unusual formation. Dr MacKie found some signs of packing stones associated with one of the boulders, but more important evidence was forthcoming from a stony layer which ran on either side. This distinctive 'paved' area ended almost immediately to the right of the boulders, but to the left of them, in a south-eastern direction, it was traced for about twenty feet, running as a remarkably

View of the main cairn and menhir at Kintraw.

level surface despite the fact that the natural ground rose rapidly over it. No artefact of any kind, nor any trace of a post or stone hole, was found on this platform.

What evidence is there against the use of this terrace, and indeed of the whole Kintraw site, as an important centre for astronomical observation? Firstly, there is the possibility that the same phenomenon could have been seen without any obstructions from the top of the hill overlooking Kintraw, or indeed from the tree-covered ridge itself. Secondly, it may be that the stony layer uncovered by MacKie is of natural origin. Similar platforms are known elsewhere in Scotland, created by conditions of extreme frost in glacial times. For such an important observatory we would have expected the observer's final position to be marked by something more distinctive than a pair of boulders. Finally, Dr MacKie has made the serious point that when the twelve-foot menhir is viewed from the platform, it seems to indicate the peak to the north-west of the notch rather than the notch itself, although this is exaggerated by the present appreciable lean of the stone in the same direction.

On the positive side, the latest reports of geologists on Dr MacKie's excavations indicate that the arrangement of stones in the layer is quite unlike that of a natural glacial feature. The absence of finds and other markers may be plausibly explained

View from the platform at Kintraw over the cairn and menhir to the Paps of Jura and the 'notch' between Ben Shiantaidh (horizon extreme left) and Ben à Chaolais. This view can be seen from only a small area of the platform.

by the use of the platform as a temporary part of the site. If the level of atmospheric refraction remained fairly uniform for several evenings close to the solstice, there is no reason why a single winter's observations might not have been sufficient to establish where the cairn was to be built. Temporary markers such as portable stones or wooden posts (removed before their bases had started to rot) could have been used to work out the basic layout of the site.

If the broad case proposed for Kintraw and Ballochroy by Thom *is* accepted, we see that at two important megalithic sites, close enough for regular communication between them to be a possibility, highly accurate alignments were set up to observe the two key dates in the solar calendar, sharing the same distinctive mountains in Jura for a very similar technique of observation. These two sites could well represent the means by which a precise calendar system, probably used in other parts of early Britain, was established and kept in phase with the sun's movements.

Such a calendar would have had obvious practical uses for domestic and farming activities in exactly the way that we rely on the operation of our own calendar today. Yet it is difficult to view the concern for accuracy suggested for

Kintraw and Ballochroy as essential for these purposes. It is certainly possible to speculate that the demand for an accurate calendar was set up by some specialist group in ancient Britain, perhaps by a ruling aristocracy or priesthood. The idea that such a calendar was an essential basis for more purely theoretical investigations of the sun and moon has been assumed by Professor Thom over many years of extraordinarily interesting research. Thom takes the concept that pure scientific investigation existed in early Britain to the point where, if he is right, prehistoric 'professors' must once have argued and proposed different theories on the critical movements of the sun and moon, four thousand years ago.

# 8: *Megalithic Mathematicians*

One of the most decisive conclusions to emerge from Professor Thom's 1967 study was that the megalith builders had made observations of the moon. At over thirty important sites, accurate alignments can be traced to either the upper or lower edge of the moon's disc as it rose or set at its extreme positions. The manner in which the observed sight-lines 'pile up' to indicate both edges of the moon in Professor Thom's analysis is remarkable, and the likelihood of these alignments falling into so clear a pattern by chance or for any other reason is remote indeed. So there seems to be a body of reliable evidence to show that at many places throughout Britain, but especially in the north-west and in Argyll and Kintyre, the people who erected stone circles and standing stones were actively interested in marking the extreme positions reached by the moon during its 18·61-year cycle.

The knowledge of the moon's movements, which must have taken a considerable length of time to acquire, was not, of course, useful as a means of time-keeping or as a basis for a calendar. We might speculate and say that this interest in the moon was the result of simple astronomical curiosity or because the moon was looked on as a deity. But in his later studies, especially in his book published in 1971, Thom takes the argument much further and suggests a practical purpose for many of the lunar observatories.

Supposing that the megalithic astronomers set up a sight-line which accurately indicated the very farthest north that the moon ever set, about once every eighteen years. By 'accurately', let us mean that they used much the same technique employed for the sun at Ballochroy and Kintraw, in other words, the method of lining up prominent natural features to coincide with the upper or lower edges of the disc. By watching the full moon rising or setting behind a natural landmark such as a 'notch', any small variations in movement would be apparent from month to month, and would produce changes in an observer's position just like those resulting from successive sunsets at Ballochroy and Kintraw.

As the moon approached its northernmost limit, the distance between monthly observing positions would become progressively smaller, until the moon would appear to set in much the same place each month, and then begin its long journey south again. This resembles the behaviour of the sun near the solstices, except that the time-scale is quite different. Instead of the few *days* when the sun's daily movement is scarcely detectable, the most northerly setting position of the moon in the month would be located at roughly the same place for *nearly a year*.

During this period, any sensitive observatory with a distant foresight might have revealed a slight variation of the moon's position from side to side on the

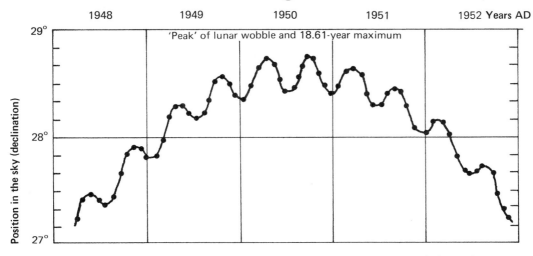

A detailed close-up of the moon's oscillating extreme positions as it passed through a recent maximum. The black dots represent the monthly extreme observations.

horizon from one month to the next. This variation is a small 'wobble' in the moon's orbit set up by gravitational forces relative to its position with the sun. The moon takes about 173 days to complete one of these cycles, moving from side to side of its average path by only about nine minutes of arc each way.

Supposing that our megalithic astronomers were aware of this variation, they would probably also begin to notice that eclipses coincided with the time when the wobble was making its greatest contribution to the moon's position (in other words, when the moon was as far north and south as it could possibly go). If they could find the date when the lunar wobble reached its maximum, an eclipse of the sun or moon would always occur at a new or full moon within a definite 'warning period' of about three weeks around this date. The observers could then count intervals of 173 days until the next danger period, and be able to make a regular check that the periods were constant every nine years, when the moon once again 'slowed down' to one of its limiting positions in the nineteen-year cycle.

But simply following these lunar cycles by monthly observation alone would present difficulties. It would be a rare event if the moon rose or set exactly at its extreme position for that month. More often than not the moon would reach its limit between two successive nightly observations. The fact that the moon had passed its extreme and had begun 'travelling' back on itself again would be obvious from the irregular spacing of observation posts on the second night. So if the megalithic astronomer wanted to follow the moon's movements with any accuracy, he had to devise some geometrical equivalent of his observations to find out where the extreme had really occurred. Today the problem can be solved by algebra, but in 2000 BC the problem would have to be worked out on the ground. If our megalithic observers had stepped back by an equal distance each night at the monthly extreme—and every month at the nine-year maximum or minimum—then they would have actually seen what they were up against; the geometry of a parabolic curve.

If this obstacle were overcome, the general technique would be a very efficient method of predicting eclipses. The forecasting of such spectacular astronomical events would surely have brought great power to the priesthood whom we may imagine to be closely involved with the observatories.

So much for the theory, and no one will deny its ingenuity. Can it be proved in practice at the megalithic sites claimed to be lunar observatories by Professor Thom?

At Callanish we saw how a number of short-length alignments have been claimed as indicators of lunar extremes. There is also a possibility that a distant foresight, Mount Clisham in Harris, was used to observe the moon at its maximum southern setting, which could be seen from several positions on the site. The slopes of Mount Clisham are about sixteen miles away from Callanish and the present average weather conditions in the Hebrides are such that no one has yet managed to produce a measurement by theodolite of the mountain profile. So we cannot be certain that Callanish was used for accurate observations of the lunar maximum or of the wobble that could also have been detected during the same period.

View over two of the three principal stones in the Callanish V alignment towards the critical range of peaks, ten miles away to the south.

But more positive evidence comes from an unimpressive row of boulders situated on a desolate hillside about two and a half miles south-east of the main Callanish monument. Professor Thom calls this megalithic site Callanish V. Here the mountain foresight is about ten miles away and Thom has succeeded in obtaining an accurate profile despite the weather. Moreover, the stones themselves quite unambiguously indicate this particular foresight and no other. Anyone visiting Callanish V under favourable conditions will at once notice an alignment of three stones which draws the eye along the edge of the hillside to a distant range of peaks lying within about ten degrees on the far skyline. When the moon was rising at its average southern maximum once every 18·61 years, the lower edge of the disc grazed the middle of this mountainous background. At the 'peak' of the lunar wobble, the moon would be seen rising nine minutes further south, at the right-hand edge of the mountains, along the summit indicated by the stones and known as Sithean an Airgid. Here, then, is an unequivocal alignment to a maximum position of the moon, apparently including the small contribution made to this maximum by the nine-minute wobble.

The site becomes more convincing still when one of the isolated stones at Callanish V, obviously not related to the main alignment, is considered. Standing at this isolated stone to the north, a sharp-eyed visitor will be able to see other megalithic sites, notably the main circle and alignments, and Callanish II. The distinctive horizon features immediately above these two monuments can be related respectively to midsummer sunset and to the northern lunar maximum. The stones of Callanish V, so clearly associated with far-off landmarks and astronomical events, present evidence of a lunar observatory almost as convincingly as the stones of Ballochroy indicate a solstitial site. Perhaps the practical work that could have been carried out here was incorporated in the much more impressive circles, cairns and alignments found elsewhere round Loch Roag.

A large number of the lunar observatories take the form of isolated standing stones, often reaching impressive heights, which are particularly common along the coast of Kintyre and throughout the Western Isles. The landscape in these areas is generally crowded with suitable mountain foresights, so that it is essential, if we are to accept the claims made for these stones, that they unambiguously indicate one prominent feature on the horizon. Two of Thom's sites may usefully be compared to illustrate the point. On a prominent hill surrounded by lochs near the coast of North Uist are the remains of a very large chambered cairn, which was much disturbed when Iron Age settlers actually built a small house in one corner of the monument. This site, known to archaeologists as Uneval cairn and to Thom by its Gaelic name, Leacach an Tigh Chloiche (The House on the Ridge) also features a large standing stone, placed a short distance from the edge of the cairn. The stone is visible on the horizon from a surprising number of other sites on the surrounding hills and coastal plain, and the sight-lines so formed apparently yield a number of accurate calendar dates and lunar alignments. The stone itself has a

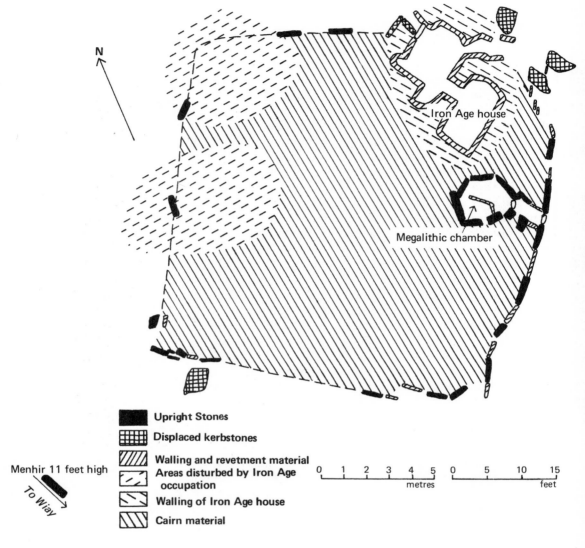

N

Iron Age house

Megalithic chamber

| | |
|---|---|
| ■ | Upright Stones |
| ▦ | Displaced kerbstones |
| ▨ | Walling and revetment material |
| ▱ | Areas disturbed by Iron Age occupation |
| ▨ | Walling of Iron Age house |
| ▨ | Cairn material |

Menhir 11 feet high

To Wiay

0 1 2 3 4 5
metres

0 5 10 15
feet

Excavation plan of the chambered cairn at Uneval, North Uist.

slightly concave right-hand face, and its front and rear edges are sharply defined. If you stand behind it, the stone indicates a small bump on the level south-east horizon, as accurately as could possibly be expected from the positioning of a single stone. The bump is in fact the island of Wiay, thirteen and a half miles away, and when the midsummer full moon rose so that its lower edge could be seen on the left-hand side of the island, this defined one limit of the wobble (to an accuracy of four minutes) and when it rose on another occasion so that its lower edge was visible on the right-hand side, this marked the other limit of the wobble (to an accuracy of two minutes). The stone is positioned perfectly 'on target' and though

View from the menhir at Uneval to the south-east, with the island of Wiay visible as a small horizon bump in the centre of the picture, $13\frac{1}{2}$ miles away.

the precision of the foresight is not as high as in other cases, the use of the site as a lunar observatory is quite plausible.

The other standing stone, some eleven feet tall, is beautifully situated in rolling pastureland high above the port of Campbeltown, on the eastern end of the Kintyre peninsula. On three sides the outlook is relatively restricted by rising ground, but to the south and south-west there is a splendid view towards a number of hills, each about a thousand feet high. The visitor's attention is certainly drawn to the slopes of Ben Ghuilean, just two miles due south of the stone across Campbeltown Loch, with its impressive, high undulating outline. There would certainly have been no difficulties encountered with atmospheric refraction using a foresight so far above ground and sea level. At its southern extreme the moon would move almost horizontally across a shallow dip (full of suitable notches) and its upper edge would pass exactly behind the highest peak of all, very nearly due south. Its absolute maximum sweep of the sky, with an extra nine minutes added to its southern limit, would make its upper edge line up behind a lower peak on the opposite side of the dip. The change in the moon's path, though small, could

The eleven-foot high standing stone overlooking Campbeltown in Kintyre. The foresight is the series of bumps on the ridge immediately to the right of the stone, due south and only two miles away.

surely have been observed against this varied skyline.

The foresight at Campbeltown is, however, not indicated by the flat side of a thin slab. There is a prominent pattern of cup-mark carvings near the top of the stone facing the foresight, but the stone itself is quite thick and if anything is turned at right angles to the required direction. Thom suggests an ingenious reason for the apparent failure of the builders to mark the Campbeltown sight-line with the flat face of a stone. Because the moon's path across the sky each month was very nearly horizontal, the observer's successive positions would not have been on a line to one side of the stone as at Leacach, but up and down the field, in line with the foresight. If a stone turned at right angles to the row of observer's stakes was usual at other sites, it could explain the very rough orientation of the Campbeltown stone. Still, the astronomical alignment is *not* indicated by the remains on the site, and while it may be perfectly true that other stones or markers in the right place could have disappeared, only excavation can prove this. Until such confirmation, the lunar observatory at Campbeltown must remain as an interesting speculation.

A consideration of these two sites shows the variations between individual megalithic observatories and the importance of carefully evaluating the evidence on the spot. Anyone who troubles to visit these impressive menhirs can judge for himself, without any knowledge of surveying or astronomy, how clearly the foresights proposed by Thom are identifiable among the local topography or are indicated by the stone itself.

In any case, the eclipse prediction theory does not rest entirely on the evidence of these single menhirs, but on the extraordinary detail with which Thom has reconstructed the work undertaken at complex sites such as Temple Wood. A full understanding of how these megalithic sites *could* have been used as observatories can only be gained from a careful reading of Thom's book, but we may note that the most accurate and astronomically useful sites do seem to coincide with the outstanding archaeological remains. For example, Temple Wood, an impressive X-shaped alignment of five standing stones, is situated close to one of the great cairns of the linear cemetery in the Kilmartin valley and about a mile from the earth circle and alignments at Ballymeanoch. The Temple Wood site refers us back to the observing technique probably used for the sun at Ballochroy, some thirty miles to the south. One of the 'arms' of the elongated X arrangement is precisely aligned on the peak of Bellanoch hill, a prominent foresight for the moon's

View of the X-shaped alignments at Temple Wood, Kilmartin, Argyll.

View towards the small observing notch on the horizon at Temple Wood, photographed here from the centre stone of the alignment. The insignificance of this notch is a key objection to the astronomical theory.

minimum position every 18·61 years. The sides of the stones themselves, however, clearly direct the eye 'forwards' to the hills immediately overlooking the site. In the same direction the observer also sees the Temple Wood stone circle, a very well preserved setting of low stones surrounding a large cist, and immediately above this circle on the hill horizon is a small and rather inconspicuous notch. The various stones in the Temple Wood alignment all indicate critical positions for an observer at the lunar maximum, including the 'peak' of the wobble, the most important sight-line of all, which is appropriately marked by the centre stone of the X, perhaps the most striking of the five megaliths. So Temple Wood could have operated as a self-contained observatory, with all the facilities necessary to observe both maximum and minimum limits of the moon about every nine years, and this unusual combination of sight-lines may account for the highly distinctive layout of the site.

But we may recall that *none* of these monuments would have been of much practical use for predicting eclipses without some means of deducing the extreme position reached by the moon each month on the basis of only two or three nightly observations. Thom has put forward complex mathematical arguments which show that what was needed at each site was a fundamental length (which he calls G) depending on how far away the foresight was from the observer, and G would enable him to discover how far to the 'left' or 'right' of previous observations the monthly extreme had actually occurred. We would expect to find evidence of this length recorded at the lunar sites, and Thom has accounted for certain features at Temple Wood in exactly this way. He develops the argument further, however, to suggest a purpose for the mysterious stone 'fans' of Caithness, including the alignments of over 200 stones at Mid Clyth. A 'grid' pattern, such as he has

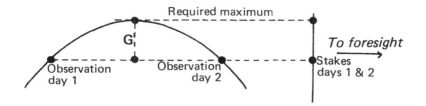

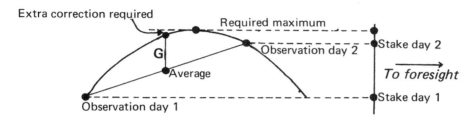

How megalithic astronomers might have found the extreme positions of the moon each month, according to Professor Thom, either by observing along one line (*right*) or spacing out successive observations (*left*). In the unlikely event of the extreme occurring exactly midway between two observations (*top*) then the required correction was the length G. More often the markers would indicate the situation shown in the bottom diagram, where an extra correction to G itself was required. Were the megalith builders capable of such systematic intellectual refinement, vital for eclipse prediction? Or were they merely interested in recording maximum and minimum lunar positions?

Average between 2 observations = EC = CB
  Required extra correction = BC−DE

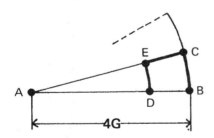

How part of a stone fan such as Mid Clyth could have been used to calculate the correction to G.

superimposed on a plan of Mid Clyth, would allow the observers to find the correction needed for the length G if the distance between successive observations was at all appreciable.

After the problems associated with the Aubrey Holes, we should perhaps beware of accepting any monuments as calculating devices, but these stone fans have rather more requirements to fulfil than any simple coincidence of numbers. The existence of a near-by lunar observatory has to be proved, this will determine the length of G recorded by the fan, and the radius of the outer perimeter of the fan must be exactly 4G. The correspondence between the six stone fans analysed

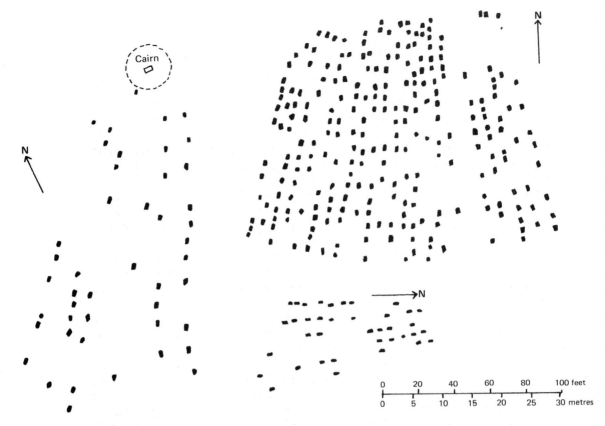

Crude nineteenth-century surveys of stone fan sites at Garrywhin (*left*) Mid Clyth (*top*) and Camster, all in Caithness. These show more stones than in Professor Thom's plans, but their accuracy, orientation and scale are not reliable.

in this way and the theoretical length of G calculated for each site is generally impressive. Once set up, these remarkable constructions would have been fairly simple to operate as calculating devices, although obviously the thought behind them was neither simple nor perhaps entirely credible, depending on how we imagine the mental capabilities of people in northern Britain about four thousand years ago.

Thom's latest work, therefore, sets forward the idea that a fairly systematic programme of lunar research was undertaken during this period for the purposes of eclipse prediction, and that this research was generally successful, otherwise we would not find the critical positions so accurately marked by observatories such as Temple Wood. Whether we agree with the theory or not perhaps depends more than anything on a factor difficult to be sure of at the best of times—the British weather. Several of the observatories, including Mid Clyth, involve small foresights over fifty miles away, and one important Welsh alignment (Parc-y-Meirw in Pembrokeshire) is linked with Mount Leinster in Ireland, 91 miles away across the Irish Sea. Can we be sure such foresights would be visible, even under ideal atmospheric conditions, for long enough periods? Consider how critical it would have been if one month's observations were obscured by cloud. Then there would probably not be enough observations to find the peak of the wobble, and in certain cases perhaps eighteen years would have to pass before another opportunity presented itself. Indeed, would the observers originally have been able to detect a regular pattern in the moon's small variations at all? It is the opinion of the Cambridge astronomer, Dr D. C. Heggie, that these difficulties would have made such a programme impractical, and that the interpretation of some of the lunar sight-lines as indications of the lunar wobble may be due to other, perhaps coincidental, factors. While the sub-Boreal period of climate in about 2000 BC was probably much warmer and drier than today, with an absence of strong westerly winds, the whole question of megalithic astronomy depends on problematical weather factors such as horizon haze which need to be carefully evaluated by the experts.

It should be obvious that the astronomical techniques summarized here demanded some degree of abstract theorizing from the megalithic observers. If we are to accept the methods for correcting observations associated with the length G and the stone fans of Caithness, the observers must also have been able to consider their problems in a purely geometrical form, based on some unit of length. Broader evidence for the geometrical skills of early Britain has been another principal focus for Professor Thom's work, and it is perhaps the most controversial one. Throughout forty years of research, he has built up a remarkable corpus of accurate surveys of stone circles, and with these he has demonstrated beyond any reasonable doubt that a large proportion of these monuments are not true circles at all. Poorly defined circles would naturally arise from the modern displacement of stones or from irregularities in the ground, but the regular distortions of outline found at dozens of sites cannot be explained away with such ease. Perhaps the best plan for someone not quite able to believe in the evidence of these surveys is to go to a well-preserved site such as Torhouse or Castle Rigg, equipped with enough string to cover the approximate radius. From the ground some of these distortions are very hard to see, but if the rough centre of the ring is found, and an attempt made with the string to 'draw' a perfect circle around the perimeter of the stones, they will in many cases immediately be apparent. Often one edge of the ring will be 'flattened' inwards (as at the two sites mentioned) or the visitor may be lucky and encounter one of the few special egg-shaped rings, where one end of the circle has been elongated outwards (as at Woodhenge or Lough Gur, Circle C). There are a number of true elliptical rings (most clearly seen at the small Nine Stones site in Dorset). Thom has also shown that more complex designs may have existed, involving various combinations of arcs, culminating in the remarkable layout proposed for Avebury, so obviously not a true circle, but (according to the Professor) an intricate arrangement of seven huge related arcs.

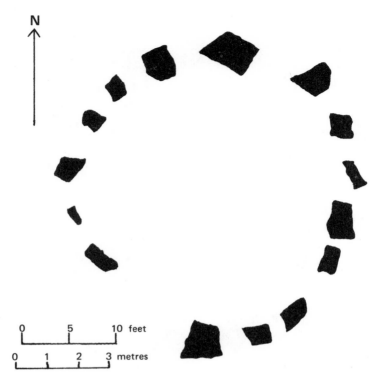

N

| 0 | 5 | 10 feet |
| 0 | 1 | 2 | 3 metres |

The ring at Lough Gur, County Limerick, consisting of large flat blocks of stone (Windle's site C). In Windle's 1912 survey, reproduced here, the stones seem to define the classic Thom egg-shape Type I.

What are we to make of the strange shapes which the megaliths mark out on the ground? The astronomy has shown that their erectors were concerned with the regular movements of the sun and moon, and that they were also in a position to detect apparent irregularities caused by refraction, by the slightly unequal periods between the solstices, and perhaps even by the lunar wobble, if its nature was imperfectly understood. Supposing that the megalith builders were interested in the most rudimentary geometrical constructions, using some unit of length. Probably the first thing they would notice would be that it is impossible to draw a circle and make all its dimensions come out as whole units. If you select a certain number of units for the diameter of a circle, the perimeter will always be almost exactly three times larger, but with some fraction of the unit left over. This, of course, is the relationship known as $\pi$, a number that can never be resolved, which might be said to be the primary 'irregularity' of mathematics. If the circle were for any reason considered as an important figure, perhaps if it had acquired some symbolic significance, the impossibility of setting out a perfectly integral circle would have been a most puzzling fact. Thom's work demonstrates that the distorted circles may be an attempt to rationalize the $\pi$ relationship, to lengthen or shorten the circumference of the figure in a symmetrical way and so produce a

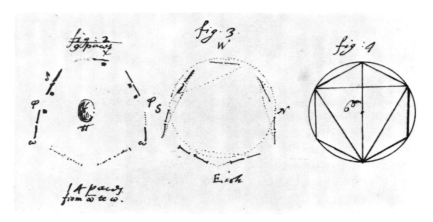

One of the first attempts to impose geometrical order on a megalithic site: John Aubrey's sketch of the trilithons at Stonehenge, from the *Monumenta Britannica*.

geometrical pattern with all the principal measurements as integral units.

This theory requires a unit of length to be used at every site, and it might be a reasonable assumption that neighbouring rings would share some common measurement. But Thom's analysis of over 150 circle diameters throughout the country concludes that there was one standard unit of length in use from the north of Scotland to the south of England, and that this unit is now known to a greater level of accuracy than any other ancient measurement. It was exactly 2·72 feet long (the megalithic yard) and the range of deviation present in the diameters analysed to support this unit is so narrow that yardsticks must have been sent out from some central source and not measured off one from another, otherwise progressive errors would have crept into the figures. Professor Thom's conclusions carry with them the inescapable picture of megalithic yard 'inspectors' who might have supervised the local setting-out and construction of stone circles.

Since the final publication in 1967 of the statistical material on which the evidence for the megalithic yard is based, the accuracy and value of this length have been the subject of considerable debate among a number of well-known mathematicians. The problem posed by Thom's measurements is to deduce the possible existence of a standard unit from an assortment of circle diameters of all sizes. Until 1956 a statistical theory for dealing with such a problem was not even known, and its application to the megalithic data is still full of difficulties. A recent study by J. Patrick examined the diameters from the circular sites according to their archaeological groupings. The results show that in some cases other values agree with the evidence better than the basic unit proposed by Thom (the 'megalithic fathom' of 5·44 feet, or two megalithic yards). Even if it is accepted that the rings *were* set out under some kind of unified geometrical system, the precision of the measurement is a critical factor and is still being debated. It is genuinely difficult for a non-statistician to decide between the arguments. The *accurate* measuring of lengths along the circumference of a circle or at the end of an egg-shape would surely have been a problem if uniform straight 'yardsticks' were in use. Instead, it could be that at each site a person's height was measured off for a rough basic unit, and that the figure of 5·44 feet which emerges from the data could represent the average height of the late Neolithic and Bronze Age population! Yet against such an attractively simplified idea, there is the apparent high accuracy of the megalithic yard as demonstrated by Thom at the Ring of Brogar and at Avebury, where a value of 2·73 feet would have made his construction fall about five feet outside the line of the stones.

Another problematical question is how the designs were set out. Professor Thom bases the construction of his elliptical and egg-shaped types on at least three different sizes of true Pythagorean triangles, that is, right-angled triangles where the lengths of all the sides are whole numbers. The mathematical sophistication implied by this knowledge may be set against an alternative theory developed from an analysis of the deviation of constructional lines by B. R. Hallam. He proposes that *all* the megalithic shapes could be drawn by various arrangements of no more than two circles or arcs, set out with comparatively little need for mathematical skill. At the present stage of research, it is difficult to decide which answer is the right one.

To illustrate this problem in greater detail, the case of Woodhenge is of special interest. Woodhenge is the name given to the pattern of post-holes first discovered

The method of constructing a megalithic egg-shape as defined by Professor Thom, based on Pythagorean triangles, and (*right*) the simpler technique proposed by B. R. Hallam. The correct answer depends on complex study of the errors between these constructions and the actual surveys.

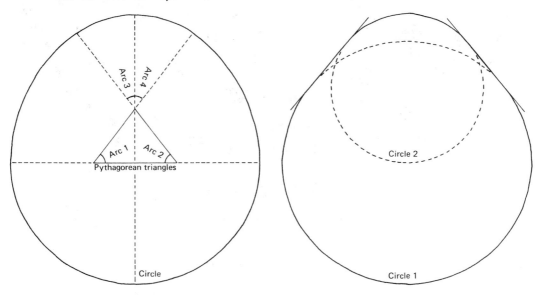

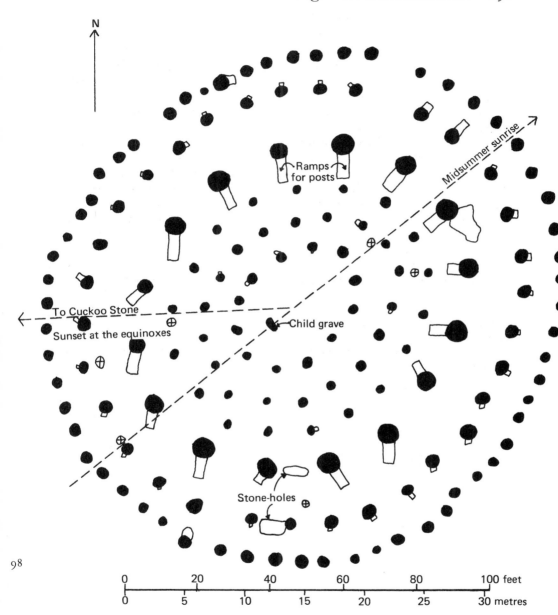

N

Ramps
for posts

Midsummer sunrise

To Cuckoo Stone
Sunset at the equinoxes

Child grave

Stone-holes

98

| 0 | 20 | 40 | 60 | 80 | 100 feet |
| 0 | 5 | 10 | 15 | 20 | 25 | 30 metres |

A copy of the Cunningtons' original survey of Woodhenge.

from the air in 1925 and subsequently excavated by Mr and Mrs M. E. Cunnington, who left small concrete posts to mark the positions of the holes. Professor Thom has accurately surveyed these posts and superimposes six egg-shaped rings to fit their outline, all based on a Pythagorean triangle with the proportions 12, 35, 37. The radius of each ring has been chosen such that successive perimeters are multiples of twenty megalithic yards, a remarkable mathematical feat.

But this conclusion poses some difficulties of interpretation. If Woodhenge had been set out simply to commemorate this geometrical exercise, we would expect high precision in the placing of posts along the circumference of each ring. In fact there are many post-holes which diverge appreciably from Professor Thom's construction. Can we be sure that the concrete posts were set up exactly in the excavated post-holes? Look at the Cunningtons' original survey (which may simply be less accurate than Thom's) and there are slight differences noticeable in the placing of certain posts. In any case, after the evidence of Marden, Mount Pleasant and neighbouring Durrington Walls, it is hard to see these large-scale settings of posts as anything other than roofed timber buildings. Dr Wainwright and Mr C. R. Musson have plausibly suggested that Woodhenge represents a two-phase timber structure, the later building (supported by the outer three post rings) an enlargement of the first. Should the vivid archaeological picture of communal activities built up át the other sites by Dr Wainwright and his colleagues be allowed to rule out the claims for megalithic mathematicians?

The Cunningtons were themselves interested in a numerical and astronomical approach to Woodhenge, and they first pointed out that the long axis of the post setting indicates midsummer sunrise. Other possible sighting directions, including an equinox line to the west, are suggested by significant gaps or displacements of posts in the rings. One is irresistibly reminded of the orientation discovered at several Egyptian temples by Sir Norman Lockyer, by which the sun must have illuminated the corridors of the building at sunrise or sunset at key points in the calendar. It was the excavator's view that the Woodhenge rings had been measured off from true circles, and this accounts satisfactorily for some of the posts which are out of line. Certainly some care *was* taken in the layout of this elongated building, since the number of posts in the six rings, counting from the centre, are respectively 12, 18, 18, 16, 32 and 60. The regularly increasing perimeters discovered by Thom are an inherent part of the structure, whether the unit used is metres, feet, megalithic yards or a person's height. Such careful proportions are arguments for a high level of architectural, if not mathematical, thinking. The remarkable ground plan recovered at Mount Pleasant must have been set out with equal deliberation, since there are exactly the same number of posts in each quadrant formed by the four corridors of the building. Whatever the subsequent uses of these timber monuments, it is probable that there was a preliminary planning stage during which the shape, numerical properties and perhaps orientation of the building were considered, either for esoteric purposes or in the interests of pleasing architecture. It should be added that a thorough analysis of the Durrington Walls post settings by Professor Atkinson fails to reveal any evidence that the megalithic yard was used in their construction.

Should some of these criticisms encourage general scepticism about the concept of megalithic geometry, it is worth studying a group of stone circles not actually surveyed by Professor Thom but by one of his colleagues, Dr A. E. Roy of Glasgow University. The circles are situated on Machrie Moor, on the west coast of the island of Arran, and two of them are related 'egg-shapes' of a type that cannot be matched up with the general categories proposed by Thom. Circle No 1 of the Machrie Moor group, however, is a classic example of megalithic geometry.

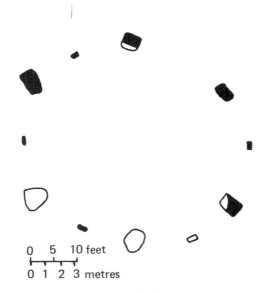

0   5   10 feet

0  1  2  3 metres

The elliptical stone ring surveyed by Dr A. E. Roy on Machrie Moor, Aran. The regular alternation of large and small granite and sandstone slabs is very striking.

A true ellipse, such as could easily be set out by a loop of rope drawn taut around two pegs not far apart, fits the eleven stones of the ring very satisfactorily. Six large granite boulders alternate with five small sandstone slabs in so regular a formation that their symmetrical placing around the ring can hardly be due to accident. A pair of granite blocks indicates the major axis of the ellipse, and it seems likely that the minor axis was once shown in a similar way by sandstone slabs, one of which has probably disappeared. Lines drawn from all the stones to the centre of the ellipse make eleven nearly equal angles of about thirty degrees. There is hardly any other conclusion to be drawn but that this stone circle was deliberately and carefully planned as a harmonious geometrical design, based on the ellipse

Professor Alexander Thom beside the Grand Menhir Brisé at Locmariaquer, Brittany.

which was not to be investigated by Greek mathematicians until well over a thousand years later.

Many equally convincing examples of specialized astronomical and geometrical knowledge can be found by anyone taking the trouble to study Professor Thom's work carefully. These new discoveries are in no sense the one solution to all the problems associated with many megalithic sites, and indeed the geometrical shapes recorded by the stone rings surely makes their function and purpose all the more mysterious. But a critical study of the astronomical theories proposed for Ballochroy or Temple Wood adds an important new dimension to our understanding of early Britain. However it may qualify his conclusions, archaeology owes an immense debt to Alexander Thom for single-handedly recovering our respect for the intellectual capabilities of Neolithic and Bronze Age people. The meticulous standard of his research, with a notable absence of the kind of speculation that beset Lockyer's work, is not likely to be repeated by many investigators in the future.

# 9: The Mystery of the Carvings

There are dozens of rock faces, cist covers and standing stones all over Britain which show evidence of the megalith builders' strange ideas. Immense labour was once expended on these stone surfaces, carving them into abstract ornamental designs that defy easy explanation. The problem is similar to that of the stone circles with which these markings are often associated: the same formal patterns occur over and over again at sites sometimes separated by hundreds of miles of land and water. Simple, apparently haphazard, arrangements of cup-marks, which could almost be the equivalent of megalithic 'doodles', are often found side by side with complex spirals and concentric circles that might have been executed by skilled craftsmen. The meaning of these symbols (if symbols they are) remains obstinately closed to us.

The cup-and-ring marks have a much shorter history of antiquarian interest than other megalithic monuments. Apart from one rather dubious early reference in the ancient Welsh annals, the *Triads of the Island of Britain*, mentioning the stones of Gwidden-Ganhebon, on which 'one could read the arts and sciences of the world' and to the 'astronomer Gwydon-ap Don' who was buried at Caernarvon 'under a Stone of Enigmas', the carvings seemed to escape the attentions of local folklore and Druid-minded scholars alike. The first drawing known of a cup-and-ring marking was made by Col. Montgomery in 1785, and showed the cover of a cist found at Coilsfield in Ayrshire, decorated with a spiral, cup and six concentric circles. In the 1820s one site at Old Bewick among the remarkable Northumberland group of carvings was discovered, but the first controversy over their date and purpose did not begin until the investigation of the Roughting Linn rocks by the well known barrow digger, Canon William Greenwell, in 1852. The famous Roughting Linn carvings are among the most spectacular in the country, for an extensive area of undulating sandstone is profusely ornamented with cup-marks and concentric circles broken and linked to one another by radial grooves. Canon Greenwell also found an unusual group of carvings, consisting of roughly triangular and rectangular 'rings' enclosing a random set of cups, superficially resembling the plans of Iron Age hill-forts. The improper understanding of the comparative date of these monuments, as well as the fact that the Roughting Linn figures as well as several other Northumberland sites lay very close to the remains of actual later forts, led Greenwell to propose the popular theory that cup-and-ring markings represented the plans of fortifications or settlements. The dramatic positioning of nearly all such carvings on prominent horizontal masses of rock, usually commanding extensive views, makes the idea of prehistoric maps less improbable

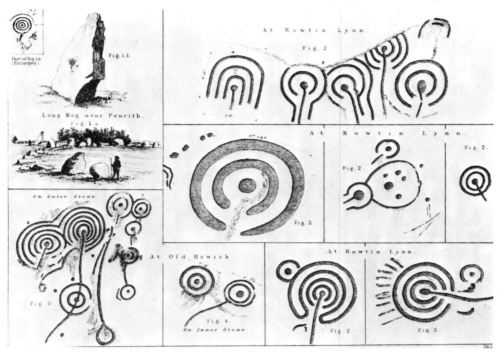

An 1860 engraving of cup-and-ring marks, mainly from the Northumberland group.

than it might at first seem. But this theory was challenged by George Tate in 1865 in a most interesting survey of the Northumberland cup-and-ring marks.

> I cannot regard them [he wrote] as the amusements of an idle soldiery, nor as plans of camps, nor as exercises of incipient engineers; for their wide distribution, and notwithstanding differences in detail, their family resemblance prove that they had a common origin and indicate that the whole of Britain was peopled by one race, who were imbued with the same superstitions, and expressed them by the same symbols.

His summary of the problem still cannot be bettered for its expression of the remarkable unity that lies behind these carvings.

> Look at the extent of their distribution, from one extremity of Britain to the other, and even into Ireland; and say, what could induce tribes, living hundreds of miles apart and even separated by the sea, to use precisely the same symbols, save to express some religious sentiment, or to aid in the performance of some superstitious rites . . .

Furthermore, Tate felt that the cup-and-ring markings were not related to the art

A cup-and-ring design rubbed from a rock on Drumtroddan Farm, Wigtownshire.

of the megalithic tombs, although he did not realize that the tombs were likely to be earlier than the cups and rings:

> The scroll, zigzac and lozenge figures at New Grange and in Brittany are probably only ornamental, and the work of a later age.

The first attempt to impose a typological sequence on British prehistoric carvings was made in the 1930s by the Abbé Breuil, the world famous expert on Palaeolithic cave paintings. He was sure that the cup-and-ring marks were closely related to the megalithic tomb art not only of Ireland and Brittany, but also of Spain and Malta. Moreover, all the carvings could be interpreted as stylized human figures or faces, and standing stones were probably put up to represent people.

> ... everything seems to show [he claimed] that after the erection of the menhir in honour of the memory of some person, elementary human faces

continued to be cut on it by succeeding generations.

While there is not much disagreement that *some* of the Brittany tomb carvings represent female figures, the case that all the prehistoric rock designs are explicable in this way is hard to accept.

Where did the cup-and-ring style originate? Did it in fact come from the art of the great tombs, which seems to have a wider range of symbol and motif? The spirals of Newgrange, so often grouped into balanced and pleasing patterns, contrast with the apparently random repetition of cups and encircling rings over large natural rock surfaces. Isolated spirals are found on cup-and-ring stones, but they are not very common and usually appear to be more regular and formal than the Newgrange series. At other major decorated tombs, however, such as neighbouring Knowth and the great cemetery at Loughcrew, there are gapped concentric circles and cups which seem much closer to common cup-and-ring motifs.

Even at Newgrange, there are less prominent carvings which usually escape the visitor's eye, and these are comparable to simple cup-marks. Dots and concentric circles have recently been found, scratched in profusion on the back faces of some of the exterior kerbstones. One of these slabs was decorated with nearly 100 motifs, mainly dots, cups and concentric circles, and was built into the mound so that these carvings would never have been seen. Much of this decoration may be the equivalent of 'doodling' by the craftsmen and builders who erected the tomb. However, if we consider, say, the cup-and-four-rings discovered on the back of a corbelling slab over the main passage to be a genuine cup-and-ring carving, then this style seems to have been current by the time Newgrange was built in 3300 BC. While the cups and rings of Cork and Kerry give a very different impression to a visitor than Newgrange and Knowth, yet these 'graffiti' may provide a connection.

Confirmation of the idea of a long tradition behind the carvings seems to come from cup-marked stones often found in Scottish chambered tombs, and from a slab recently uncovered in a long barrow at Dalladies, Kincardineshire, probably dating from the start of the fourth millennium. These simple markings, then, seem to go right back to the days of the early farmers.

The development of the cup-and-ring marks, however, was not as widespread as this might suggest. Their distribution in Ireland roughly overlaps with the pattern of stone circles through Wicklow, Waterford, Cork, Kerry and Donegal. Similarly, some major Scottish concentrations appear side by side with the important megalithic monuments, especially in the Kilmartin valley, and sometimes on the stones themselves, such as the spiral at the Temple Wood stone circle. But in many other regions it has been observed that the location of the carvings corresponds more closely to that of later Bronze Age sites rather than to the pattern of standing stone monuments. Despite the obvious importance of centres such as Callanish, no carvings are found in the Western Isles (except for a few isolated cup-marks on North Uist) and their absence from the south of Britain is even more puzzling. At Came Down on the Dorset ridgeway, a barrow was

12 inches

30 centimetres

The Swastika Stone, Wood-
house Crag, and (*right*) patterns
on the Hanging Stones, Ilkley
Moor, West Yorkshire.

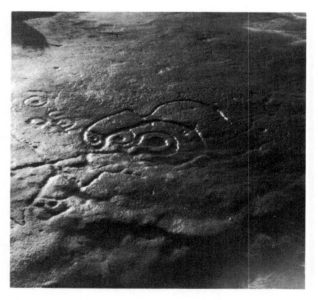

opened in the last century which contained two flat slabs placed over successive cairns, both marked with concentric circles. Small cup-marked stones are quite frequently encountered in West Country barrows, but if these carvings symbolized the religious thought of the megalith builders, where are the great designs we would expect to find at Stanton Drew, Avebury or Stonehenge?

In some previous studies, too much has been made of fortuitous resemblances between carvings in different regions or other countries, but anyone comparing the most elaborately ornamented rocks in Northumberland, the Yorkshire West

Riding or the mid-Argyll region can hardly fail to be impressed by the correspondence in the basic motifs—the cup, concentric rings and radial grooves, which appear time after time. Yet definite regional styles and variations are detectable; for example, there are the distinctive 'ladder' patterns diverging from the central cup, which characterize some of the Ilkley Moor carvings. They can be seen all around the edge of the moor, usually on the flat millstone grit outcrops which project forward over the slopes with dramatic views of the Wharfe and Aire valleys below. Some of the markings are close to the nine ring cairns or stone circles scattered over the moor. Here and there, interspersed with the familiar concentric circle patterns, are rocks with surprising variations on the cup-and-ring motifs, such as the famous Swastika Stone on Woodhouse Crag, with a symmetrical layout so unusual that it has often been attributed to the Iron Age despite the presence of imitations on other rocks in 'classic' cup-and-ring style. Also perched high over the town of Ilkley are the bizarre patterns recorded on the Hanging Stones, while by contrast, the visitor to Rivock Edge, on the other side of the moor, can find next to some simple cups a remarkable four-feet long 'comet' marking. These examples give some idea of the variety present within any one area of cup-and-ring carving, which makes any attempts to relate the rocks in a stylistic sequence very difficult (especially when some of the more complex designs have weathered badly enough to make their outlines uncertain or deceptively simple).

The main interest for anyone studying the West Yorkshire group, however, is the relationship between the diverse Ilkley Moor patterns and the clusters of simple cup-marks found at the neighbouring hill-tops of Baildon and Snowden Moors. Both of these concentrations seem to be different in character from the Ilkley markings, although they are only about three miles away and some common motifs can certainly be identified. But the Baildon Moor carvings are all on small, unimpressive boulders, laid almost flush with the surrounding turf on the flat hill-top, and they consist mainly of cups inside roughly executed rings or enclosures. These markings may be contemporary with a small number of cairns built round the hill, which probably have a date well into the Bronze Age. On Snowden Moor, north of the River Wharfe, the cup arrangements are generally similar, although in two cases they are linked by curving lines which have given rise to vivid local nicknames—the Tree of Life Stone and the Death's Head Stone. The skull-like Death's Head marking may be an attempt to produce a symmetrical pattern, based on a triangle, fairly similar to the Swastika Stone. Are these outlying cup-and-ring marks therefore decadent and degenerate copies of the Ilkley Moor rocks, or could they be primitive early attempts? If all the West Yorkshire markings are roughly contemporary with one another, there must be some reason for the local differences. Even more marked variations of style are to be seen in the Kilmartin valley in Argyll, between the Cairnbaan rocks and the relatively crude Kilmichael Glassary carvings.

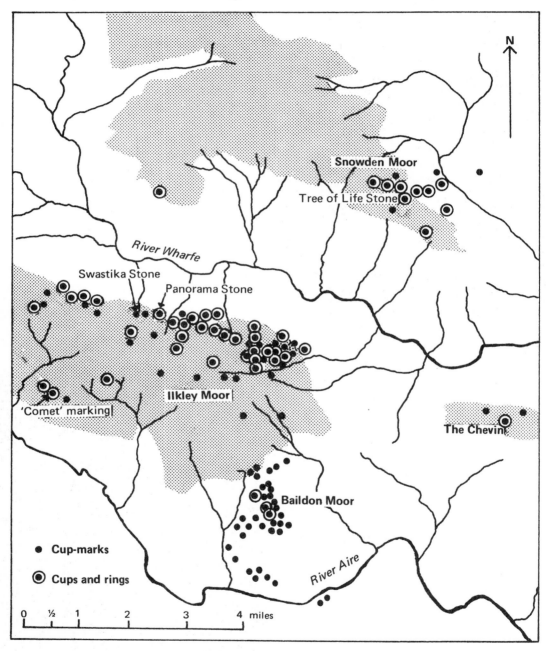

Cup-and-ring marks in the Aire and Wharfe districts of the Yorkshire West Riding.

Cup-mark patterns at Baildon Moor and (*right*) the Tree of Life Stone, Snowden Moor.

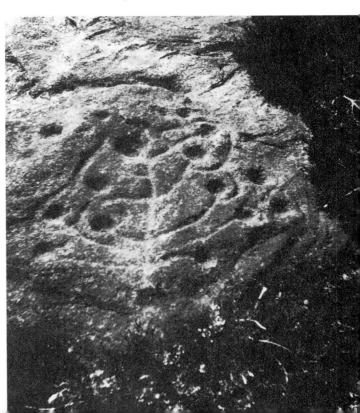

Is it possible to make any informed guesses about the purposes of the cup-and-ring marks? The use of the designs on cist covers makes it clear that they were connected with religious beliefs in some way. The presence of the markings on standing stones such as those at Temple Wood and Long Meg shows that they were never devised to contain liquids such as blood, and indeed the fact that the radial grooves frequently lead away from the cup and ring down the slope of the rock has suggested their use as drains to keep the carving surface clean. They could certainly have been painted, and any number of close anthropological parallels may be found to account for their symbolic significance. For example, Australian aborigines still produce ceremonial ground drawings with concentric circles and spirals, recreating the journey of their ancestors' spirit into the physical world. Bronze Age Scandinavian rock art, although it is rather unlikely to have been influenced by the ideas of British cup-and-ring carving, may provide a clue since it sometimes features representational scenes with circles that appear to stand for the sun. Pilgrims in East Tibet still make cup-marks by grinding a pebble as they walk round and round a rock, always in the same direction, and after which they pick up the stone dust with a finger and lick it.

Mr Ronald Morris has studied the southern Scottish groups for many years, and produced one of the first comprehensive surveys of the scores of markings in this area. Perhaps the most significant result of his analysis is that the distribution of the carvings coincides to a remarkable degree with deposits of copper and gold in the district. Professor Stuart Piggott has independently suggested that they represent metal prospectors' magic or else their trade-marks, an idea reinforced by the axe carvings found with cups on a cist cover from the Kilmartin linear cemetery. But the spread of the cup-and-ring marks might equally well coincide

An intriguing contrast in patterns between two rocks only a few hundred feet apart at Derrynablaha, County Kerry.

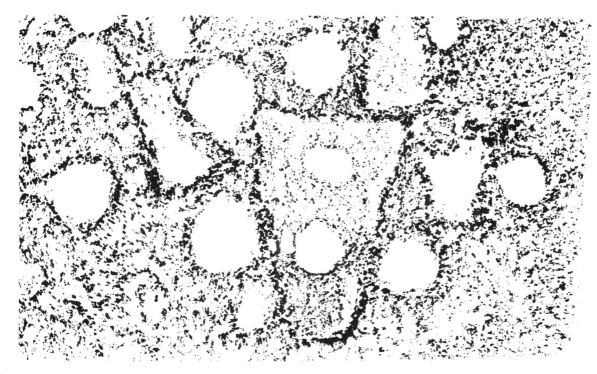

Detail from the lower surface of a cist cover in Nether Largie North Cairn, from the linear cemetery near Kilmartin. Carvings which almost certainly represent flanged bronze axes appear alongside ordinary cup-marks.

with the pattern of prehistoric settlement, if only we knew the picture more fully than we do. In any case, everyone has a private explanation for the carvings. Mr Morris's study lists what might be thought to be fifteen 'sensible' different possibilities that have been suggested to him by other publications and by private individuals (including the idea of the markings as tattooists' show-cases) and then lists 'at least ten other theories—more or less fanciful' which include 'adder lairs, knife-sharpening holes, moulds for metals, sex-rites, masonic marks, grinding mills, anvil stones, lamps, early writings, and the druids'.

Not surprisingly, recent studies have revived geometrical and astronomical interpretations that are in fact quite old. One of the nineteenth-century accounts of the Panorama Stones on Ilkley Moor by Nathan Heywood proposes that simple cup-marks represent the fixed stars, and the concentric circle designs the planets, with the rings intended to give the appearance of motion. The 'ladder' patterns on the Panorama Stones,

> . . . may have been intended as emblematical of some mysterious connection
> of the earth with the heavens or planets . . . The markings . . . perhaps were
> utilised to explain the motion of the planets round the fixed stars.

Dr Ludovic Maclellan Mann obtained rubbings of a number of the southern Scottish carvings and wrote a pamphlet in 1915, linking the geometry of the

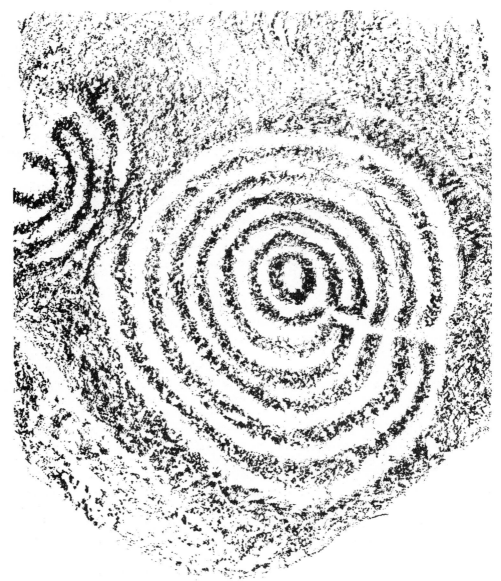

The magnificent spiral carved on a block of whinstone not far from the stone circle and cairn cemetery at Cauldside Burn, Kirkcudbright.

cup-and-ring marks with the arcs and ellipses he had observed in the layout of the 'horned' Caithness cairns.

> The positions of these curved figures were studiously prearranged . . . The apparently isolated cairns, the groups of standing stones far distant from each other, and the detached sets of rock carvings well removed from each other, may all form part of one widely spread design; and the surveyor of prehistoric monuments should endeavour to show this relationship in his charts.

But the relationships which Mann discovered in his rubbings were based on what was surely the fortuitous lining up of cup-and-ring features when radiating lines were drawn from one or two fixed points on the plan. The astronomical approach was tried with greater success by G. F. Browne in one of the most remarkable of all the speculative books on megalithic monuments, published by Cambridge University Press in 1921. This was a detailed study of the Aberdeenshire stone circles and also of the cup-marks found on the recumbent stones at various sites. The pattern traced from the seventeen-feet-long Sunhoney stone showed the correct relationships of the principal stars in the Hercules, Corona, Little and Great Bear constellations, forming an 'instruction chart on which the magician could teach his apprentice, instead of teaching him by pointing with his finger to the stars in the sky'. This suggestion, perhaps not altogether improbable in itself, was reinforced by a splendid shuffling of the evidence from the Rothiemay circle. Here no less than 107 cups may be counted on the flat stone, of which eight are surrounded by a single ring. If one of these eight, situated in the middle of the pattern, was regarded as the Pole Star, then the constellations and first magnitude stars (the other seven ringed cups) all appeared in their correct places *when the pattern was reversed in a mirror*. The explanation? The stone was used to 'print off' star charts onto skins laid face downwards with some adhesive colouring material, for the benefit of neighbouring magicians.

This and other less inspired speculations advise caution where the subject of cup-and-ring geometry is concerned, but Professor Thom's initial studies are characterized by his usual care and precision. From an examination of nearly sixty rubbings made by Ronald Morris and his colleague Mr D. C. Bailey, Professor Thom applies the same statistical tests as he used with the stone circles, this time deducing the existence of the megalithic inch, which has a value of ·816 inches, or exactly 1/40th of a megalithic yard. The results of the analysis show that in all cases the figures were set out measuring from the middle of the groove forming the ring. The shapes that Thom finds recorded in over a dozen exceptional non-circular designs all obey the rules that govern the geometry of the stone circles. They are based on Pythagorean triangles and the resulting constructions have perimeters with integral lengths. To set out designs of this accuracy, Thom proposes that the carving surfaces would be polished beforehand, and that trammels or beam compasses were used with points adjustable to within a few thousandths of an inch.

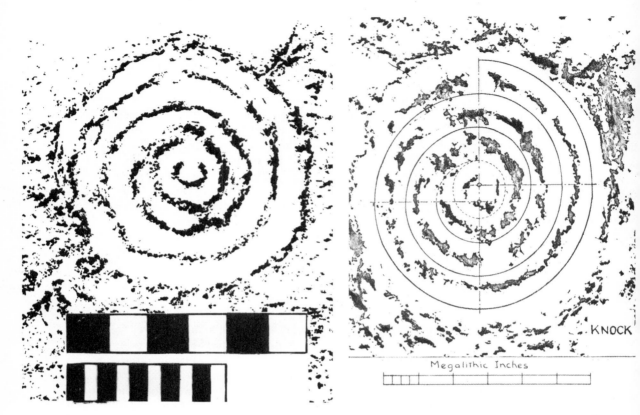

Megalithic Inches

KNOCK

The author's rubbing of the spiral at Knock, Wigtownshire, and the same carving (*right*) rubbed by Mr R. W. B. Morris, with a construction of half-ellipses superimposed by Professor Thom.

Anyone at all acquainted with cup-and-ring marks will probably find himself in two minds over such a theory. Professor Thom was kind enough to superimpose his elliptical construction over the author's rubbing of the Knock spiral, and the way in which the design 'sprang to life' and became clear, the construction accurately fitting the grooves in the stone, was very striking indeed. But the construction lines *do* determine the way we 'see' the rubbing, and on this small scale there is perhaps an element of subjectivity in choosing the right design to fit the rubbing that is usually absent from the large scale surveys of well-preserved stone circles. A slightly damaged ring or an error in rubbing (since it is very easy to 'interpret' the same feature of a cup-and-ring mark in different ways by various angles of rubbing) and the theoretical positioning of the middle of the groove will alter. This is a crucial consideration for the determining of values such as the megalithic inch and for superimposing constructions even as apparently successful as the case of the Knock pattern.

Yet it seems quite obvious to the author that many of the most complex of these

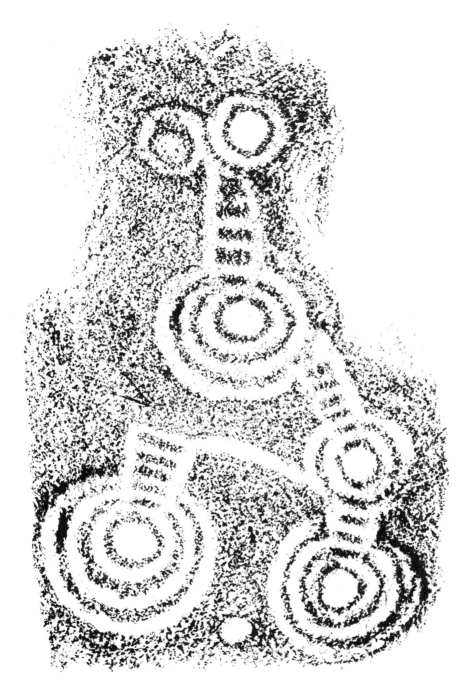

The strange design on one corner of the Panorama Stone, now enclosed by railings opposite St Margaret's Church, Ilkley. Note that the upper complex ring appears to be a spiral.

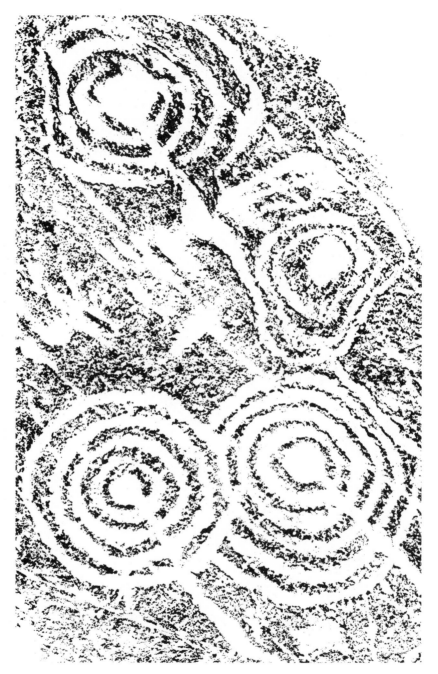

The huge concentration of carvings at Achnabreck, mid-Argyll, presents a bewildering range of form and workmanship. In this detail, well-executed patterns appear side-by-side with cruder carvings.

carvings *were* set out with geometrical skill of one kind or another, as in the case of the remarkable spiral at Cauldside Burn, curling outwards to meet a secondary gapped concentric circle motif beside it. Would it have been difficult to achieve the regular spacing of the rings by eye alone? Simple compasses might well have been used for drawing circular patterns on some other rocks. The regularity of the elongated designs on the Panorama Stone or at Cairnbaan may yet convince the sceptic that more complex geometrical techniques were being practised.

Whatever we think of the concept of mathematically precise rock carvings, the cup-and-ring marks do demonstrate the limits of a theory based on a purely mathematical interpretation of the past. Side by side with formally constructed patterns covering the huge rock surface at Achnabreck in Argyll (its Gaelic name is 'The Rock of the Host') are many cup-and-rings which have all too obviously been the result of 'freehand' work. Their outlines are sometimes deformed to avoid crevices and irregularities in the rock. Cup-mark arrangements such as characterize the Baildon and Snowden Moor groups are unlikely to have any plausible geometrical solution. The concentric circle motif must have had a significance beyond that of a mathematical puzzle or a geometrically pleasing design. It is the symbol of much that will never be known about early Britain.

# 10: 'That Regiment of Stones...'

The town of Carnac on the southern coast of Brittany is associated with a group of the most surprising and impressive ancient monuments in Europe. A visitor leaves the old town along a minor road to the hamlet of Le Menec, where a cluster of whitewashed cottages is encircled by an almost continuous ring of seventy large granite stones, forming an oval enclosure nearly 300 feet across. On the rocky ground to the east of this ring is the starting point for eleven lines of standing stones, and from this position the visitor has a view of 1,099 megaliths sloping away from him almost as far as the eye can see. The first glimpse of these alignments, since extensive restorations were carried out in the late nineteenth century, is now even more striking than it was for an early antiquary, the Chevalier de Fréminville, who described it in 1827:

> As I reached the top of the hill, the plain of Karnac suddenly spread itself out below me, and its wild heathland, the horizon fringed with pine woods, and above all the extraordinary view of that regiment of stones, the startling army of shapeless rocks so symmetrically aligned, filled me with astonishment.
>
> Surely nothing offers a greater, stranger or more singular spectacle than the assembly of these massive and gigantic monuments. Vainly the observer searches for some word to describe them, and when he has failed, is bound to confess that any idea or picture which he may previously have formed does not bear any relation to what is here before him. The numbers of these stones in their bizarre arrangements, the height reached by their long, grey, mossy outlines rising from the black heather in which they are rooted, and finally the absolute stillness that surrounds them, all astound the imagination and fill the soul with a melancholy veneration for these ancient witnesses of so many centuries.

As the visitor wanders among the Le Menec stones, perhaps sharing the thoughts and impressions of Fréminville, he may also become aware of less obvious features of the alignments: for example, the fact that the distance between the rows seems to increase towards the centre, while the rows themselves, in their present state, are not parallel at all. Individual lines wander appreciably from a straight path, perhaps as a result of faulty restoration. The most striking feature of all the Carnac alignments, however, is the way in which the megaliths decrease in size quite regularly from the enormous boulders that form the start of each series of avenues until, right at the end of the rows, the visitor is flanked by stones which are only two or three feet high. Another remarkable point is the overall gentle 'curve' of the alignments to the north-east, which cannot be explained by

A romantic lithograph of alignments at Carnac, from Godfrey Higgins' *The Celtic Druids* of 1829, based on the engravings of Cambry a quarter of a century before.

The alignments of Le Menec, looking west towards the hamlet and the cromlech.

any local irregularities in the terrain. The Le Menec lines eventually lead to the few probable remains of another stone ring, over half a mile from the starting point by the village.

Continuing up the road for a few hundred yards, the visitor arrives at the head of the Kermario alignments, which begin on an even grander scale than before. The stone ring that probably stood here has been obliterated by a modern car park, but the well-preserved chamber and passage of a megalithic tomb to the south have escaped destruction. All the Carnac stones are balanced almost on the bedrock, or else in the thin soil on which only heather and thick gorse bushes thrive, so that the erection of megaliths nearly twenty feet high at the beginning of the Kermario alignments must have been a considerable feat. After a short distance, the size of the stones rapidly diminishes as they run down into the valley close to La Petite-Métairie farm, and here three large menhirs interrupt the southern edge of the alignments, standing at right angles to their course. On the other side of the farm stands the tower of the old windmill, and from the top of its crumbling walls there is perhaps the strangest view in the whole of the Carnac region. At the foot of the tower and in each direction, east and west, lines of menhirs stretch away as far as the enveloping screen of pine forest. From this

Looking south-west from the tower of the old windmill along the alignments of Kermario.

distance, the scale of the rows on the other side of the valley is so diminished that irregularities in their course suggest the serpentine symbolism that was one common explanation of the monuments during the nineteenth century.

Towards the end of the Kermario group, the stones actually run over the top of a long earth mound which was excavated by Zacharie Le Rouzic in 1922. He discovered that the mound contained many arrangements of small stones in the form of cists or rings, filled with blackened earth and charcoal fragments, together with pieces of pottery and flint flakes, but without trace of human remains. The monument was surmounted by a standing stone much larger than the alignments all around it, and orientated in a quite different direction. Just below ground level, the excavators discovered five wavy lines carved near the base of the stone and close by were five small polished stone axes. These wavy lines have traditionally been interpreted as serpents, and seem to link the mound with the megalithic tomb art displayed at Gavrinis and elsewhere. Whether or not this gives us any clue to the date of the mound, the Kermario alignments are obviously later than this monument, and were perhaps deliberately directed towards it.

The next group of megaliths lies a little further to the east of Kermario, near the village of Kerlescan. At the edge of the forest clearing there is a most unusual setting of stones in the form of a 'square' with slightly rounded sides, and not far from this enclosure are thirteen alignments comprised of 540 standing stones. The Kerlescan rows may once have had some link with the arrangement of nearly 100 stones at Petit Menec, again a short distance away to the east.

Not surprisingly, these extraordinary monuments offered scope for every kind of inspired guess or speculation from the earliest days of antiquarian interest. Indeed, the local folklore associated with the alignments must have originated many centuries ago. The attractive church front in the town of Carnac bears the date 1639 together with a statue of the patron saint, St Cornély, blessing two paintings at his feet. The paintings depict bulls standing on fallen megaliths, while menhirs and 'dolmens' loom in the background. The story goes that St Cornély was once the Pope at Rome, until he was chased all the way to Brittany by Roman soldiers. When St Cornély saw that the ocean blocked his flight, he transformed the Roman army into stone. The part played by his baggage-carrying oxen in the story led pilgrims to bring their diseased cattle to Carnac to be cured. The early origins of this story and of the beliefs behind it (no doubt given a Christian basis by the Celtic missionaries who came to Brittany in the fifth century AD) were seemingly confirmed when Zacharie Le Rouzic and James Miln found the statue of a bull in the Gallo-Roman villa at Bosseno near Carnac. Further evidence came from the animal remains often found by them with burials of the prehistoric period. The saint's fair is still held on September 13, when cattle are drawn up in front of the church to be blessed and are then driven through the streets of the town in procession.

But this shadowy region of half-remembered folklore and superstition is far removed from the wild assumptions and heated academic debates of the last century, scornfully summarized in an essay by Gustave Flaubert in 1858:

> Those who like mythology see them as the Pillars of Hercules; those who like natural history see here a symbol of the Python. . . . Lovers of astronomy see a zodiac like M. de Cambry, who recognizes in these eleven lines of stone the twelve signs of the zodiac 'because it must be (he adds) that the ancient Gauls only had eleven signs of the zodiac'.
>
> Then a member of the Institute has speculated 'that this could well be the cemetery of the Veneti' who lived at Vannes six leagues away . . . Finally one man has come forward, a man touched with genius for antiquarian matters . . . to recognize the remains of a Roman camp, and to be precise the camp of Caesar, who raised these stones for the sole purpose of *propping up the tents of his soldiers and to prevent them from being blown away by the wind*. What squalls there must once have been on the Brittany coasts!

The fact that speculations on the purpose and date of the alignments have in any way advanced from this period of guesswork is mainly due to the activity of James Miln (a Scotsman) and to later excavations by Zacharie Le Rouzic, who established the basis of our knowledge about the Carnac megaliths and tombs.

Miln was able to show that the alignments belonged to an earlier period than the Gallo-Roman villa at Bosseno, which incorporated fragments of menhirs in its construction. However, there is still no precise evidence of the relationship between the alignments and any other kind of monument, with the exception of the Kermario long mound. The radiocarbon dates now available for Brittany have in any case considerably shaken confidence in quite long established suppositions such as those once made about the time-span of the megalithic tombs (the 'dolmens') and of the Neolithic occupation. We have seen that the Kercado tomb was apparently built a few centuries after 6000 BC, one of the earliest dates in Europe for such a monument. Yet it seems that megalithic tombs of a similar kind were continuously built and re-used at least well into the third millennium if not later, which is a far longer period of development than had previously been assumed.

If we overlook some important examples of stone settings in Finistère, alignments do seem to be a speciality of the Carnac region. So, too, is a particularly impressive form of large burial mound known to the archaeologist as the 'Carnac' type and to the tourist as the 'tumulus'. The first stop for anyone newly arrived at Carnac is the St-Michel Tumulus, situated on the outskirts of the town, which is nearly 350 feet long and 40 feet high. A chapel has been built on its summit, and there are extensive views over the coast and inland towards the megalith country. First opened in 1862, the Tumulus can now be explored along a narrow and eerie underground passageway, which takes the visitor into the middle of the mound. Here he can inspect part of a long stone cairn overlying numerous cists, including several at the centre surrounded by a ring of small stones. Most of the burials consisted of burnt or partly burnt bones, while spectacular grave goods were

These objects are typical of the rich grave-goods from the 'Carnac' type mounds in Brittany. The ring-disc and large polished axe are of chloromelanite; at the top is another axe of jadeite. At the bottom are pendants and a bracelet made from the stone known as callaïs.

recovered here and at the other large mounds, which were almost all excavated during the last century. The characteristic finds from these digs were huge polished axes, perfectly shaped from blocks of jadeite or fibrolite. It is obvious that these axes of local semi-precious stone were made purely for ornamental and perhaps religious use, and very often seem to have been deliberately broken in two when deposited with the burial. They have been found in great numbers: there were 39 of them at St-Michel, while the record seems to be held by the Mané-er-Hroech mound near Locmariaquer, which yielded 106. Among the items from this mound were several magnificent ring-discs, perhaps worn as bangles, made from serpentine rock imported from Alpine regions. A further characteristic find was the remains of necklaces and pendants made from an attractive local bluish stone known as callaïs. There is a notable absence of pottery and metal objects from the mounds. When these remarkable grave goods are considered as a whole, they form convincing evidence for a special concentration of wealth and power in the Carnac region, exactly the kind of social conditions which we might expect to be associated with a great communal undertaking like the alignments.

The large mounds seem to have had quite a complex internal history, the most bizarre evidence of all coming from Mané-Lud, near Locmariaquer. Here excavators revealed a central elongated round cairn, bounded on its eastern side by a slightly curved double row of menhirs, with a horse's skull balanced on the top of each stone. In most cases the mounds were built next to or on top of earlier

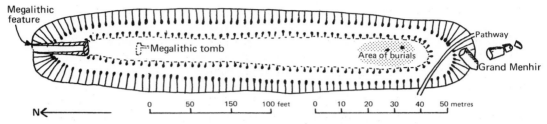

The tumulus of Er Grah, based on Le Rouzic's excavation plan of 1909.

megalithic chamber and passage tombs, so that in general a date later than the main period of tomb building would seem highly probable—perhaps around the time 2500 BC. This is also about the date which might be assumed for the Carnac alignments simply judged by comparison with British stone circles and avenues. The apparent association between the great stone monuments and the mounds is even more evident from the fact that the 'Grand Menhir', to be described later, probably stood on one end of the covering mound of a 'tumulus'.

But in this problem as in so many others, the radiocarbon dates have upset all our expectations. The only 'Carnac' mound to be dated so far is St-Michel, where four tests on the central ring of cists gave results in the sixth and fifth millennia, with an average of about 5000 BC. This date may, if confirmed from other sites, alter much of the traditional way of looking at the prehistory of Brittany. The exact relationship between the megalithic tomb, the great 'tumulus' associated with semi-precious objects, and the avenues of stone is now a completely open question. Perhaps the alignments are really as old as the St-Michel tumulus, and date back to 5000 BC. Or if we agree that the long mound *underneath* the Kermario alignments, with its stone cists and polished axes, is just a 'tumulus' on a less grand scale, then perhaps the alignments are much later than the traditions of the wealthy mound-builders. The people who erected the alignments may be difficult to identify; we could be wrong to associate them with obvious signs of material prestige and power.

What was the connection between standing stones in Britain and in Brittany? With such intensive building of megalithic monuments on both sides of the Channel, it is hard not to believe that there were intimate communications between the peoples of Carnac and Wessex. Yet the archaeological evidence from the Breton menhirs and alignments is generally rather different from excavation results at British stone circles and rows. In the first place, the concentration on the circular (or near-circular) pattern so evident in this country is not nearly as marked a feature of the Carnac culture. If we discount the rings which probably stood at both ends of the Le Menec and Kermario alignments, there are only five other sites with circular settings, and in most of these cases the original outline of the monument is far from certain. In fact, square or rectangular megalithic enclosures are just as common in the Carnac area, but comparable sites have yet to be found in Britain.

The isolated menhir and the alignments are both frequently associated with small cists discovered at the foot of the stone, usually showing evidence of burning, together with fragments of pottery and flint. These 'ritual fires' must have been an important element in the Breton megalithic tradition, because frequent later depositions during the Iron Age and Gallo-Roman period are also found at the foot of the menhirs. This practice is usually absent from British monuments.

The spectacular stone rings of Er-Lannic are a good illustration of the differences between superficially similar kinds of monument from the two cultures. Er-Lannic is a small round island just to the south of the great tomb of Gavrinis in the Gulf of Morbihan, and was the site of a famous excavation by Le Rouzic during the 1920s. Today the motorboat visiting Gavrinis will sometimes make a detour around the tiny island, where the tourist is rewarded by the extraordinary sight of a stone circle running into the sea. The half-submerged menhirs lead to a southern ring which is now completely covered by water, as a result of significant changes in sea level probably during the Gallo-Roman period.

Le Rouzic found that the stones of the northern circle were set up in a supporting bank, and on either side of each menhir, he uncovered the familiar small stone boxes charred by fire. Inside these boxes were their characteristic contents: cattle

The half-submerged stone rings at the island of Er-Lannic, seen from the Gulf of Morbihan.

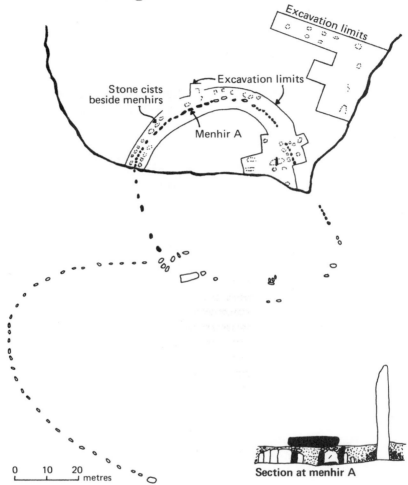

A plan of Le Rouzic's excavations at Er-Lannic in the 1920s.

bones mixed with charcoal, flint flakes, polished stone axes, often broken in two, and a large number of small pottery objects known as 'vase supports' attractively decorated with '*pointillé*' or dotted decoration.

While this plentiful evidence for at least partly ceremonial activity—quite absent from many British stone circles—helps to emphasize the distinctive character of the Brittany sites, it is the little pottery objects that provide the first archaeological clues of direct links with southern Britain. In the Wessex area, mainly concentrated in the rich Stonehenge barrow burials, small pottery vessels have been found which in many cases are perforated with holes and cannot have had any obvious functional use. They are generally known as 'incense cups' and the decoration on certain varieties is almost identical with the Er-Lannic pottery 'vase supports'.

Throughout coastal and central Brittany, round barrows are found with roughly similar proportions to those in Wessex, and they contain inhumations usually accompanied by several bronze daggers and finely worked flint arrowheads. Not only can the general characteristics of these daggers be paralleled in the English barrows, but the decoration on the hafts of at least two famous examples provides added evidence of trading or imitation. We may recall that when Colt-Hoare's workmen dug into Bush Barrow in 1808, they salvaged the

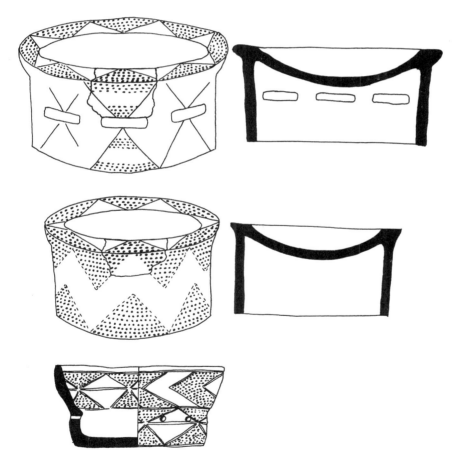

Typical 'vase supports' from Er-Lannic and (*below*) an 'incense cup' from Camerton, Somerset, with similar decorative techniques.

remains of a dagger haft decorated with thousands of gold pins in a *pointillé* technique. No fewer than eight of these elaborately ornamented dagger hafts have been found in Brittany. These and other factors argue for close contact between Brittany and the Wessex area in the Bronze Age (or else actual invasion, as Professor Piggott proposed in his famous study of the problem). If the megaliths of Carnac and Wessex really are connected in some way with a common source of ideas, we may well prefer to think of the alignments as belonging to the period of the Bronze Age and contemporary with the construction of the sarsen ring at Stonehenge.

There is, of course, another field of evidence for continuity between the two cultures, and that is astronomy. Once more it is in this area of knowledge that dramatic new possibilities have been presented in recent studies by Professor Thom and other investigators. Since the turn of the century there have been a number of French enthusiasts of orientation such as Marcel Baudouin, whose work was mainly concerned with megalithic tombs. Recent inventories of these monuments have indicated that most tombs are orientated with their passages facing east and the rising sun. Even so, there is no particular uniformity about the precise direction selected, which in any case cannot be found with any accuracy because of the short length of most passageways.

A number of curious facts about other types of monuments have been known for a long time, however. For instance, most of the long 'Carnac' mounds seem to be positioned with their major axis running east and west. An exception is the elongated mound of Er Grah, which appears to lie due north of the 'Grand Menhir' that probably stood on one end of it. The rectangular arrangement of menhirs at Crucuno is one of the most interesting of all the Brittany monuments, because it seems to record a symmetrical relationship between solar observations that can only be found at the latitude of Carnac, in a way reminiscent of the Station Stones at Stonehenge. The sides of the rectangle refer to the four cardinal points, while the diagonals coincide with the solstices. The proportions of the figure so formed are 3:4:5—the classic Pythagorean triangle. Unfortunately the enclosure was restored in the last century, so that no reliance can be placed on these remarkable facts.

Professor Thom and his colleagues first visited Carnac at the suggestion of Dr Glyn Daniel in the summer of 1970. The task before them was nothing less than a complete and accurate survey of the megaliths in the Le Menec and Kermario alignments in an attempt to recover the original geometry. The first significant finding was that the positions of stones in the Le Menec ring corresponded to the layout of a typical egg-shaped figure such as the Professor had found at Wood-henge, based on a 3:4:5 triangle and with a calculated perimeter of almost exactly 305 megalithic yards. Only about four or five of the seventy stones in the Le Menec ring were found without the small plug of red cement indicating restoration, although these four or five stones in fact lay exactly on the theoretical

Blair and Ronalds measuring the height of menhirs in the Ste Barbe alignments in 1834. A print from their *Sketches at Carnac*, published in London two years later.

construction line.

The main sections of the Le Menec alignments were only just well-enough preserved to enable the Professor to apply statistical analysis in the hope of revealing a unit of length employed in setting out the distances between the stones and between the rows. Complicated calculations have allowed him to discover the original plan outlined by the alignment builders, and to conclude that the 'megalithic rod' (a unit $2\frac{1}{2}$ times the megalithic yard, and often found at British stone circles) was used for accurate surveying throughout the immense task of raising the megaliths. 'Accurate surveying' means that the builders used measuring rods exactly 6·80 feet long, with their ends probably splayed for accurate registration. The distances must have been measured off 'on the level', despite the irregularities of the ground, just as in modern surveying practice.

Professor Thom has tentatively suggested a purpose behind the alignments, although it is a rather complicated solution. First of all there is convincing evidence that lunar and solar observations were made in the immediate vicinity of the alignments. Four substantial menhirs, including the famous twenty-feet-high 'Giant of Manio', are related to one another to give a number of critical sight-lines. Thom proposes that the alignments may have been built as a device for correcting and predicting lunar phenomena (somewhat similar to the operation of the Caithness 'fans') on the basis of three consecutive nights' observation near the monthly extreme. This theory deserves serious attention because striking evidence of interest in the moon is forthcoming from a quite different type of monument.

In 1659, a naval lieutenant sent a report to the French admiralty concerning the loss of a small ship off the Morbihan coast. The report makes a reference to 'the great stone of Locmariaker' that could be seen from the place where the ship was wrecked. Today the remains of an enormous menhir can be seen close to Locmariaquer alongside the famous megalithic tomb known as La Table des Marchands. It is broken into four pieces, and the papers of Président de Roubien,

The Grand Menhir Brisé.

who was a wealthy landowner in the area and was actively interested in the monuments, include a sketch of the menhir in exactly its present state, drawn in 1727. His own opinion was that the stone had fallen sometime around the year 1722. Ever since, there have been conflicting theories accounting for the collapse of the menhir. The most popular idea is that the stone was struck obliquely by lightning, although some think that it fell as the original builders were struggling to erect it. Le Rouzic considered that the different direction taken by the lower fragment as the stone collapsed indicated a violent rocking motion such as could only have been produced by an earth tremor.

Whatever the cause of the accident, Er Grah (The Stone of the Fairies) or the 'Grand Menhir Brisé', now lies in four pieces on the end of an almost obliterated long 'Carnac' mound. Most estimates of the original length of the stone are between 65 and 70 feet, while the base at its broadest point is a little over thirteen feet across. The weight of the menhir is probably in the region of 340 tons. The rock of which the Grand Menhir and the Table des Marchands are composed is a quartzite granite not found locally. Indeed, the nearest outcrop of this type of stone today is at Pont-Aven in Finistère, at least fifty miles away. It is hardly conceivable that so huge a mass could have been transported by sea, no matter how large and unmanoeuvrable a raft was built to carry it. Since glacial action cannot have been responsible, the only conclusion left is that there is a local outcrop of the quartzite granite now submerged by the sea. The stone's movement over land for any great distance must have presented engineering problems on an unprecedented scale. The normal techniques of raising megaliths, probably using beams, levers and rope harnesses, must have been modified to deal with the enormous weight of the Grand Menhir; a huge earth ramp seems to be the only practical way of imagining how such a stone could have been manoeuvred towards an upright position.

But according to Professor Thom, the months or years spent on erecting the menhir were only the culmination of *decades* of astronomical work directed toward finding the right location for such a marker. What the builders may have been looking for was an accurate lunar foresight that could provide complete information about the moon's behaviour during its 18·61 year cycle, in both its rising and setting positions. Natural outcrops and peaks that may have been used for distant observations in Western Scotland are not a feature of the Carnac landscape, and in any case it would be nearly impossible to make one 'notch' or outcrop serve in *both* directions for rising and setting. But a very large stone, seen from some miles away (presumably with some kind of illumination on or near it) could be lined up against the moon's disc from one direction as it rose, and the same night from another direction as it set. The difficulty, of course, would be to find a location where a huge stone would remain visible from every side at a range of several miles. This is exactly the topographical situation of the Locmariaquer site, sur-

One of a number of menhirs dotted along the west coast of the Quiberon peninsula. Perhaps frost was responsible for the curious shape of this stone.

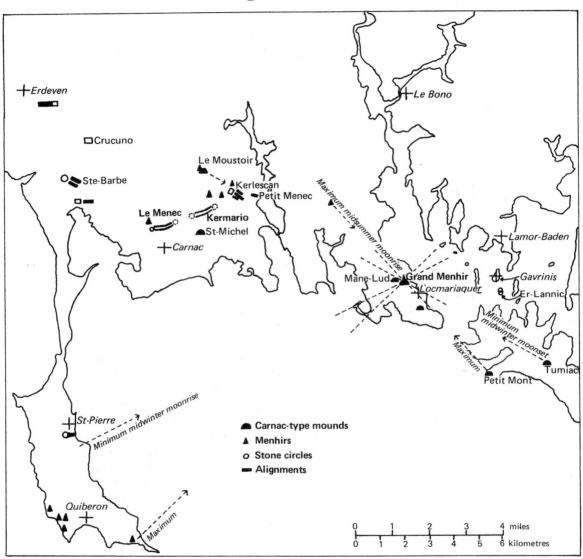

Map of the principal sites in the Carnac region, showing Professor Thom's alignments to the Grand Menhir.

rounded by water on three sides, but with peninsulas of land (such as Quiberon and Presqu'île de Rhuys) available at just the right angles.

If this should at first seem a fantastic explanation of the Grand Menhir, the Professor has gone a long way in answering possible objections. The sites of most of the possible eight lunar observing positions have been identified, and the contours of land traversed by the sight-lines have been carefully plotted so that strong evidence of the former visibility of the Menhir from each place can be presented. Some of the locations, however, have been extensively interfered with in recent times. At the tip of the Quiberon peninsula, only one of several menhirs formerly present now remains, and this shows one of the lunar maxima with an error of 42 minutes that Thom considers to be unacceptably high. At St Pierre, the position for a minimum lunar backsight was assumed to have been obliterated by the houses and gardens of the town, until in 1972 Thom discovered a large fallen slab lying on the beach. A standing stone at Kerran to the north-west of the Menhir gives another lunar extreme with great precision. The same sight-line reversed to indicate the maximum point of the moon's setting position could have been observed on or near the 'Carnac' mound known as Petit Mont to the south-east. A final highly convincing backsight is another 'tumulus', the well-known Le Moustoir site, where two menhirs (one on top of the mound) are very close to the critical lunar angles.

In order to correct their observations, the builders may have used the main Carnac alignments as a kind of 'stone fan' or computing grid. In fact, two less conspicuous groups of alignments at Petit Menec and on the beach at St Pierre were surveyed by Thom, and, although both are in a poor state of repair, enough stones remain to suggest that they actually were stone fans, with a radiating pattern of megaliths just as at Mid Clyth. The presence of these fans quite close to the probable locations of two backsights strengthens Thom's argument. So, too, does the extreme care with which the theory has been set out: for example, most of the sight-lines were not measured from a map but calculated from theodolite observation of a reference point close to the Grand Menhir. The explanation of the Menhir accounts both for its position and its great size, and in the absence of any other sensible suggestion, the theory may be some help towards an understanding of why the great Carnac monuments were erected. It is a hypothesis that is at once highly ingenious and provocative. Can it be that megalithic astronomers from Carnac and Caithness once met to discuss the problems associated with their observations of the moon?

# 11: Who Were The Druids?

Searching for some clue to the nature of society in early Britain, we may be strongly tempted to turn to the Greek and Roman literary sources where we inevitably encounter the Druids. The legendary powers of the Celtic priesthood, distorted by centuries of interest and enthusiasm from antiquaries, poets and mystics, naturally became associated with British megalithic remains. Despite the fact that there is no single early written source mentioning Druidic ceremonies at stone circles, one does not have to travel far to find local nicknames such as Druids' Stones, Rings, Temples, Altars and Beds, sometimes associated with entirely natural rock formations. Obviously the Druids provided an immensely popular and comfortable explanation for the bewildering variety of monuments that have survived into modern times. There are still many people who would like to think that the Druids inherited the system of Bronze Age religion, magic and perhaps even astronomy, guarding ancient secrets in a desperate nationalistic resistance against their Roman conquerors. In spite of their fame, however, remarkably little is known about the Druids. What has come down to us through literary sources of varying reliability needs careful evaluation.

The written evidence begins with Posidonius, a Greek who lived at Apamea in Syria during the end of the second century BC, and extends to numerous philosophers and commentators of the third century AD and later. During this period the Roman world was torn by the civil disorders and military campaigns leading to the establishment of the Empire, and at the same time came into increasing contact with the peoples beyond its borders, especially the Celtic tribes in Gaul and north of the Alps. Trading centres such as the Greek colony at Massalia (Marseilles) must have been important meeting points between the classical and Celtic worlds. In any case, the values of the 'barbarians' cannot have been entirely alien. There is ample literary evidence to suggest that the Gauls practised auguries and animal sacrifices not very far removed from the superstitious beliefs of many Romans. Indeed, through all the classical sources there runs an element of nostalgia for the simplicity of rural Celtic society, freed from the corrupting influence of urban life and practising its religion in a purer form. Certainly the human sacrifice carried out by the Druids was abhorrent to the Roman world (although the Romans were still engaged in it when Posidonius was alive). But as time passed and the Druids were suppressed under successive measures taken by Augustus and later emperors, the unpleasant aspects of the early accounts could be easily overlooked. Seneca says that Posidonius himself believed in a 'golden age' when leadership had been 'confided to the wise', so that from the very start our literary sources are slanted

One of the many sites to be linked with the Druids in local folklore was this curious alignment known as the 'Wren's Egg', Wigtownshire. The wren was the bird popularly associated with the Druids.

towards an idealizing view of the Druids which may conceal part of the truth. As Professor Stuart Piggott has shown, the classical interest in the Druids provides a perfect example of the impact of a simple society upon a more highly organized culture, displaying the idealizing tendencies so apparent when the eighteenth-century world encountered the South Sea islanders, and its antiquaries 'discovered' the temples and artefacts of early Britain.

Posidonius, none the less, was a much-respected scholar who had travelled in Gaul and used sources from Massalia in his account of the country. This forms one of the fifty-two books of his *Histories*, which we only know from quotations by later writers, such as Caesar in his *Gallic Wars* and Strabo in his *Geographica*. Caesar, describing the organization of the eleven tribes of Gaul under their ruling chieftain, attributes substantial legal and religious power to the Druids, and places them on an equal social footing with the *equites* or nobles. They were exempt from many of the feudal duties and taxes normally owed to the chief, and they decided the most serious law cases. Ritual questions were interpreted, sacrifices performed and they were held in great awe ('a large number of young men gather around them for the purpose of instruction'). Caesar discusses a supreme Druid authority, presumably outside the tribal organization, at whose death a successor was chosen by 'vote' or sometimes by 'armed force'. Every year they met at a consecrated spot at what was believed to be the centre of Gaul, and a high court for all disputes evidently took place. At least one Irish legend, *The Exile of the Sons of Uisliu*, confirms Caesar's picture of the Druids' power and influence, for it describes the Druid Cathbad as 'a prince, a diadem great and mighty, who is magnified through the wizardries of Druids . . .'.

From the classical sources it is clear that the Celtic world already considered Druidism to be a long-established institution by 200 BC. The later texts, together with other Irish tales, perhaps indicate that under the Roman repression their status had degenerated to the level of magicians or fortune tellers without any of the civil authority and hierarchical organization credited to them by Caesar. In this context we can set the most famous of all the ancient descriptions of the Druids, which is to be found in Pliny the Elder's *Natural History*, dating to about AD 77. Here we have the image of the Druid in his white robe collecting mistletoe that was to form the basis of most of the Druidic fantasies and misconceptions of the past two centuries. The Druids, Pliny believed, held that everything that grew on the sacred oak tree had been sent from heaven, and when mistletoe was found growing on it, the plant was gathered with

> . . . due religious ceremony, if possible on the sixth day of the moon (for it is by the moon that they measure their months and years, and also their *ages* of thirty years). They choose this day because the moon, though not yet in the middle of her course, has already considerable influence. They call the mistletoe by a name meaning, in their language, the all-healing. Having made preparation for sacrifice and a banquet beneath the trees, they bring thither two white bulls, whose horns are bound then for the first time. Clad in a white robe, the priest ascends the tree and cuts the mistletoe with a golden sickle, and it is received by others in a white cloak. Then they kill the victims, praying that God will render this gift of his propitious to those to whom he has granted it. They believe that the mistletoe, taken in drink, imparts fecundity to barren animals, and that it is an antidote for all poisons. Such are the religious feelings that are entertained towards trifling things by many peoples.

Pliny also echoes one of Caesar's most interesting remarks that the original source of Druidism was Britain. 'It is believed', Caesar writes, 'that their rule of life was discovered in Britain and thence transferred to Gaul; and today those who would study the subject more accurately, travel, as a rule, to Britain to learn it.' It is therefore surprising that Caesar makes no mention of the Druids in his

Ancient Britons and Druids, wearing the white robes and wielding the golden sickle and mistletoe of Pliny, in a plate from Edward King's *Munimenta Antiqua* of 1799–1805.

account of the campaigns in Britain, although the rites connected with the rebellion of Boudicca (Boadicea) make it clear that some similar system was functioning. Indeed the only direct picture of Druids in Britain to come from the classical texts is the undignified incident in Suetonius Paulinus' raid of AD 60, recorded by Tacitus, where dishevelled Druids howl curses on the Roman army, temporarily paralysing the soldiers with fear. But it seems that the Druid priesthood in Britain was not powerful enough to draw comment from the earlier classical commentators of the second and first centuries BC.

Is it then wise to assume that the Druids had ancient origins rooted in the religious traditions of the Neolithic and Bronze Age periods? The archaeological evidence is scanty, but highly interesting. No one has yet dug up the grave of a man, and showed it to be that of a Druid. But in 1834 a barrow was opened at Gristhorpe in Yorkshire that must have sent scholars back to re-read their Pliny. The massive coffin which contained the body had been hollowed from an oak trunk, while across its top had been laid oak branches, presumably part of some funerary ritual. With this burial the original excavators *thought* that they found traces of mistletoe. One apparent case of the sanctity of the oak tree is far from convincing evidence that 'Druidic' beliefs were current in the Bronze Age.

The general form of some types of Iron Age monument do have a curious resemblance to those of earlier periods, however. The Celtic word for a sanctuary was 'nemeton', and the sacred identity of several locations in Gaul and Britain seems to be preserved in their place-names. We have Medionemetum in southern Scotland (perhaps the name for Cairnpapple Hill, which was a persistent centre for religious activity during the Neolithic and Bronze Ages) and another typical example is Nemetodunum, the modern Nanterre, in France. Unfortunately the place-names alone do not help in determining what form the sanctuary took. Besides simple clearings in the forest, Pliny's sacred 'groves' could conceivably be taken to refer to long rectangular enclosures, two of which have been excavated. One is at Aulnay-aux-Planches in the Marne department, and the other at Libenice in Czechoslovakia, which dates to the third century BC. Both sites consist of an elongated rectangular ditch about 300 feet in length, at Aulnay enclosing numerous burials and at Libenice a kind of sunken shrine, containing a stone stele and two large post-holes, perhaps supporting wooden idols. Both infant and animal sacrifices seem to have been performed at Libenice. Caesar's account of the more gruesome religious practices of the Druids does seem to be confirmed from such a site. The rectangular sanctuaries inevitably remind us of the cursus monuments and the long mortuary enclosures constructed in Britain 2000 years before, but to suggest that the same tradition underlies both is a very long shot indeed.

Slightly more reliable evidence for continuity is forthcoming from the excavation of Romano-British temple sites in Britain, dating from the third century AD and earlier. In at least two cases, Frilford in Berkshire and Brigstock, Northamptonshire, these temples overlie circular enclosures broken by a single entrance of

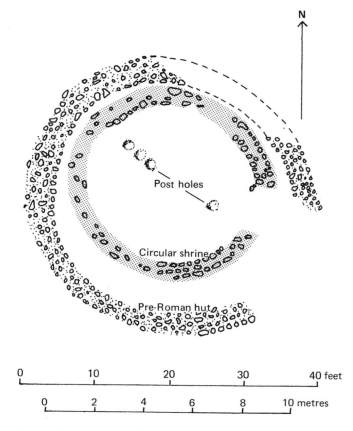

N

Post holes

Circular shrine

Pre-Roman hut

| 0 | 10 | 20 | 30 | 40 feet |

| 0 | 2 | 4 | 6 | 8 | 10 metres |

At Maiden Castle, Dorset, an oval Roman shrine (with central post-holes, probably for wooden images) lay over an Iron Age hut. One example, perhaps, of persisting native traditions of circular temple-building.

pre-Roman, Iron Age date. Inside the ditch at these and other pre-Roman sanctuaries, traces remain of isolated, shallow post-holes to support the general conclusion (amply confirmed by archaeological and literary evidence) that wooden effigies were once set up at such sites for veneration, presumably protected by some kind of roofed structure or hut. Once again it is conceivable that the tradition of building circular enclosure ditches and round shrines may derive remotely from the earth circles of the second millennium. These Iron Age structures are in marked contrast to the square or rectangular Romanized temples which superseded them.

The phrase 'ritual pit' is something of an archaeological joke, since excavation features of unidentifiable purpose used to be explained away by this term. Caution is still required in the case of a number of sites where 'ritual shafts' have been found singly or in groups. In 1971 Dr Geoffrey Wainwright uncovered a Neolithic settlement at Eaton Heath near Norwich, and found 21 clay-lined shafts, the deepest of which were sunk to over 25 feet. The modern water-table occurs a few feet higher than this level, and Dr Wainwright has suggested that the shafts in fact represent wells repeatedly dug into the extremely unstable sandy subsoil. Nevertheless we have seen that rings of pits within earth circles built before about 2500 BC, such as Stonehenge I, Dorchester-on-Thames and Maumbury, cannot easily be explained without recourse to some non-functional, religious concept.

The most remarkable of all the 'ritual shafts', dated to about 1650 BC, was located at Wilsford, about two miles from Stonehenge. Paul Ashbee undertook excavations in 1960 and found that the shaft had been dug about 110 feet down through the solid chalk, terminating in a well and containing the remains of buckets, ropes and Bronze Age pottery. A purely utilitarian function is unlikely to be the explanation for the Wilsford Shaft. The extraordinary effort required to drive a pit down to this level, and the closeness of the site to Stonehenge, suggest a communal or religious undertaking. There may be some sort of relationship between the Wilsford Shaft and other more obviously non-functional pits dating to two or three centuries later. One of these, excavated at Swanwick in Hampshire, has close similarities to an Iron Age shaft at Holzhausen in Bavaria. Both sides feature a large wooden post set upright at the bottom of the pit, together with traces of dried animal blood and flesh, again reminding us of the traditions of augury and sacrifice recorded by the classical writers. Quite a number of deep wells or shafts, usually packed with animal bones and Roman pottery, have been discovered in the South of England and on the Continent.

It will be seen that in the case of three representative types of Iron Age religious monuments—the long rectangular enclosures, the circular ditches surrounding shrines, and the ritual shafts—superficial links can be found with the period of the stone circle builders. Whether we can refer to the priests presiding at the ceremonies at Libenice or Swanwick as Druids is quite another matter. Indeed, the general links between Britain and the Continent during this period are not at all good, centring mainly on the evidence of a few wealthy 'chariot burials' found on both sides of the Channel. One wonders how much of past religious tradition can have been remembered or even cared for under the aggressive leadership of rival chieftains based at the great southern hill-forts such as Hambledon or Maiden Castle. The scraps of evidence on the side of continuity are perhaps too tenuous for the claim that some kind of distorted tradition of religious ideas persisted from the second millennium right down to the Roman conquest of the Celtic areas.

Our inquiry becomes even more speculative when we turn back to the Classical sources to see why the ancient Greeks and Romans were so interested in these religious ideas. We find repeated reference to the fact that the Druids followed the 'Pythagorean' philosophy, a belief that the soul is transferred after death into another body, human or animal. Strabo, however, mentions a simpler creed of the Druids 'that mens' souls, and also the universe, are indestructible, although both fire and water will at some time or other prevail over them'. To the Classical mind, with a much gloomier concept of the progress of the soul after death, this Celtic belief was a continual source of fascination. The excavation of aristocratic burials of the Iron Age, where a chief would usually be interred complete with his possessions and sometimes his chariot, indicates a crude belief in a literal reproduction of the living world after death. The Classical writers, in seeking a parallel among their own philosophers by which to express this concept, probably made the association with Pythagorean doctrine themselves.

However, the insistence on the Pythagoras link (usually by the later and more unreliable writers) raises the question of whether it was merely the philosophical teachings of Pythagoras which the Druids appeared to imitate. In the first century AD Clement of Alexandria even claimed that Pythagorean and other Greek philosophy was actually learned from the Gauls, and Hippolytus, writing in the third century AD, said that 'the Celts believe in their Druids as prophets because they can foretell certain events by the Pythagorean reckoning and calculations'. This calls to mind the rather fanciful picture of geometrical ideas together with more commercial items passing through a trade centre like Massalia.

Caesar's account of the Druids is more specific on the practical side of their philosophy, for he tells us that 'they have many discussions concerning the stars and their movements, the size of the universe and of the earth, the order of nature, the strength and power of the immortal gods, and hand down their learning to the young men'. Another writer drawing directly on Posidonius, Pompeius Mela, claims for them 'knowledge of the heavens and of the stars'.

The interest in a calendar recorded both by Caesar and Pliny was confirmed when the remains of what could have been an actual Celtic calendar were discovered at Coligny, in the Ain district of France, at the turn of the century. This calendar was once a large bronze plate, nearly five feet square, and was found close to a Roman road and the pieces of a bronze statue dated to the first century AD. Although the names of the months are written in Gaulish, the lettering and numerals are Roman. The calendar reckons by nights (which is how Caesar says the Celts counted time) and by lunar months. The insertion of two 'intercalary' months every $2\frac{1}{2}$ and 3 years alternately shows that the calendar was an attempt to reconcile the lunar count with the solar year, probably on the basis of the familiar 18·61-year cycle.

The most we might claim from this evidence of rudimentary scientific skills among the Celts is that it presents a typical example of the interests displayed by many communities with a relatively low level of technology. The astronomical and navigational skills of today's Pacific islanders are another well-known case, and many other instances can be found in the surprisingly large volume of literature on the subject. The awareness of fundamental cycles like the nineteen-year lunar swing was the sort of knowledge that might be lost and recovered again among a non-literate people; we do not necessarily have to think in terms of an unbroken tradition of ideas transmitted from generation to generation.

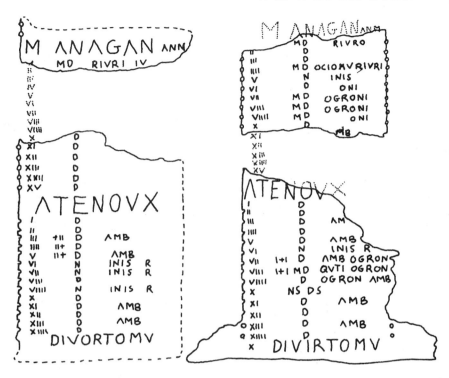

The month Anagan from the second and fourth years spanned by the Coligny calendar. The word 'Atenoux' divides the months in two corresponding to the waxing and waning of the moon, while lucky and unlucky days are also recorded. The calendar was probably the product of local craftsmanship, but in a number of ways reflects Roman practice.

We can imagine how some of the regular cycles and less predictable events might be explained in terms of mythology. For example, a powerful god might be responsible for 'swallowing up' the sun or moon at the time of an eclipse. Just such an idea seems to be present in Plutarch's remarkable account of the Pythagorean theories, where one explanation is that '. . . the shadow of the earth, into which they believe the moon to fall when eclipsed, is called Typhon . . . the Pythagoreans look upon Typhon as a demoniacal power, for they say he was produced in an even proportion of numbers: to be exact, in that of 56'. Here we have the number of the eclipse cycle supposedly commemorated by the Aubrey Holes at Stonehenge. Alternatively, the nineteen-year swing of the moon might be thought of as the god 'returning' to the same place in the sky. This could be one implication of the last and most tantalizing of the Classical texts we have to consider, which may at last bring us into some kind of contact with traditions about Bronze Age Britain.

In the seventh century BC a Greek traveller called Aristeas seems to have made a journey into Scythian territory, roughly where Romania is situated today. He finally reached the edge of the Carpathian mountains, where he hoped to find a race called the Hyperboreans, whom, it was rumoured, were specially blessed by Apollo and lived in a golden age of peace and contentment. When Aristeas reached tribes who had some contact with central Asia, he seems to have once again encountered stories of a prosperous and virtuous people living far away. There is a possibility that the myth could have originated from nomadic contact with the highly civilized Chinese under their Eastern Chou dynasty. At any rate, Aristeas' return meant that the Hyperboreans came into assured existence in the text-books of Classical geography, living beyond the Scythians and the Rhipaean mountains, where the Danube was supposed to have its source. Herodotus regarded the Hyperboreans as a mythical race, but he too put their country of origin beyond Scythian territory. Yet he also asserted, correctly, that the Danube rose in the Alps, and so a most interesting geographical confusion seems to have taken place. Posidonius and most later writers thought that the Rhipaean mountains were the Alps and placed the Hyperboreans beyond them in Celtic territory. When Rome was sacked by northern tribes in about 390 BC, it was attributed to the Hyperboreans. By the time Hecateus of Abdera came to write about the Hyperboreans, it seems that they had become associated with Britain. All we have of Hecateus' fourth-century account are fragments quoted by Diodorus Siculus in his *Histories*, probably written in about 8 BC. These fragments, however, are worth reading in full for their fascinating mixture of a 'golden age' tradition and what may be half-remembered 'travellers' tales' of early Britain. The island in the account cited by Diodorus,

> . . . is at least the size of Sicily, and lies opposite the land inhabited by the Celts, out in the Ocean. This is in the far North, and is inhabited by the people called Hyperboreans from their location beyond Boreas, the North Wind. The land is fertile and produces every sort of crop; it is remarkable for the excellent balance of its climate and each year it affords two harvests. The story goes that Leto [Apollo's mother] was born there. It is for this reason that Apollo is honoured above all the gods. There are men who serve as priests of Apollo because this god is worshipped every day with continuous singing and is held in exceptional honour. There is also in the island a precinct sacred to Apollo and suitably imposing, and a notable temple decorated with many offerings, and looking like a globe. There is also a community sacred to this god, where most of the inhabitants are trained to play the lyre and do so continuously in the temple and worship the god with singing, celebrating his deeds.

> . . . There is a story that some Greeks visited the land of the Hyperboreans and left costly offerings inscribed with Greek letters. In his turn Abaris came

to Greece from the Hyperboreans a long time ago to renew the friendship
and family ties with the Delians. They say that from this island the moon is
seen only a little above the earth and has certain definite prominences on its
surface, just like the earth. It is said that the god returns to the island every
nineteen years, the period when the stars complete their cycle ... During
this appearance the god plays on the lyre and dances continuously by night
from the Spring Equinox till the rising of the Pleiades, enjoying his own
triumphs. The men called Boreads are in charge of this city and over the
sacred precinct, and appointment to authority is always a matter of birth.

A great deal of debate has naturally centred on whether the Hyperboreans'
'spherical' temple is a genuine reference to Stonehenge. Whatever trust can be
placed on this remarkable account, it does reflect a number of themes which may
be relevant to our picture of early Britain: the apparent knowledge and interest
in astronomy displayed by a simple people; the concentration of such knowledge
within the hands of a few; and finally, the distortion of the evidence by a more
sophisticated culture and a 'golden age' outlook.

# 12: Christianity: Conflict or Continuity?

A remarkable variety of lore and legend is associated with megalithic sites. As we have seen, there is very little direct evidence for the survival of Bronze Age beliefs into later times, yet the folk-tales show that in every period superstitions of one kind or another were linked to the stones.

Many of the stories are very odd indeed and caution is necessary if they are to be interpreted. For example, the Cornish legends that the 'Hurlers' and 'Merry Maidens' are really people turned into circles of stone for breaking the sabbath are not likely, in their present form, to be earlier than Puritan times. Another story connected with the Hurlers is that the stones could never be counted until a baker had placed penny loaves on each one and calculated the result. Versions of this story of the countless stones are known from Stonehenge, Stanton Drew, Rollright, Castle Rigg, Long Meg, and from the megalithic tomb called Lower Kits Coty in Kent. A possibility that this tradition has quite an early origin might be considered. The muddled Welsh chronicle of Nennius, probably compiled in the early ninth century, includes a section on 'marvels' in which the burial mound of Licat Anir, apparently a Saxon barrow at Archenfield, Hertfordshire, is reported to change its dimensions every time it is measured. There may be quite a simple explanation for these stories (rather than folk-memories of megalithic yards and the incommensurability of $\pi$). It is in fact not always easy to count the stones at a ruined megalithic site, and conflicting totals from the same circles were actually reported by various antiquaries. In the eighteenth century, it seems that tallying up the stones was a firmly established popular pastime, since William Stukeley tells us that at Stonehenge, this was the 'argument . . . of vulgar incogitancy' with which 'the infinite numbers of daily visitants busy themselves'.

Another popular idea with a remarkably wide distribution is that at certain times of the day or year the stones spring to life and go down to the stream to wash or drink. This is told of the Carnac alignments, of the Four Stones, Radnor, of Stanton Drew, Rollright and many other sites. A typical version of the story concerns a stone at Banbury which *hears* the church clock strike twelve, the signal for its nightly drink down by the Avon. While these traditions are doubtless no more than the product of colourful local imagination, it is interesting that so many cursus monuments, earth circles and stone rings do seem to be sited close to fresh water.

A further immemorial association of megaliths is with powers of fertility or healing. Contact or propitiation of the stones will correct barrenness or ensure an easy childbirth. The smearing of menhirs with butter, honey or oil so that people

Knowlton church and barrow at sunset.

Le Menec is an eerie place at nightfall. At certain times of the year the stones are reputed to walk down to the local stream to drink, and kill anyone in their path.

Culliford Tree Barrow, Came Down, Dorset, which according to local legend emits music at noon.

could slide down the sticky coating was apparently widespread in Brittany. At Plouarzel, for example, there was a round boss on a menhir about three feet from the ground, against which a husband and wife were supposed to rub themselves, the husband hoping to be the father of boys and the wife hoping to rule the husband. Similar customs, including the propitiation of cup-and-ring marks with milk, are known from all over Britain. The healing power of megaliths is emphasized in a famous legend of Stonehenge contained in Geoffrey of Monmouth's *History of the Kings of Britain*, finished in about the year 1136. Geoffrey was probably a Welshman who succeeded to various ecclesiastical posts and almost certainly lived in Oxford. The *History* seems to have been based mainly on his own highly imaginative interpretation of traditional material, such as early Welsh chronicles which provided the book with its legendary genealogies. The story of the 'Giant's Ring' is connected with the victory over the Saxon invaders by Aurelius Ambrosius, king of the Britons. To commemorate the men who had fallen in the battle, Ambrosius asks the advice of Merlin, prophet of the Gewissei tribe. He tells him to send for the Giant's Ring

> . . . which is on Mount Killaraus in Ireland. In that place there is a stone construction which no man of this period could ever erect, unless he combined great skill and artistry. The stones are enormous and there is no one alive strong enough to move them.

Ambrosius ridicules Merlin's project but is sharply corrected.

> ... 'Try not to laugh in a foolish way, your Majesty,' answered Merlin. 'What I am suggesting has nothing ludicrous about it. These stones are connected with certain secret religious rites and they have various properties which are medicinally important. Many years ago the Giants transported them from the remotest confines of Africa and set them up in Ireland at the time when they inhabited that country. Their plan was that, whenever they fell ill, baths should be prepared at the foot of the stones; for they used to pour water over them and to run this water into baths in which their sick were cured.'

Inspired by Merlin's idea, the Britons gather an army and invade Ireland. Winning a battle against the brave and down-to-earth Irish leader Gillomanius ('Who ever heard of such folly? Surely the stones of Ireland aren't so much better than those of Britain . . .') Ambrosius' men are unable to dismantle the Giant's Ring until Merlin derides their brute force and takes the stones down himself 'more easily than you could ever believe'. Then the Britons set sail again and arrive in Britain. Ambrosius summons the bishops and people to the monastery of Mount Ambrius, which was probably Avebury and was constantly confused by Geoffrey with the site of Stonehenge. It is on this spot that the Giant's Ring is re-erected. 'Merlin obeyed the King's orders' Geoffrey concludes,

A 'bullaun' or holy stone lying in the street at Dingle, County Kerry.

. . . and put the stones up in a circle around the sepulchre, in exactly the same way as they had been arranged on Mount Killaraus in Ireland, thus proving that his artistry was worth more than any brute strength.

Whatever details of the story were invented by Geoffrey, the journey of the megaliths from Ireland corresponds closely enough to the transportation of the bluestones from Mount Prescelly to suggest that Geoffrey may have elaborated on some very ancient and authentic piece of Welsh folk tradition.

If this intriguing tale has some basis of truth, there are countless others which appear to belong firmly in the realm of the popular imagination. Take, for instance, one of the many remarkable stories attached to the Callanish stones, as it is told in the latest anthology of Hebridean legends:

Once there was a great King who was also a Holy Priest; he came to Lewis with many ships and in the ships were lesser priests and great stones and black men to handle them. It was these black men who set up the Circle. While the black men were so employed, many died and were buried with ceremony inside the circle. When the stones were all in place, some of the priests and the remaining black men sailed away, but the Great Priest stayed and with him lesser priests and he invited men from other Isles to come and serve him, and some came. The priests wore robes made of the skins and feathers of birds, that of the Chief Priest being white with a girdle made from the neck feathers of mallard drakes; the other priests wore feather cloaks of mixed colours. The Chief Priest never appeared without wrens (or a wren) flying near him.

Until the last century certain families in Lewis were held in secret esteem as 'belonging to the stones', although no one knew exactly why. Indeed, up to a few generations ago, the local people still secretly congregated at the Callanish stones on May Day and midsummer morning, and the custom probably accounts for the old Gaelic name for the site, Turusachan, which apparently means 'the place of pilgrimage'. On midsummer morning it was believed that 'something', perhaps a deity, came to the stones and walked down the avenue, heralded by the call of the cuckoo.

What these beliefs suggest is that the folklore associated with megaliths was not always invented for a frivolous purpose, but sometimes reflected the considerable community feeling which these monuments once evoked, an attitude of mind that must ultimately have had very ancient roots indeed. A common Gaelic phrase used by Scottish people to ask each other if they were going to church was 'Am bheil thu dol d'on clachan?' (Are you going to the stones?) which may be a relic of gatherings at stone circles. A few centuries ago festivals in the pre-Roman calendar were still observed by the widespread lighting of fires. It is this tradition to which Thomas Hardy alludes in the celebrated passage on Rain Barrow in *The Return of the Native*. The Reverend Donald McQueen, writing in Ireland in 1782, described how during the night before midsummer morning the country was lit up for miles by fires 'in honour of the sun'.

A woodcut of 1823 showing local customs associated with the area around the Ring of Brogar, Orkney, some forty years previously and perhaps originating from the time of the Norse settlement. The lettered features are as follows: A—Stenness church, B—Maes Howe, C—The Ring of Stenness, or 'temple of the moon', at which a woman is invoking Odin to keep a promise of betrothal, D—Swearing an oath through the Odin Stone, E—The Watch Stone, F—The Ring of Brogar, or 'temple of the sun', G—The Watch Hill, H—The Loch of Stenness.

Moreover, barrows and stone circles were often the judicial and administrative focus of a community. Prominent mounds were sometimes chosen as meeting places for local moots and hundreds. When the hundred of Stone met in Somerset, its members opened the proceedings by emptying a bottle of wine over the megalith from which the hundred's name originated. As late as the fourteenth century, courts were still being held at stone circle sites in Perthshire and Aberdeen. The swearing of an oath or marriage by clasping hands through a stone with a hole in it was a serious matter. In 1781 a young man who had broken such an agreement made through the hole in Odin's Stone, near the Ring of Brogar, was severely reprimanded by the elders of the Orkney sessions for 'breaking the promise of Odin'.

Not surprisingly, the traces of paganism associated with the monuments that still lingered in the popular mind met with disfavour and opposition from the Church. Mr Leslie Grinsell has recently drawn attention to several cases of witchcraft associated with barrows and other prehistoric sites. In 1699 a man was brought before the Kirk session at Elgin, Morayshire, charged with idolatry in setting up a stone and removing his cap to it. The strong local feelings attached to megaliths must at times have been a matter of concern for the authorities.

It is well known that Christianity absorbed quite a number of pagan beliefs (including the main pre-Christian festival at midwinter) and occasionally churches were even sited on ancient earthworks. The suggestion that this was a systematic policy is principally based on a letter quoted by Bede, written by Pope Gregory to Abbot Mellitus on the occasion of his departure for Britain in 601, to assist the Augustinian mission at Canterbury. 'We have been giving careful thought to the affairs of the English', Pope Gregory writes,

> . . . and have come to the conclusion that the temples of the idols among that people should on no account be destroyed. The idols are to be destroyed, but the temples themselves are to be aspersed with holy water, altars set up in them, and relics deposited there. . . . And since they have a custom of sacrificing many oxen to demons, let some other solemnity be substituted in its place, such as a day of Dedication or the Festivals of the holy martyrs whose relics are enshrined there. On such occasions they might well construct shelters of boughs for themselves around the churches that were once temples, and celebrate the solemnity with devout feasting. . . . If the people are allowed some worldly pleasure in this way, they will more readily come to desire the joys of the spirit.

Such was the attitude of compromise apparently adopted by the early missionaries in their work among the pagan Saxons. The conversion of King Edwin of

In the shadow of paganism: a Christianised menhir in Brittany.

The Rudston megalith.

Northumbria and his council in 627 is described in detail by Bede, and the chief priest, Coifi, supposedly accepted the new faith because it was 'better and more effectual'.

It is quite clear that certain church sites were deliberately chosen to assert Christian authority over ancient remains. The presence of the tallest standing stone in the country within the churchyard at Rudston, East Yorkshire, can hardly be fortuitous, and the dramatic positioning of the Norman church at Knowlton, Dorset, in the middle of a large circular earthwork, even less so. In Cardiganshire, it appears that a circular churchyard wall at Yspytty Cynfyn was built on top of a ring of megaliths, while there is a likelihood that a large menhir was incorporated into the church fabric at Llandysiliogogo. From Wales also comes the proverb 'Da ywr maen gyda'r Efengyl' (Good is the stone together with the Gospel).

In Brittany, superstitious beliefs were absorbed by churches dedicated to St Méen, whose name is probably derived from the Breton word for 'stone'. These examples of Christian compromise could be multiplied, and the case supported in particular by cross-inscribed menhirs which are frequently encountered in

Brittany. The author was surprised to find a simple cross carved on the huge rock known as Clach ant Sagairt in North Uist, which was perhaps artificially erected or moved in some way, and which Professor Thom thinks may have been used for megalithic observations. Stones of a more obviously pagan character attracted carvings of crosses throughout Britain.

If much of this evidence appears to favour a peaceful continuity between Christianity and the beliefs attached to the stones, there are equally convincing signs that at times there was genuine conflict and hostility. Indeed, antagonism of this kind may have had a long history. Professor Atkinson found that at a time probably between AD 50–400, a number of Stonehenge megaliths had been broken up, and the resulting rubble was distributed in an even layer all over the site. Since it is difficult to conceive of a practical reason for this action, it may have been a symbolic or deterrent gesture, although of course we can only speculate about who was responsible (the Roman administration or early Christians?). At a later stage demolition work was also carried out at Avebury. The Saxon church was built away from the centre of the village, outside the western bank of the ring, which could suggest (among several possible interpretations) that the pagan sanctuary was thought to be unfit ground for a churchyard. In the fourteenth century some of the stones were pulled down and buried, while a deliberate breach was made in part of the bank close to the church and the material was thrown into the main ditch. During these operations one of the megaliths fell accidentally, completely burying a man who was carrying a barber or surgeon's scissors and probe, together with coins from the reign of Edward I. Although most of the Avebury stones were overthrown in the eighteenth century to clear land for agriculture, the presence of a barber in these medieval operations suggests that religious icono-clasm was the chief motivation during this period. It is interesting to note that a stone circle on the island of Iona was deliberately destroyed in 1560 because offerings were still being made there.

On the Continent, from the fifth century onwards, various ecclesiastical councils issued edicts condemning the worship of stones. At the Council of Nantes in 658, an order directed 'bishops and their servants to dig up, remove and hide' heathen stones. In 789, Charlemagne took active steps to suppress paganism, and forbade the practice of barrow burial, while similar measures were later organized in England by Canute and others.

These fragments of historical evidence can be supplemented by a mass of folk-lore which seems to echo the conflict. At Callanish, for example, the giants met once a year for a parliament on the site, and there they convened to discuss how Christianity could best be countered. When St Kiaran arrived to preach and the giants refused to be christened or build a church, he turned them into stone. The Irish story of St Patrick destroying the idols at Magh Slecht has been shown to be a medieval invention, accounting for the features of a particular stone circle, but perhaps it reflects the struggles of the conversion. A crude sixth-century 'Life' of

St Samson tells of similar confrontations at an idol in the hundred of Trigg in Cornwall, where idolaters indulging in a 'lewd play' were converted and the idol destroyed.

The widespread feeling that the megalithic monuments were to be avoided as symbolic of dark and evil powers could have originated at any time, but is surely most likely to have received popular currency through the Christian conversion. There are countless names and stories connecting ancient sites with giants and devils, such as the Devil's Arrows alignment at Boroughbridge, Yorkshire, or the name Devil's Quoits associated with Stanton Drew. The devil played a hand in the building of both Stonehenge and Silbury Hill. The devil attempted to destroy Rudston church by throwing the huge megalith at it, but he missed. There are twenty stories of giants known from Cornwall alone, mainly associated with megaliths or topographical features, while in Brittany there are at least sixty-three different menhirs on record with individual legends of the devil.

One story occurs so persistently in these cases that it may be a lasting reflection of the struggle between old and new beliefs. At well over twenty individual churches, scattered through almost every county in England from Cornwall to Northumberland, the story describes how the building of a church is constantly hindered by the devil. During the night either the devil or an agent (a pig at Winwick and a cat at Leyland) carries off the building materials to another site, which is usually higher or lower than the original church. In some cases the devil's site is an ancient monument, as in the case of Rodmarton in Gloucestershire and its long barrow. The evil powers are generally defeated with the help of a saint. A proportion of the tales may have been concocted to account for churches oddly situated as a consequence of a declining manorial system or of a drift of settlement. Some could also reflect genuine attempts to build churches on pagan sites which met with local opposition, resulting in the church being built elsewhere.

While these old traditions are certainly entertaining, it is obvious that their historical value must be limited, and indeed the same stories can be interpreted in different ways to supply contradictory evidence. Any kind of theory which is even partially founded on this folklore therefore runs the risk of generalizing from an inadequate and half-understood basis. The best-known example of such a theory was explained in a book published in 1925 by Alfred Watkins, called *The Old Straight Track*. Watkins was a brewer's representative whose business took him on long rides across the Herefordshire countryside, and it was here that he conceived his idea that most prehistoric monuments were laid out intervisibly, according to an elaborate system of straight trackways, to provide travellers on foot with landmarks. This basic theory (to some extent developed from Lockyer's ideas) deserves serious attention if only because in most cases barrows *do* seem to have been carefully sited to appear as landmarks, and would certainly have been noticeable in chalk country soon after being dug. All this is based on the assumption that forest cover did not seriously restrict possibilities for long-distance views. It would be rather surprising if Bronze Age travellers had *not* used their conspicuous monuments for establishing paths or routes, and perhaps straight tracks were once cleared to link them. Today the linear cemeteries at Kilmartin or Lambourn seem to suggest the existence of pathways, although the mounds were demonstrably not laid out along precise bearings. However, Watkins' main argument involved the positions not only of earthworks of every period but also of Christian churches, lying along lattices of straight lines constructed across Ordnance Survey maps, supplemented by investigation on the ground. There are obvious questions of method, and even of statistics, involved in this argument, and their consideration is not entirely relevant here. Supporters of this theory are convinced that nearly *every* church, irrespective of period, was systematically positioned on an ancient site. This exceeds the limited evidence available and in any case is surely a distinct improbability.

It has also been suggested that authentic megalithic traditions were somehow secretly transmitted into historical times when they were incorporated into Christian sanctuaries. Among these supposed traditions was the practice of orientation which determined the long axes of churches and cathedrals. The Freemasons are favourite candidates for this rôle, and in fact there *is* some highly interesting evidence to connect them with church architecture and with the simple layout of buildings to face the rising sun. But the subject of church orientation is a complex one, which has been fully investigated by several authorities. Some of the earliest church buildings in Italy seem to face east and still earlier examples of orientated temples are described in the Hebrew scriptures of the Old Testament. There is some reason, then, to think that orientation was associated with very early Christian beliefs and that its application in England was an exclusively Christian affair.

An extension of these ideas is implicit in a more recent theory of Professor Lyle B. Borst, an astronomer and physicist of the State University of New York, which received wide publicity in many newspapers. According to Borst, English cathedral and church plans were laid over the sites of stone circles or late Neolithic timber buildings, incorporating the same geometry and the megalithic yard in their layout. Borst's superimposed constructions mainly involve egg-shapes that do not seem to be very common in megalithic geometry, and quite a variety of Pythagorean triangles (usually of very large dimensions). Besides churches, these are set to work on the outlines of long barrows and on a curiously conceived plan of Stonehenge. The deviations present in the long axes of many cathedrals are explained by stellar orientation, successive building phases and the precession of the equinoxes. It is enough to ask how medieval architects could possibly have had accurate surveys of timber or stone circles in the first place, remembering that most of the regular distortions of these monuments are not at all obvious on the ground.

As surely as musical barrows or the Callanish 'black men' belong to the popular imagination, so megalithic Masons or Pythagorean cathedrals must be consigned to the folklore of science.

# 13: The Druid Revival

'I never saw the Country about Marleborough, till Christmas 1648' wrote the author of *Brief Lives*, John Aubrey; it was at that time,

> . . . the morrow after Twelf day, Mr Charles Seymour and Sir William Button of Tokenham (a most parkely ground, and a Romancy-place) Baronet, mett with their packs of Hounds at the Greyweathers. These Downes looke as if they were Sown with great Stones, very thicke; and in a dusky evening they looke like a flock of Sheep: from whence it takes its name. One might fancy it to have been the Scene where the Giants fought with stones against the Gods. 'Twas here that our Game began: and the chase led us . . . through the Village of Aubury, into the Closes there: where I was wonderfully surprised at the sight of those vast stones, of which I had not heard before; as also at the mighty Banke and Graffe about it. I observed in the Inclosures some segments of rude circles, made with these stones, whence I concluded, they had been in old time complete . . .

For centuries people had lived beside the alignments of Callanish or within the great circle at Avebury, content with their traditional, superstitious explanations for the ruins around them. Sometimes by accident, the monuments of early Britain

John Aubrey, 1626–1697.

etiam curiofus indagator de fimilibus faxis, tam folitudines, quàm apertos campos fcrutādi gratia peragrare uoluerit, infinita fpectacula comperiet, quæ præfentibus haud opus eft tædiofius infinuare. Vna tamen caufa promptior effe pofsit, quòd non longa diftantia ab ea uetuftifsima urbe Scareli erat arx regia Aaranes dicta(de qua fpecialiter alibi dicet)circa quā fuccefsiuis feculis,et generationibus,committebatur acerrima bella: de quibus charilsimus frater & anteceffor meus Archiepifcopus Vpfalenfis mirifica fcripfit. Sunt & apud Oftrogothos itidem, & fuperiores Sueones, magnatum ac nobilium arces latè per regiones in locis natura munitis extructa:penes quarum muros,& agros,ueterum ingentia faxa cuneato,rotundo,oblongo,& erecto fitu ter

De bellicis Gothorum obelifcis,& erectis faxis.

CAP. XXIX.

Veterum Gothorum,ac Sueonum antiquifsimus mos erat,ut ubi acriores in cāpis,feu montibus inftituiffent,& perfeciffent pugnas,illic erectos lapides,quafi Aegyptiacas pyramides collocare foliti fint:quibus huiufmodi præclara gefta breuifsimo aliquo titulo infculpentes,memoriam nominis,& geftorum fuorum perpetuari putabant, prout eorundem temporum ufitatæ cantiones rhythmaticis compendijs compofitæ,continuatifqùe feculis in

One of the first appearances of prehistoric monuments in a printed book was in Olaus Magnus' *Historia de gentibus septendrionalibus*, which depicted Scandinavian megaliths alongside Runic stones of the Viking age.

now began to be 'discovered' by the inquiring rationalists and philosophers of the seventeenth century. When as keen an observer as Aubrey rode into Avebury ring without the foreknowledge of local legends or of any important historical reference, it is scarcely surprising that his sense of admiration and curiosity was aroused. 'This old monument' he wrote, 'does as much exceed in greatness the so renowned Stoneheng, as a Cathedral doeth a parish Church: so that by its grandure one might presume it to have been an Arch-Temple of the Druids.'

How did Aubrey reach this conclusion? The 'so renowned' Stonehenge had, of course, been a great deal more conspicuous than Avebury, and Geoffrey of Monmouth's legend was firmly rooted in the popular mind. Most Elizabethan visitors to Stonehenge would probably have thought the monument to be about a thousand years old, a British memorial to those slain in battle against the Saxons under Hengist and Horsa. Even William Camden, in his great work the *Britannia* of 1586, felt obliged to record Geoffrey's story, although he was 'not curious to argue and dispute' the origins of Stonehenge, 'but rather to lament with much grief, that the authors of so notable a monument are thus buried in oblivion'. His speculation was limited to an idea that the stones were formed in moulds from a kind of cement. Other writers were ready to join in lamenting the 'oblivion' of Stonehenge's history, and were equally unwilling to advance any serious alternative to Geoffrey's story. Most of them painted a moral, like Michael Drayton in his topographical poem, *Poly-Olbion,* of 1612—

Ill did those mighty men to trust thee with their story.

Thou hast forgot their names, who rear'd thee for their glory:

For all their wondrous cost, thou that hast serv'd them so,
What 'tis to trust to tombs, by thee we eas'ly know.

The beginnings of serious speculative inquiry into the subject were the result of a visit which King James I paid to the monument early in the seventeenth century. He was so interested in what he saw that he ordered his architect, Inigo Jones, to prepare a plan of Stonehenge and find out its origin. Jones' notes and plans were finally published many years later in 1655 by his son-in-law John Webb, in a volume called *The most notable Antiquity of Great Britain, vulgarly called Stone-heng, Restored*. As the champion of courtly neo-classic taste, Jones 'restored' Stonehenge in the form of a Roman temple, dedicated to the sky-god Coelus because its stones stood on a broad plain, unroofed and open to the sky. The choice of the Roman period was not solely dictated by Jones' own architectural interests, since he carefully considered and eliminated other possibilities. The classical texts, he reflected, made no reference whatever to architectural skills practised by the ancient Britons, who were doubtless a 'savage and barbarous people, knowing no use at all of garments', incapable of erecting the 'stately structures' of Stonehenge. The Romans had carefully selected the proportions of the temple, and in particular the plain Tuscan order of pillar because it was most appropriate for the 'rude, plain, simple nature of those they intended to instruct'.

Inigo Jones had initiated the popular interpretation of megalithic remains as temples, but his attribution of Stonehenge to the Romans did not pass unchallenged for long. In 1663 a small book appeared written by Dr Walter Charleton, physician to Charles II and a friend of John Aubrey, vigorously refuting Jones' entire theory. The substance of Charleton's impressively titled book, *Chorea Gigantum, OR the most famous Antiquity of Great Britain, vulgarly called STONE-HENG, Standing on Salisbury Plain, Restored to the DANES* is given in the prefatory verse by John Dryden:

The *Circling* ſtreams, once thought but pools, of blood
( Whether Life's fewel , or the Bodie's food )
From dark Oblivion *Harvey*'s name ſhall ſave ;
While *Ent* keeps all the honour that he gave.
Nor are *You* , Learned Friend , the leaſt renown'd ;
Whoſe Fame, not circumſcrib'd with *Engliſh* ground ,
Flies like the nimble journey; of the Light ;
And is, like that , unſpent too in its flight.
Whatever *Truths* have been , by *Art* , or *Chance* ,
Redeem'd from *Error* , or from *Ignorance* ,
Thin in their *Authors* , ( like rich veins of Ore )
Your Works unite , and ſtill diſcover more.
Such is the healing virtue of Your Pen ,
To perfect Cures on *Books* , as well as *Men*.
Nor is This Work the leaſt : You well may give
To *Men* new vigour , who make *Stones* to live.
Through You, the *DANES* ( their ſhort Dominion loſt )
A longer Conqueſt than the *Saxons* boaſt.
*Stone-heng*, once thought a *Temple* , You have found
A *Throne*, where Kings, our Earthly Gods, were Crown'd.
Where by their wondring Subjects They were ſeen ,
Joy'd with their Stature, and their Princely meen.
Our *Soveraign* here above the reſt might ſtand ;
And here be choſe again to rule the Land.

These Ruines ſheltred once *His* Sacred Head ,
Then when from *Worʼſters* fatal Field *He* fled ,
Watch'd by the Genius of this Royal place ,
And mighty Viſions of the Daniſh Race.
His *Refuge* then was for a *Temple* ſhown :
But, *He* Reſtor'd , 'tis now become a *Theatre*.

*John Driden.*

On at least one point, however, the studies of Inigo Jones concurred with Charleton's theory that Stonehenge was a Danish *'Court Royal*, or Place for the *Election* and *Inauguration* of their *Kings*': the complicated equipment and skills required to erect the structure meant that it could not possibly have been the work of ancient Britons, 'a rude and barbarous people, utterly ignorant of such Machines and artificial helps'. Not long after the publication of *Chorea Gigantum*, John Webb determinedly re-stated his father-in-law's views, and so the controversy continued. By the end of the seventeenth century, most megalithic sites had emerged from the obscurity of folklore, and were variously regarded as temples, 'forums' or 'sepulchral monuments', built by Romans, Saxons or Danes.

Such conflicting views might have clashed for centuries if John Aubrey had not exerted a crucial, though indirect, influence in the development of theories about the stones. 'Fate', wrote Aubrey, 'dropt me in a countrey most suitable for such enquiries'; he was born in the village of Easton Pierse, thirty miles from Stonehenge, in 1627, and was a schoolfellow of Thomas Hobbes. It was Hobbes who concluded in the *Leviathan*, published in 1651, that the life of primitive man was 'solitary, poore, nasty, brutish, and shorte', and the reasoning on which Aubrey's ideas were based was equally free from any tendency to idealize the ancient Britons. In an essay written in 1659, Aubrey thought that they were 'almost as savage as the Beasts whose skins were their only raiment'. Throughout the seventeenth century, the spirit of 'hard' primitivism is often apparent in writings and illustrations of the Druids, usually concentrated on the gruesome side of Caesar's descriptions. This emphasis is best represented by one of the famous engravings included in Aylett Sammes' *Britannia Antiqua Illustrata* of 1676, which depicts writhing victims trapped within a fantastic cage, and was inspired by Caesar's mention of mass human sacrifices burnt alive in wicker images by the Druids.

Despite their barbarities, Aubrey cautiously concluded that these were the people responsible for the building of stone circles. He was finally sure that he had identified 'Druid's temples' when he encountered the place-name Kerrig y Drewen assigned to a group of monuments in Denbighshire in Camden's *Britannia*. The origin of 'Drewen' has long since been shown to have no connection with Druids, but at the time of another of Aubrey's essays in 1663, it was enough to convince him that his theory was plausible. His 'presumption' was

> . . . That the Druids being the most eminent Priests, or Order of Priests, among the Britaines; tis odds, but that these ancient monuments, sc. Aubury, Stonehenge, Kerrig y Druidd &c, were Temples of the Priests of the most eminent order, viz, Druids, and it is strongly to be presumed, that Aubury, Stoneheng &c, are as ancient as those times. This enquiry, I must confess, is a gropeing into the dark: but although I have not brought it into a cleer light yet I can affirm that I have brought it from an utter darkness, to a thin mist, and have gonne farther in his essay than any one before me . . .

The changing Druid. Aylett Sammes' engraving of 1676 (*left*) was based on a contemporary description of six statues found in Germany and thought to represent Druids by antiquaries of the period. By 1815, Meyrick and Smith's Druid (*right*) had acquired a range of improbable accessories, notably a Bronze Age lunula ornament worn upside-down as a crown.

Aubrey's opinion was supported by careful observation, including the fact that the main ring at Avebury was not a true circle at all, which eluded or was ignored by several of his successors in fieldwork there. When Dr Charleton told Charles II of Aubrey's conviction that Stonehenge was a mere parish church compared to the 'cathedral' of Avebury, the King paid a visit to Marlborough and inspected the monument. 'His Majestie commanded me to digge at the bottom of the stones . . .' Aubrey wrote in a margin, 'to try if I could find any human bones: but I did not doe it'. As the King left Avebury to catch up with the Queen who was on her way to Bath, 'he cast his eie on Silbury-hill, about a mile off: which he had the curiousity to see, and walkt up to the top of it . . .'.

A royal visit alone was not sufficient to popularize Aubrey's theory, and, as with most of his literary projects, the jumble of notes which expounded it were never collected into a book. Extracts were printed in a 1695 edition of Camden, and two years later Aubrey was dead. It is conceivable that the popular view of Stonehenge and Avebury might have remained in confusion, had not a young man of thirty examined and taken notes from a transcript of Aubrey's original manuscript in 1717.

William Stukeley had first visited Stonehenge two years previously, and after that he paid regular annual visits to Wiltshire in order to carry out an extensive programme of investigation. He arrived at Avebury just before a major season of demolition of the stones by the village farmers 'for a little dirty profit', as he commented, but was able to record the position of many stones since broken up or buried. Many of his observations at ancient sites were landmarks on the road to systematic archaeology: for example, he was the first to note the composition of the various layers in the barrows which he excavated. Yet with powers to observe and analyse more accurately than any before him, Stukeley combined a reckless streak of imaginative speculation. Scarcely acknowledging Aubrey's original

A plate from Stukeley's *Stonehenge, A Temple Restored to the British Druids*, printed in 1740.

suggestions on Druidism, Stukeley developed them to fantastic and unsubstantiated extremes. Stonehenge, he declared in his 1740 study, was 'the metropolitical Church of the chief Druid of *Britain* . . . This was the *locus consecratus* where they met at some great festivals of the year, as well to perform the extraordinary sacrifices and religious rites, as to determine causes and civil matters.' An interesting example of Stukeley's imagination at work follows his mention of the Heel Stone (or Bowing Stone, as he referred to it):

> The use of it I can't certainly tell; but I am inclined to think that as part of the religious worship in old patriarchal times, consisted in a solemn adoration, or three silent bowings: the first bowing might be perform'd at this stone, just without the ditch. Then they turn'd by that stone to the left hand, as the manner was, in procession round the temple, both the priests and animals for sacrifice. At those two stones and water-vases, probably there were some washings, lustrations, or sprinklings with holy water and other ceremonies, which I don't pretend to ascertain. Then upon the entry into the temple, perhaps they made the third bow, as in presence of the Deity. After this, in the *court*, we suppose the priests prepar'd the hecatombs and customary sacrifices. If that great stone just within the ditch, always lay, as it does now, flat on the ground, and *in situ* (which I am not unwilling to believe) then, I apprehend, it was a table for dressing the victims . . . I suppose only the priests and chief personages came within the *area*, who made the procession with the sacrifices along the avenue. The multitude kept without, on foot or in their chariots . . .

With Stukeley's volume on Avebury, published three years later, the Druidic theory was expanded still further to account for a whole prehistoric landscape. The area of the Kennet valley, he wrote, 'was entirely sacred ground, under the care and custody of the Druids, one of their great seminaries or academies, every where a fine turf, cover'd over with an infinite variety of barrows . . .' Linking Biblical iconography with the 'serpent's eggs' described by Pliny in connection with the Druids, Stukeley conceived the idea that the two avenues emerging from Avebury were the symbolic expression of a snake cult. The Druids, he explained, had made the whole countryside of hills, valleys and rivers contribute to a great serpentine hieroglyph three miles long, from the 'head' at the Sanctuary to the 'tail' at Beckhampton. Within the 'serpent's egg', the great temple of Avebury itself, 'the highest part of the religion was to be perform'd by the archdruid and the upper order of priests before the magnificent cove of the northern temple, together with hymns, incense, musick and the like.'

It is scarcely surprising that this fanciful concoction, so vividly illustrated by Stukeley's own engraved drawings, became widely accepted as an explanation of the monuments. Yet the popularity of the Druids was a measure of something more than the success of one man's theory. It was a symptom of the growing tastes for the primitive and the exotic, which conveyed the reader of Joseph

Warton's *The Enthusiast* of 1744 from coastlines 'when wild tempests swallow up the plains', over forests from which 'spires emerge' and the 'ruin'd tops' of 'Gothic battlements', to the oak groves dear to 'bards of old, Fair Nature's friends'. The 'pre-romantic' poets such as Gray and Collins responded not only to the uncivilized world of ancient Britain, as re-created by Stukeley, but also to the simple communities still existing in remote parts of the country, as they were encountered and reported in a growing number of travel books. For example, Martin's *Description of the Western Isles*, in which the first crude plan of Callanish appeared, furnished Collins with material for his *Ode on the Popular Superstitions of the Highlands*, notably for the stanza describing the people of St Kilda whose lives are 'yet sincere and plain' and 'blest in primal innocence . . .' The eighteenth-century reading public's extraordinary appetite for the Celtic wilderness and its heroic past, evident in the success of Macpherson's fabricated translations of Ossian, or Gray's versions of Nordic and Welsh poetry, partly explains why the Druids became so firmly fixed in the popular imagination.

The discovery of primitive societies in North America made a profound impact even before the time of Aubrey's essays on ancient Wiltshire. John White, the illustrator on Raleigh's voyage of 1585, portrayed Britons and Picts modelled on the Virginian tribes which the expedition had encountered. The influence of these pictures is apparent in John Speed's *Historie* of 1611 and its representations of

Proud savages from John Speed's *Historie* of 1611, based partly on illustrations of American Indians and on classical references to the tattooed Picts.

ancient Britons, complete with severed heads and bizarre body painting. Aubrey wrote that 'they were 2 or 3 degrees I suppose less savage than the Americans . . .'.

However, from the time of the earliest New World voyages, there were always writers with a quite different response, who compared the simplicity and lack of sophistication in the life of native communities to the golden age. This attitude—'soft' primitivism—became increasingly common, especially after Cook's voyages and their contact with the South Sea islanders. Just as rumours of a golden land of contentment initiated the classical legend of the Hyperboreans, so numerous travel books of the late eighteenth century appeared with descriptions of Pacific paradises. In an Oxford Prize Poem of 1791, George Richards perfectly caught the romantic image of the heroic, isolated native Polynesian; British sailors had

> View'd on the coast the wondering Savage stand
> Uncouth, and fresh from his Creator's hand;

just as in Britain long ago . . .

> Rude as the wilds around his sylvan home,
> In savage grandeur see the Briton roam;
> Bare were his limbs, and strung with toil and cold
> By untam'd nature cast in giant mould.

If the 'Noble Savage' was to be found in Polynesia, then it was natural to conclude that he had once lived among the oak groves and Druid temples of Britain.

Religious controversies were an even stronger stimulus toward the creation of an idealized picture of prehistoric times, and these theological issues were in turn partly provoked by the discovery of American Indians and South Sea Islanders. Were such non-Christian communities condemned to suffer eternal damnation, or did they exist in some state of primal innocence and pure faith? The exponents of 'Natural Religion' were anxious to show that the ancient Britons had shared in universal spiritual values and that their Druid priests, far from practising barbarities such as human sacrifice, were the proud national defenders of true religion against Roman paganism.

The only pre-classical background available to antiquaries was the received truth of the Biblical narrative of the Deluge, and the peopling of the earth by the sons of Noah, Shem, Ham and Japheth. Through complicated and false etymological studies of Welsh words and Hebrew names that sounded similar, the majority of scholars became convinced that Europeans were descended from Japheth's son, Gomer. The Druids had to be placed somewhere within this framework of Biblical authority, so the oaks on the Plain of Mamre recorded in the Old Testament were soon associated with the Druidic groves. Such reasoning provoked the exclamations of a scholar, Edmund Dickinson, in 1655: 'Lo the *Oke Priests*! Lo the *Patriarchs* of the *Druides*! From these sprang the *Sect* of the *Druides*, which reached up at least, as high as *Abraham's* time'. Stukeley's own two volumes were intended as only the first instalments of a vast projected work to be called *Patriarchal Christianity, or a Chronological History of the Origin and Progress of true*

'Grand Conventional Festival of the Britons': a Druidic extravaganza from Meyrick and Smith's *The Costume of the Original Inhabitants of the British Islands* (1815).

*Religion, and of Idolatry*. In 1729 Stukeley had abandoned his medical career to enter Holy Orders, and became convinced that the Druids learned of 'patriarchal' religion from eastern contacts (probably Phoenician traders) and believed in a future Messiah. Until old age he continued to preach sermons based on the contention that the Druids were 'of *Abraham's* religion intirely', and that the symbolic plan of Avebury, the snake emerging from the sacred circle, prefigured 'the eternal procession of the Son from the first cause'.

However, it would be wrong to conclude that Stukeley was only an isolated and eccentric enthusiast. A vigorous theological controversy was generated by those free-thinkers and Deists, such as John Toland, who interpreted the ideas of 'Natural Religion' in an extreme form that threw doubt on the doctrines of Revelation and on the miracles of the Bible. Stukeley was not the only clergyman prepared to defend the Druids against the heretical charge that they had practised anything other than the true faith. The Reverend William Cooke in his *Enquiry into the Druidical and Patriarchal Religion* of 1754 exceeded even Stukeley's claims for Avebury by asserting that it was 'without Question the most glorious Temple of the Kind which the World has ever heard of'. Stukeley and many other antiquaries inclined towards religious orthodoxy would no doubt have agreed with Cooke when he wrote,

> . . . it is evident that the *Patriarchs* were acquainted with the true Nature of the Deity and the Means of their Own Redemption; that JESUS CHRIST is the *Alpha* and *Omega*, and the Christian Scheme the *One Religion* given to Mankind, the *first* and the *last* . . .

Cooke even attempted to blame the matter of human sacrifice (which was simply ignored by most participants in the controversy) on Caesar's bad reporting, and on his literal misinterpretation of a symbolic belief in the redemption of sins:

> . . . Yet [how] easy was it for a *Roman* to mistake the *imputed* for the *real* Sacrifice of a Man? How Natural for a Stranger, and one wholly unacquainted with Revelation to make wrong deductions from such a Principle, and to conclude that, because they were convinced that the Deity would not be appeased without the Sacrifice of a Man, therefore they themselves, in Order to appease him, offered, not bestial but, human Sacrifices . . .

Such were the lengths to which many eighteenth-century theorists on early Britain were prepared to argue, in order to create a race of virtuous and enlightened prehistoric men.

One of the chief interests of what now seems an obscure theological dispute is the transformation of 'patriarchal' religion into the visionary art of William Blake. Behind the extraordinarily complicated mythology of the prophetic books lies a conviction that the origins of humanity arose in the age of the Titans, when the world was populated from 'Albion', which stands not only for Britain but for the lost perfection of humanity itself, when 'Man anciently contain'd in his mighty limbs all things in Heaven & Earth'. The spread of the Druids across the earth preceded and inspired the Hebrew prophets, as some bolder antiquarian speculators such as Edward Davies had seriously claimed. In an address 'To the Jews' from the symbolic book *Jerusalem*, Blake writes:

> Your Ancestors derived their origin from Abraham, Heber, Shem and Noah, who were Druids, as the Druid Temples (which are the Patriarchal Pillars & Oak Groves) over the whole Earth witness to this day.

The children of Albion, he explains in his *Descriptive Catalogue*, were once archetypal figures of the 'golden age'.

> The Britons (say historians) were naked civilized men, learned, studious, abstruse in thought and contemplation; naked, simple, plain in their acts and manners; wiser than after-ages . . .

But at some remote era, the patriarchs degenerated into the Druids of history. The abuse of reason and intellect, which Blake saw as corrupting the free-thinkers and rationalists of his own day, led to an increasingly rigid social structure and finally to the practice of human sacrifice. Far from symbolizing the ancient spirit of true religion, Stonehenge represented the product of a monstrous tyranny—

> —a wondrous rocky World of cruel destiny,
> Rocks piled on rocks reaching the stars, stretching from pole to pole.
> The building is Natural Religion, and its altars Natural Morality,
> A building of eternal death, whose proportions are eternal despair.

This poetic inversion of the central ideas which the antiquaries of a previous century had held with such deep conviction is unique in the literature of Stonehenge. Most writers and artists of the romantic age were content simply to invoke

Stonehenge was the subject of distortion and exaggeration long before the conventional beginning of the romantic period in the arts. The first known sketch (*above*) from a Dutch MSS of 1574, inspired a long line of progressively less faithful copies, from Camden's *Britannia* through to this engraving from a French atlas (*below*) as yet unidentified, but probably dating to the mid-seventeenth century.

the 'Gothic' atmosphere of megalithic remains and to magnify the impressions created by the stones. Even Stukeley's views of Stonehenge, though carefully observed, are drawn on a much exaggerated scale in relationship to the human figures surrounding the stones, while Silbury Hill is distorted to appear with the proportions of a steep-sided Christmas pudding. Yet the element of the picturesque in Stukeley's work is negligible compared to the 'gigantism' which began to influence depictions of megaliths, and which reached its heights in Cambry's *Monumens Celtiques* of 1805. In this volume, the alignments of Carnac are scarcely recognizable as artificially raised blocks of stone, but instead have become massive fingers of rock sprouting out of the ground, towering over full-grown trees. If the stones themselves were not always enlarged, then the same effects could be created by stormy backgrounds or dramatic lighting, outlining the cracks and fissures in the rocks, such as characterized Stonehenge studies by Turner and Constable, as well as many other less distinguished artists.

Besides Blake, only one major nineteenth-century poet connected Stonehenge with the currents of speculation created by the antiquaries of the period. In August 1793 William Wordsworth was left alone on Salisbury Plain after the carriage in which he had been travelling met with an accident. It was a crucial period in the poet's life, a few months after the declaration of war between Britain and France, the shattering of all his hopes for the French Revolution, and of his relationship with Annette Vallon. In his autobiographical poem of 1805, *The Prelude*, Wordsworth describes the deep impact made on his imagination by his three-day walk across the Plain. The Wiltshire landscape first of all induces a 'reverie' of the past, in which the 'barbaric majesty' of Aylett Sammes' engravings seems to be called to his mind,

> . . . the sacrificial Altar, fed
> With living men, how deep the groans, the voice
> Of those in the gigantic wicker thrills
> Throughout the region far and near, pervades
> The monumental hillocks . . .

But a second mood overtakes the poet, and the heroic image gives way to a mystical 'antiquarian's dream' of the primitive astronomer, shaping the landscape to symbolize his skill,

> . . . the work, as some divine,
> Of infant science, imitative forms
> By which the Druids covertly express'd
> Their knowledge of the heavens . . .

If we look at this passage in *The Prelude* from a narrow historical point of view, it does seem to balance both the 'hard' and 'soft' images of ancient Britain which were inherent in serious speculative thought on the monuments from the beginning.

Artists still continue to be inspired by megalithic remains, even in the field of music. For example, Sir Michael Tippett's experience of Avebury played a part in the creation of his opera *The Midsummer Marriage*. Writing of the instinctive nature of the artistic drive, Tippett describes Avebury as

—a strange, strange place, full of magic, where certainly art and religion were practised together. . . . Could we go back to that time and see the people moving about, we would find that they danced to music and sang and dressed themselves in particular clothes, and that at that time the religion and the art were absolutely together . . .

Whether or not we would share such a picture of Avebury, Tippett's response to it is perhaps one more example of the way these monuments have always excited an idealizing or simplifying vision of their builders. The image of the circles as places where the conflicting ideas and values of men were drawn together either in ritual harmony or in a scientific system continues to fascinate both artistic and technical minds to this day.

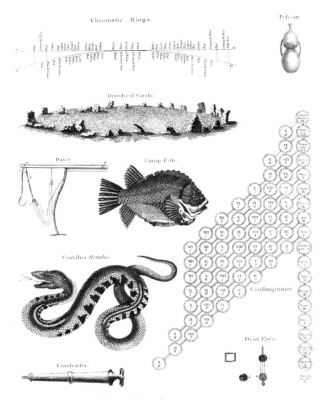

From an encyclopaedia of 1795.

# 14: The New Hyperboreans

By the early nineteenth century curators of museums and private collections had begun to accumulate increasing quantities of prehistoric implements, pottery and ornaments. What inferences could be drawn from the comparison of museum objects? For instance, did the contrast between bronze and iron tools indicate their respective use by distinct classes, or was there a chronological difference involved? The far-sighted curator of the National Museum of Denmark, Christian Thomsen, recognized a practical and theoretical need for some organizing structure or 'model' as a basis for classifying and arranging the material in the collections. His guide-book to the National Museum at Copenhagen, published in 1836, included the first serious attempt to devise such a system, and his proposal of successive 'Ages' of Stone, Bronze and Iron was a turning point in archaeology. Once the idea of technological progression had taken root, other Scandinavian theorists, such as Sven Nilsson, developed the picture further. Nilsson suggested four stages of civilization, from the savage to the herdsman, agriculturist and finally to the growth of specialized ranks or professions, which (as he wrote in 1843) enabled society

> . . . to fulfil more and more completely its allotted mission—to attain the highest degree of culture and the highest state of civilization.

Clearly the concept of technological and cultural progress was relevant not only to the past, but reflected the social beliefs of many people in nineteenth-century Europe.

Charles Darwin's *The Origin of Species*, published in 1859, finally overthrew a literal Biblical framework for prehistory, but Darwin was at first reluctant to apply the theory of natural selection to human society; indeed, in the closing paragraphs of *The Origin*, he was prepared only to say that 'light will be thrown on the origin of man and his history'. Less cautious theorists, such as Herbert Spencer, who invented the phrase 'the survival of the fittest' in 1852, envisaged a process of *social* selection operating throughout human history, which was especially evident in the development of man's tools and technology. Spencer believed this process was not only inevitable but that it fully justified the social order of his own times. He opposed any state interference on behalf of the poor because such actions would obstruct the 'natural selection' of the upper classes at the expense of the lower. In other words, for Spencer and his followers, the broad outline of the archaeological 'three-age' classification provided a background for a highly individualistic and competitive theory of society, past and present.

Obviously, in the self-confident atmosphere of mid-Victorian Britain, it was

A highly impressive megalithic monument was built in the 1820s under the directions of William Danby of Swinton Hall, near Masham, Yorkshire, to give work to local unemployed people. They produced a number of dolmens and avenues and this large temple, with its Druidic grotto and sacrificial altar (*above*) and central precinct with standing stone (*below*).

immensely comforting for many well-educated people to believe that they represented the peak of a naturally ordered society. There was no urge to believe in a 'golden age' when men were bound together in corporate values and harmony. Early men were thought of not as 'patriarchs', or as superior prophets of a lost epoch, but rather as 'toolmakers', since there was an emphasis on the technology which seemed to demonstrate so clearly man's inexorable rise to civilization. In the popular literature at least, we return to the spirit of 'hard' primitivism, evident in the titles of books on prehistoric Britain such as *Man the Primaeval Savage* by Worthington G. Smith (published in 1894) or in imaginative descriptions of ancient ceremonies, like the 'eye-witness' account of a long barrow burial at Ogbury Down, Wiltshire. This appeared in an 1891 book of essays by Grant Allen rather inappropriately titled *Falling in Love*:

> I saw the fearful orgy of massacre and rapine around the open tumulus, the wild priest shattering with his gleaming tomahawk the skulls of his victims, the fire of gorse and low brushwood prepared to roast them, the heads and feet flung carelessly on the top of the yet uncovered stone chamber, the awful dance of the blood-stained cannibals around the mangled remains of men and oxen, and finally, the long task of heaping up above the stone hut of the dead king the earthen mound that was never again to be opened to the light of day till, ten thousand years later, we modern Britons invaded with our prying,

Last rites at a burial cairn: the frontispiece from Bateman's *Vestiges of the Antiquities of Derbyshire*, published in 1848.

sacrilegious mattock the sacred privilege of the cannibal feast.

A harsh and strongly materialistic vision of our ancestors persists among the general public to this day. Even in the academic world, we should recall that a decade ago it was widely believed that Stonehenge was inspired and built under Mycenaean influence. One of the subsidiary reasons for such a theory was that a 'barbarian' community was incapable of so refined and calculated a design. In any case, modern archaeologists are naturally cautious of speculating beyond the limitations of their own skills and the material evidence. In an excellent general book on English prehistory published in 1940, Professor Grahame Clark summarized a scholarly view of the difficulties attached to megalithic sites:

> Even if we could visit Bronze Age Britain and study at first hand the rites and practices associated with them, it would still be difficult to comprehend their underlying meaning: to probe the innermost consciousness of men who lived thousands of years ago by measuring and classifying stones, however meticulously, is manifestly vain.

Many ordinary visitors to Stonehenge or Avebury would still conclude that the meaning and purpose of these monuments is forever lost in primitive and barbaric obscurity.

Yet the 1960s saw a concentration of attempts by people, usually outside the field of academic archaeology, to recover new information from the stones. This work implied not only that we could 'probe the innermost consciousness' of Bronze Age men and discover the main purposes of the monuments, but that the scientific capabilities and interests of these men were very similar to our own. Professor Thom has wisely avoided general speculation about the people who built Temple Wood or Callanish, but in his book on the lunar sites he speaks of the 'genius' who must have been responsible for solving the problem of correcting observations. The stones were not 'orientated for some ritualistic purpose' but seemed to represent 'the remnants of a scientific study of the Moon's motion'. The work of Thom and Hawkins assumes that religion still played an important part in the building of monuments, but that the driving force behind them was scientific curiosity.

The recent application of techniques such as computer analysis or photogrammetry to recover and test new kinds of information partly explains why so much interest has been focused on the possible existence of an astronomer priesthood. Yet underlying the work of some theorists is a more general feeling that the image of the past presented to them from archaeological sources is inadequate. One case is *The Roots of Civilisation*, published in 1972, which proposed that simple lunar observations were recorded by tally-marks scratched on many objects from Palaeolithic times. Its author, Alexander Marshack, was a professional writer at the outset of his researches, and in his Introduction he describes his sense of 'something missing' in the picture of primitive man conveyed by text-books. It is surely as interesting to ask why this emphasis on the 'missing' rational capabilities of early man has arisen in recent years as to determine whether the theories themselves are right or wrong.

Perhaps it is easier to understand why the astronomical theories of Thom and Hawkins have been so enthusiastically taken up by many young people who reject any conventional concept of the past. The hypothesis which can claim to project the modern student into the mind of a megalithic observer, and show just where he stood on a certain evening, to fulfil a scientific and religious purpose, has an obvious appeal to the romantic and occultist imagination.

The views of two writers in particular have generated much enthusiasm. T. C. Lethbridge was a well-known Cambridge archaeologist who specialized in the Anglo-Saxon period and taught many of the generation who were later to become distinguished scholars in their own right. Throughout his life, Lethbridge was not only absorbed by academic questions, but by his own experiences of extra-sensory perception, dowsing and other phenomena. In his last book, published posthumously in 1972 and called *The Legend of the Sons of God*, he described how he and his wife were able to 'date' the Merry Maidens circle to 2450 BC by the turns of a pendulum.

> . . . The hand resting on the stone received a strong tingling sensation like a mild electric shock and the pendulum itself shot out until it was circling nearly horizontally to the ground. The stone itself, which must have weighed over a ton, felt as if it were rocking and almost dancing about. This was quite alarming, but I stuck to my counting . . .

Lethbridge was another person who felt that the archaeological record was somehow inadequate, failing to explain the presence of monuments in what are (now) remote parts of the country such as Dartmoor or the Hebrides. Yet he rejected any environmental or astronomical explanation, and instead suggested that the alignments of Callanish or Carnac were devised as signal beacons to be seen from some kind of extra-terrestrial craft.

The most widely read exponent of unorthodox theories about the past is John Michell, who in a recent work is concerned with the revelation of a 'sacred' and eternal canon of numbers which he claims is detectable in Stonehenge and other ancient religious structures. Briefly, Michell seeks to recover not merely the practical astronomical functions of the monuments but also the entire spiritual and magical system in which the astronomy played its part. Indeed, Michell believes that to interpret the megalithic religion as a 'pure' science, with a priesthood modelled on the scientific establishment of the present day, is a fundamental mistake.

At the moment perhaps the most widely circulated idea, derived from Watkins and developed by Michell and others, is that all early sites were related to one another by a network of alignments (called ley-lines) which marked the presence of some kind of force, now detectable by dowsing and other methods. It would be unusual to go to any current archaeological dig and not find a surprisingly

Earth's first civilisation reawakens in

# Gandalf's Garden

### Mystical Scene Magazine

issue 6

3/-

The re-awakening of a mystical interest in the past: cover from
a 1969 issue of *Gandalf's Garden*.

large group of people dedicated to discovering and discussing the secret force fields of ancient monuments. It may be added that some reputable excavators actually use dowsing rods to find buried features in conjunction with electronic surveying devices. What is of interest is not so much these half-understood forces but their interpretation as evidence for a system which brought universal harmony to early Britain. The literature associated with these ideas is of an unmistakably 'golden age' character. Extracts from writings by Anthony Roberts are typical:

> At points such as Stonehenge [or] Callanish . . . injection of solar energy into the Ley system would occur when the sun rose over the alignments—now preserved as Saints' days, the Equinoxes and Solstices—celebrated by the priesthood and used for levitation, flight and other forgotten powers . . . The geometrically straight lines of the leys rearranged the flow of terrestrial current, imparting a pattern of fertility and harmony to the land . . .

An architect, Keith Critchlow, who has interested himself in the proportions of Stonehenge, takes the scarcity of occupation evidence in southern England to indicate that the prehistoric inhabitants were perfectly integrated with their natural environment, and he stresses the lessons which may be learned for our own wasteful and polluting society. In magazines such as *The Ley Hunter* or *Arcana*, articles of this nature appear side-by-side with explanations of radiocarbon chronology and the work of Professor Thom.

At a time when many young people are reacting against a society increasingly dominated by science and technology, it is perhaps not surprising that the scientists and technologists of early Britain, glimpsed over a comfortable time-span of four thousand years, offer an alternative, escapist vision.

The archaeological record has broadened significantly in the past decade. Fundamental problems seem on the point of solution, even if more puzzles arise to take their place. Dramatic evidence has shown the probable meeting places of Neolithic communities and where their domestic remains are likely to be found. The prehistoric environment can now be reconstructed in detail from plant and pollen traces recovered from an excavation. The great monuments of standing stones have emerged from total obscurity to the point where a few seem to be explicable by plausible and rational scientific theories. It is surely ironic, just as new evidence may prompt some of us towards an entirely reasonable view of our ancestors, that once again 'rumours', this time of mathematical research understood clearly by only a few, have created for many others a Hyperborean dreamland of primitive science.

# *Appendix One*

## List of Conventional Radiocarbon Dates

The following uncorrected dates are from sites mentioned in the text, and are given there in a corrected form (see 'A Note on Dates'). They are all derived from *Archaeological Site Index to Radiocarbon Dates for Great Britain and Ireland*, published by the Council for British Archaeology, 1971–. The Brittany dates in the text are based on P. R. Giot, 'The impact of radiocarbon dating ... in *Proceedings of the Prehistoric Society* XXXVII Part II, 1971, p. 208.

| | | |
|---|---|---|
| *Antofts Windypit* | BM—62 | 1800 BC ± 150 |
| *Arminghall* | BM—129 | 2490 BC ± 150 |
| *Barford* (last phase) | Birm—7 | 2416 BC ± 64 |
| *Durrington Walls* material from base of | BM—400 | 2050 BC ± 90 |
| main enclosure ditch | BM—399 | 2015 BC ± 90 |
| | BM—398 | 1977 BC ± 90 |
| Packing of south circle, last phase | BM—396 | 2000 BC ± 90 |
| | BM—395 | 1950 BC ± 90 |
| | BM—397 | 1900 BC ± 90 |
| *Hembury* | BM—138 | 3330 BC ± 150 |
| *Newgrange* | GrN—5463 | 2465 BC ± 40 |
| | GrN—5462 | 2550 BC ± 40 |
| *Silbury Hill* | I—4136 | 2145 BC ± 95 |
| *Star Carr* | Q—14 | 7607 BC ± 210 |
| | C—353 | 7538 BC ± 350 |
| *Stonehenge* I | I—2328 | 2180 BC ± 105 |
| II (abandonment) | I—2384 | 1620 BC ± 110 |
| IIIb/IIIc transition | I—2445 | 1240 BC ± 105 |
| *Wayland's Smithy* (phase II) | I—2328 | 2820 BC ± 130 |
| *Wilsford Shaft* | NPL—74 | 1380 BC ± 90 |
| *Windmill Hill* | BM—74 | 2580 BC ± 150 |

# *Appendix Two*

## Further Reading

The following selection of works which the author has found useful is divided into groups related to the content of each chapter. The sub-headings should provide further help in tracing a reference. The more common archaeological periodicals are abbreviated as follows:

| | |
|---|---|
| *Ant* | Antiquity |
| *AntJ* | Antiquaries Journal, Society of Antiquaries of London |
| *Arch* | Archaeologia |
| *ArchJ* | Archaeological Journal |
| *CA* | Current Archaeology |
| *JCorkHAS* | Journal of Cork Historical & Archaeological Society |
| *JRSAI* | Journal of Royal Society of Antiquaries of Ireland |
| *PPS* | Proceedings of the Prehistoric Society |
| *PRIA* | Proceedings of the Royal Irish Academy |
| *PSAS* | Proceedings of the Society of Antiquaries of Scotland |
| *TrGlasgAS* | Transactions of the Glasgow Archaeological Society |
| *UJA* | Ulster Journal of Archaeology |
| *WiltsAM* | Wiltshire Archaeological Magazine |
| *YAJ* | Yorkshire Archaeological Journal |

Most of the publications listed here can be studied (on written application to the librarian) at large museums or libraries; the author found the Society of Antiquaries, London, and the Institute of Archaeology, London, invaluable for research.

## Introductions to European Prehistory

Childe, V. G., *The Dawn of European Civilization*, Routledge 1957.
  *The Prehistory of European Society*, Pelican 1958.
Clark, J. G. D., *Prehistoric Europe: The Economic Basis*, Methuen 1952.
  and Piggott, S., *Prehistoric Societies*, Pelican 1970.
Daniel, G. E., *The Origins and Growth of Archaeology*, Pelican 1957.
  *From Worsaae to Childe: the Models of Prehistory*, in *PPS* Vol 37 part 2 1971, p. 140.
Piggott, S., *Ancient Europe*, Edinburgh University Press 1965.
Roe, D., *Prehistory*, Paladin 1971.

# Radiocarbon Dating

Libby, W. F., *Radiocarbon Dating*, University of Chicago Press 1955.

Olssun, I. U. (ed), *Radiocarbon Variations and Absolute Chronology,* Proc. 12th Nobel Symposium, John Wiley, New York 1969.

*The Radiocarbon Revolution*, in *CA* No 18 Jan 1970, p. 180.

Renfrew, C., *The Tree-Ring Calibration of Radiocarbon: An Archaeological Evaluation,* in *PPS* Vol 36 1970, p. 280.

   *Revolution in Prehistory*, in *The Listener* Vol 84 Dec 31 1970, p. 897 and Jan 7 1971, p. 12.

   *Before Civilization*, Jonathan Cape 1973.

# Megalithic Tombs and Malta

Borlase, W. C., *The Dolmens of Ireland*, Chapman and Hall 1897.

Childe, V. G., *Maes Howe*, in *PSAS* Vol 88 1956, p. 155.

Daniel, G. E., *The Megalith Builders of Western Europe*, Pelican 1963.

   *The Prehistoric Chamber Tombs of France*, Thames and Hudson 1960.

   *Northmen and Southmen*, in *Ant* 41 1967, p. 313.

   and ÓRíordáin, S. P., *New Grange,* Thames and Hudson 1964.

Eogan, G., *Excavations at Knowth, Co. Meath, 1962–1965*, in *PRIA* Vol 66 Sectn. C, p. 299.

Evans, J. D., *Malta*, Thames and Hudson 1959.

Giot, P. R., *Brittany*, Thames and Hudson 1960.

   *The Impact of Radiocarbon Dating . . .*, in *PPS* Vol 37 part 2 1971, p. 208.

Henshall, A. S., *The Chambered Tombs of Scotland*, Edinburgh University Press, Vol I 1963, Vol II 1972.

L'Helgouach, J., *Les Sépultres Mégalithiques en Armorique*, Faculté des Sciences, Rennes 1965.

O'Kelly, C., *Guide to Newgrange*, 2nd edtn., John English, Wexford 1971.

Powell, T. G. E., and others, *Megalithic Enquiries in the West of Britain: a Liverpool Symposium*, Liverpool University Press 1969.

# CHAPTER TWO

## Introductions to Early Britain

Childe, V. G., *The Prehistory of Scotland*, Kegan Paul 1935.

Clark, J. G. D., *Excavations at Star Carr*, Cambridge University Press 1954.

   *Prehistoric England*, Batsford paperback 1962.

Crampton, P., *Stonehenge of the Kings*, John Baker 1967.

Foster, I. Ll., and Daniel, G. E., *Prehistoric and Early Wales*, Routledge and Kegan Paul 1965.

Piggott, S., *The Neolithic Cultures of the British Isles*, Cambridge University Press 1954.

Place, R., *Introduction to Archaeology*, Newnes paperback 1968.
Raftery, J., *Prehistoric Ireland*, Batsford 1951.
Stone, J. F. S., *Wessex Before the Celts*, Thames and Hudson 1958.

## Long barrows

Ashbee, P., *The Earthen Long Barrow in Britain*, Dent 1970.
Atkinson, R. J. C., *Wayland's Smithy*, in *Ant* Vol 39 1965, p. 126.
*CA* No 34 Sep 1972 (Megaliths issue).
Piggott, S., *The West Kennet Long Barrow: Excavations 1955–56*, HMSO 1962.

## Cursus monuments

Atkinson, R. J. C., *The Dorset Cursus*, in *Ant* Vol 29 1955, p. 4.
Dymond, D. P., *Ritual Monuments at Rudston, E. Yorks*, in *PPS* Vol 32 1966, p. 86.
Stone, J. F. S., *The Stonehenge Cursus and its Affinities*, in *ArchJ* Vol 104 1948, p. 7.

## Causewayed enclosures

Curwen, E. C., *The Archaeology of Sussex*, Methuèn 1937.
Piggott, S., *The Neolithic Cultures of the British Isles*, Cambridge University Press 1954.
Smith, I. F., *Windmill Hill and Avebury* (booklet), The Clover Press 1959.
    *Windmill Hill and Avebury: Excavations by Alexander Keiller 1925–39*, Clarendon Press 1965.
    *Windmill Hill and its Implications*, in *Palaeohistoria* Vol 12 1966, p. 469.

# CHAPTER THREE

## Late Neolithic enclosures

Atkinson, R. J. C., and others, *Excavations at Dorchester, Oxon.*, Ashmolean Museum, Oxford 1951.
Bartram, W., *Travels through North and South Carolina . . .*, London 1792.
Case, H., and others, *Excavations at City Farm, Hanborough, Oxon.*, in *Oxoniensa* Vol 29–30 1964–65, p. 1.
Clark, J. G. D., *The Timber Monument at Arminghall and its Affinities*, in *PPS* Vol 2 1936, p. 1.
Cunnington, M. E., *Woodhenge*, Simpson, Devizes 1929.
    *The Sanctuary on Overton Hill, near Avebury*, in *WiltsAM* Vol 45 1931, p. 300.
Gray, H. St. G., various reports on Maumbury Rings in *Proc. of Dorset Field Club*.
Houlder, C., *The Henge Monuments at Llandegai*, in *Ant* Vol 42 1968, p. 216.
Piggott, S., *Timber Circles: A Re-examination*, in *ArchJ* Vol 96 1940, p. 193.
    *The Excavations at Cairnpapple Hill*, in *PSAS* Vol 82 1947–8, p. 68.

Wainwright, G. J., *Durrington Walls: a Ceremonial Enclosure of the Second Millennium BC*, in *Ant* Vol 42 1968, p. 20.

*A Review of Henge Monuments in the Light of Recent Research*, in *PPS* Vol 35 1969, p. 112.

*Woodhenges*, in *Scientific American* Vol 223 No 5 1970, p. 30.

*Mount Pleasant*, in *CA* No 12 1970, p. 320.

*The Excavation of a Late Neolithic Enclosure at Marden, Wiltshire*, in *AntJ* Vol 51 1971, p. 177.

and Longworth, I. H., *Durrington Walls: Excavations 1966–1968*, Society of Antiquaries, London 1971.

*Waulud's Bank*, in *CA* No 30 1972, p. 173.

# CHAPTER FOUR

## Megalithic sites in England and Wales

Atkinson, R. J. C., *Stonehenge*, Pelican 1960.
*Stonehenge and Avebury*, HMSO Guidebook 1959.
*The Stonehenge Bluestones*, in *Ant* Vol 48 1974, p. 62.
Fowler, P. J., *Wessex*, Heinemann 1967.
Gray, H. St. G., *The Avebury Excavations 1908–1922*, in *Arch* Vol 84 1935, p. 99.
Grimes, W. F., *The Stone Circles and Related Monuments of Wales*, in *Culture and Environment*, ed I. Ll. Foster and L. Alcock, Routledge and Kegan Paul 1963.
Helm, P. J., *Exploring Prehistoric England*, Robert Hale 1971.
Longworth, I. H., *Yorkshire*, Heinemann 1965.
Painter, K. S., *The Severn Basin*, Cory, Adams and Mackay 1964.
Smith, I. F., *Windmill Hill and Avebury* (booklet), The Clover Press 1959.
*Windmill Hill and Avebury: Excavations by Alexander Keiller 1925–39*, Clarendon Press 1965.
Thomas, N., *A Guide to Prehistoric England*, Batsford 1960.
Worth, R. H., *Worth's Dartmoor*, David and Charles 1967.
For Silbury Hill, see Atkinson, R. J. C., *Silbury Hill 1968*, in *Ant* Vol 42 1968, p. 299.
*The Date of Silbury Hill*, in *Ant* Vol 43 1969, p. 216.

## Scottish sites

Anderson, J., *Scotland in Pagan Times* Vol I, David Douglas 1868.
Burl, H. A. W., *The Recumbent Stone Circles of N.E. Scotland*, in *PSAS* Vol 102 1969–70, p. 56.
Feachem, R., *A Guide to Prehistoric Scotland*, Batsford 1963.
Ritchie, J. N. G. and A., *Edinburgh and South-East Scotland*, Heinemann 1972.
Scott, J. G., *South-West Scotland*, Heinemann 1966.

## Irish sites

Davies, O., *Stone Circles in Northern Ireland*, in *UJA* Vol 2 1939, p. 2.

Evans, E. E., *Prehistoric and Early Christian Ireland: A Guide,* Batsford 1966.

Flanagan, L., *Ulster*, Heinemann 1970.

Harbison, P., *Guide to the National Monuments of Ireland*, Gill and MacMillan, Dublin 1970.

Mahr, A., *New Aspects and Problems in Irish Prehistory*, in *PPS* Vol 3 1937, p. 262. For Timoney Hills, see p. 363.

Norman, E. R., and St Joseph, J. K. S., *The Early Development of Irish Society*, Cambridge University Press 1969.

ÓRíordáin, S. P., *Lough Gur Excavations: The Great Stone Circle* (B) *in Grange Townland*, in *PRIA* Vol 54 1951, p. 37.

    *Antiquities of the Irish Countryside*, University Paperback 1965.

Somerville, B., *Five Stone Circles of West Cork*, in *JCorkHAS* Vol 35 1930, p. 70.

## CHAPTER FIVE

### Domestic evidence

Bradley, R., *Where Have All the Houses Gone?*, in *CA* No 21 1970, p. 264.

Childe, V. G., *Skara Brae*, Kegan Paul 1931.

Clarke, D. L., *Beaker Pottery of Great Britain and Ireland*, Cambridge University Press 1970.

ÓRíordáin, S. P., and O'Donachair, *Lough Gur Excavations: Site J, Knockadoon*, in *JRSAI* Vol 77 1947, p. 39.

    *Lough Gur Excavations: Neolithic and Bronze Age Houses on Knockadoon*, in *PRIA* Vol 56 C 1954, p. 297.

    For Lough Gur summary, see *PPS* Vol 12 1946, p. 147.

Simpson, D. D. A., *Economy and Settlement in Neolithic and Early Bronze Age Britain*, Leicester University Press 1971.

## Round barrows

Annable, F. K., and Simpson, D. D. A., *Guide Catalogue of the Neolithic and Bronze Age Collections in Devizes Museum*, Wilts. Arch. and Nat. Hist. Soc., Devizes 1963.

Ashbee, P., *The Bronze Age Round Barrow in Britain*, Phoenix House 1960.

Coles, J., and Taylor, J., *The Wessex Culture: A Minimal View,* in *Ant* Vol 45 1971, p. 6.

Colt Hoare, R., *The Ancient History of Wiltshire*, Vols I and II, 1812–19.

Crawford, O. G. S., and Keiller, A., *Wessex from the Air*, Oxford University Press 1928.

Fox, C., *Life and Death in the Bronze Age*, Routledge 1959.

Grinsell, L. V., *The Ancient Burial Mounds of England*, Methuen 1953.

McKerrell, H., *On the Origins of British Faience Beads . . .*, in *PPS* Vol 38 1972, p. 286.

Piggott, S., *The Early Bronze Age in Wessex*, in *PPS* Vol 4 1938, p. 53.

Renfrew, C., *Wessex as a Social Question*, in *Ant* Vol 47 1973, p. 221.

Scott, J. G., *South-West Scotland*, Heinemann 1966.

Stone, J. F. S., *Wessex Before the Celts*, Thames and Hudson 1958.

# CHAPTER SIX

## Stonehenge and astronomical theories

Atkinson, R. J. C., *Stonehenge*, Pelican 1960.

    *Stonehenge and Avebury*, HMSO Guidebook 1959.

    *Moonshine on Stonehenge*, in *Ant* Vol 40 1966, p. 212.

Colton, R., and Martin, R. L., *Eclipse Prediction at Stonehenge*, in *Nature* Vol 221 1969, p. 1011.

Duke, Rev. E., *The Druid Temples of the County of Wilts*, London 1846.

Harrison, W. J., *Bibliography of Stonehenge and Avebury*, in *WiltsAM* Vol 32 1902, p. 1.

Hawkins, G. S., *Stonehenge Decoded*, in *Nature* Vol 200 1963, p. 306.

    *Stonehenge: a Neolithic Computer*, in *Nature* Vol 202 1964, p. 1258.

    *Sun, Moon, Men and Stones*, in *American Scientist* Vol 53 1965, p. 391.

    *Astro-Archaeology*, in *Vistas in Astronomy* Vol 10, ed Beer, A., Pergamon Press 1968.

    *Stonehenge Decoded*, Fontana paperback 1970.

    *Photogrammetric Survey of Stonehenge and Callanish*, National Geographic Society Research Reports, 1965 Projects, Washington DC 1971.

    *Beyond Stonehenge*, Hutchinson 1974.

Hawley, W., *Excavations at Stonehenge*, various references in *AntiqJ*.

Hoyle, F., *Speculations on Stonehenge*, in *Ant* Vol 40 1966, p. 262.

    see also *Hoyle on Stonehenge: some comments*, in *Ant* Vol 41 1967, p. 91

Lockyer, N., *Stonehenge and other British Stone Monuments Astronomically Considered*, Macmillan 1909 (2nd edtn).

Newham, C. A., *The Astronomical Significance of Stonehenge*, John Blackburn, Leeds 1972.

Sadler, D. H., *Prediction of Eclipses*, in *Nature* Vol 2111 1966, p. 1119.

Smith, J., *Choir Gaur*, Salisbury 1771.

Stukeley, W., *Stonehenge, a Temple Restored to the British Druids*, London 1740.

Thomas, H. H., *The Source of the Stones of Stonehenge*, in *AntiqJ* Vol 3 1923, p. 239.

Trotter, A. P., *Stonehenge as an Astronomical Instrument*, in *Ant* Vol 1 1927, p. 42.

## CHAPTER SEVEN
## Calendar theories for other megalithic sites

Barber, J., *The Orientation of the Recumbent-Stone Circles of the South-West of Ireland*, in *Journal of Kerry Arch. and Hist. Soc.* 1972, p. 26.

Lockyer, N., *Some Questions for Archaeologists*, in *Nature* Vol 73 1906, p. 280.
  *Stonehenge and other British Stone Monuments Astronomically Considered*, Macmillan 1909 (2nd edtn).

Lockyer, T. M. and W. L., *Life and Works of Sir Norman Lockyer*, Macmillan 1928.

MacKie, E. W., *Archaeological tests on supposed prehistoric astronomical sites in Scotland*, in *Phil. Trans. R. Soc.* A. 276 1974, p. 169.

Patrick, J., *Midwinter sunrise at Newgrange,* in *Nature* Vol 249 1974, p. 517

Thom, A., *The Solar Observatories of Megalithic Man*, in *Journal of British Astronomical Association* Vol 64 1954, p. 397.
  *Megalithic Astronomy: Indications in Standing Stones,* in *Vistas in Astronomy* Vol 7, ed. Beer, A., Pergamon Press 1966.
  *Megalithic Sites in Britain*, Clarendon Press 1967.
  *Megalithic Lunar Observatories*, Clarendon Press 1971 (see Chapter 4).

Simpson, D. D. A., *Excavations at Kintraw, Argyll*, in *PSAS* Vol 99 1968, p. 54.

Somerville, B., *Orientation*, in *Ant* Vol 1 1927, p. 31.

Windle, B. C. A., *On Certain Megalithic Remains Immediately Surrounding Lough Gur, County Limerick*, in *PRIA* Vol 30 1912, p. 283 (but see modern excavations under **Irish sites**).

## Callanish

Callender, H., *Notice of the Stone Circle at Callernish, in the Island of Lewis*, in *PSAS* Vol 2 1854–7, p. 380.

Hawkins, G. S., *Callanish, a Scottish Stonehenge*, in *Science* Vol 147 1965, p. 127.
  *A Photogrammetric Survey of Stonehenge and Callanish*, National Geographic Society Research Reports, 1965 Projects, Washington DC 1971.

Innes, C., *Notice of the Stone Circle of Callernish*, in *PSAS* Vol 3, p. 110.

James, H., *Plans and Photographs of Stonehenge and Turusachan in the Island of Lewis*, Ordnance Survey 1867.

Macchulloch, J., *A Description of the Western Isles of Scotland* Vol 3 1819, p. 49.

Martin, M., *A Description of the Western Islands of Scotland*, 1716.

Somerville, B., *Prehistoric Monuments in the Outer Hebrides, and their Astronomical Significance*, in *Journal of Royal Anthropological Institute* Vol 42 1912, p. 23 (includes 1912 survey).
  *Astronomical Indications in the Megalithic Monument at Callanish*, in *Journal of British Astronomical Association* Vol 23 1912, p. 83.

Stuart, J., *Notes of Incised Marks . . .*, in *PSAS* Vol 3, p. 212, see Plate XXV (sketch of Callanish III).

Thom, A., *Megalithic Sites in Britain,* Clarendon Press 1967, see pp. 122–8.
   *Megalithic Lunar Observatories,* Clarendon Press 1971, see pp. 68–70.

# CHAPTER EIGHT
## Lunar sites

Anderson, J., *Scotland in Pagan Times,* Vol 1, David Douglas 1868, see p. 126 for stone fans.

Heggie, D. C., *Megalithic Lunar Observatories: an Astronomer's View,* in *Ant* Vol 46 1972, p. 43.

Hewat Craw, J., *Excavations at Dunadd and Other Sites,* in *PSAS* Vol 64 1929–30, p. 111.

Kendall, D. G., review of Thom 1971 in *Ant* Vol 45 1971, p. 310.

Scott, L., *The Chambered Tomb of Unival,* in *PSAS* Vol 82 1947–8, p. 1.

Thom, A., *The Lunar Observatories of Megalithic Man,* in *Vistas of Astronomy* Vol 11, ed Beer, A., Pergamon Press 1969.
   *Megalithic Lunar Observatories,* Clarendon Press 1971.
   *A Megalithic Lunar Observatory in Orkney: The Ring of Brogar and its Cairns* in *Journal for History of Astronomy* Vol 4 1973, p. 111. Other papers forthcoming in the *Journal for History of Astronomy.*

## Megalithic geometry

Atkinson, R. J. C., *The Southern Circle at Durrington Walls—a Numerical Investigation,* in *Durrington Walls: Excavations 1966–1968,* Society of Antiquaries, London 1971, p. 355.

Broadbent, S. R., *Quantum Hypotheses,* in *Biometrika* Vol 42 1955, p. 45.
   *Examination of a Quantum Hypothesis Based on a Single Set of Data,* in *Biometrika* Vol 43 1956, p. 32.

Burl, A., *Dating the British Stone Circles,* in *American Scientist* Vol 61 1973, p. 167.

Case, H., and others, *Excavations at City Farm, Hanborough, Oxon.,* in *Oxoniensa* Vol 29–30 1964–65, see p. 16.

Cunnington, M. E., *Woodhenge,* Simpson, Devizes 1929.

Hammerton, M., *The Megalithic Fathom: a Suggestion,* in *Ant* Vol 45 1971, p. 302.

Hogg, A. H. A., review of Thom 1967 in *Archaeologia Cambrensis* 1968, p. 207.

Kendall, D. G., *Hunting Quanta,* in *Phil. Trans. R. Soc. A.* 276 1974.

MacKie E. W., *Stone Circles: for Savages or Savants?,* in *CA* No 11 1968, p. 279.

Thom, A., *A Statistical Examination of the Megalithic Sites in Britain,* in *Journal of Royal Statistical Society* Vol 118 1955, p. 275.
   *The Geometry of Megalithic Man,* in *Mathematical Gazette* Vol 45 1961, p. 83.
   *The Egg-Shaped Standing Stone Rings of Britain,* in *Arch. Int. d'Hist. des Sciences* Vol 14 1961, p. 291.

*The Megalithic Unit of Length*, in *Journal of Royal Statistical Society* Vol 125 1962, p. 243.

*The Larger Units of Length of Megalithic Man*, in *Journal of Royal Statistical Society* Vol 127 1964, p. 527.

*Megaliths and Mathematics*, in *Ant* Vol 40 1966, p. 121.

*Megalithic Sites in Britain*, Clarendon Press 1967.

Roy, A. E., and others, *A New Survey of the Tormore Circles*, in *TrGlasgAS* Vol 15 1963, p. 56.

# CHAPTER NINE
## Cup-and-ring marks

Anati, E. G., *New Petroglyphs at Derrynablaha, County Kerry, Ireland*, in *JCorkHAS* Vol 68 1963, p. 1.

Browne, G. F., *On Some Antiquities in the Neighbourhood of Dunecht House, Aberdeenshire*, Cambridge University Press 1921.

Cowling, *Cup and Ring Markings to the North of Otley*, in *YAJ* Vol 33 1937, p. 291.
   *A Classification of West Yorks. 'Cup and Ring' Markings*, in *ArchJ* Vol 97 1940, p. 114.

Hadingham, E., *Ancient Carvings in Britain*, Garnstone Press 1974.

Mann, L. M., *Archaic Sculpturings*, Hodge 1915.

Morris, R. W. B., *The Cup-and-Ring Marks and Similar Sculptures of S. W. Scotland*, in *Transactions of Ancient Monuments Society* Vol 14 1966–67, p. 77, Part II (S. E. Scotland) in Vol 16 1969, p. 37.
   and Bailey, D. C., title as above, in *PSAS* Vol 98 1964–66, p. 150.

Raistrick, A., *'Cup and Ring' Marked Rocks of W. Yorks.*, in *YAJ* Vol 32, p. 33.

Simpson, D. D. A., and Thawley, J. E., *Single Grave Art in Britain*, in *Scottish Archaeological Forum* 4 1972.

Simpson, J. Y., *Archaic Sculpturings*, 1867.

Tate, G., *The Ancient British Sculptured Rocks of Northumberland*, 1865.

Thom, A., *The Metrology and Geometry of Cup and Ring Marks*, in *Systematics* Vol 6 1968, p. 173.
   *The Geometry of Cup-and-Ring Marks*, in *Transactions of Ancient Monuments Society* Vol 16 1969, p. 77.

# CHAPTER TEN
## Carnac

Blair, A., and Ronalds, F., *Sketches at Carnac*, London 1836.

Charriere, G., *Typologie des Orientations Mégalithiques et Protohistoriques*, in *Bulletin de La Soc. Preh. Fr.* Vol 61 1964, p. 160.

Daniel, G. E., *The Hungry Archaeologist in France*, Faber 1963.

Giot, P. R., *Brittany*, Thames and Hudson 1960.
   *The Impact of Radiocarbon Dating . . .*, in *PPS* Vol 37 part 2 1971, p. 208.

Hülle, W., *Steinmale der Bretagne*, Ludwigsburg 1967.

Le Rouzic, Z., *Tumulus à Dolmen Er-Grah et Le Grand Menhir Brisé*, Vannes 1909.
  *Les Cromlechs d'Er Lannic*, Vannes 1930.
  *Tumulus du Mont St-Michel*, Vannes 1932.

Miln, J., *Excavations at Carnac*, Edinburgh 1877.
  *Les Alignements de Kermario*, 1881.

Roche, D., *Carnac*, Tchou, Paris 1969.

Rollando, Y., *La Préhistoire du Morbihan*, Société Polymathique, Vannes 1965.

Thom, A., and Thom, A. S., Carnac articles in *Journal for History of Astronomy* Vol 2 1971, p. 147; Vol 3 1972, p. 11; and Vol 3 1972, p. 151.

Worsfold, T. C., *The French Stonehenge*, Bemrose 1901.

## CHAPTER ELEVEN

### The Druids

Ashbee, P., *The Wilsford Shaft*, in *Ant* Vol 37 1963, p. 116.
  *The Dating of the Wilsford Shaft*, in *Ant* Vol 40 1966, p. 227.

Chadwick, N. K., *The Druids*, University of Wales Press 1966.

Kendrick, T. D., *The Druids*, Frank Cass reprint 1966.

Piggott, S., *The Druids*, Thames and Hudson 1968.

Ross, A., *Pagan Celtic Britain*, Routledge and Kegan Paul 1967.

Wainwright, G. J., *Ritual Shafts and Wells . . .*, in *Ant* Vol 46 1972, p. 231.

## CHAPTER TWELVE

### Folklore and the early Church

Borst, L. B., *English Henge Cathedrals*, in *Nature* Vol 224 1969, p. 335.

Bowen, E. G., *Menhir in Llandysiliogogo Church*, in *Ant* Vol 45 1971, p. 213.

Daniel, G. E., *Megaliths in History*, Thames and Hudson 1972.

Dexter, T. F. G., *The Sacred Stone*, New Knowledge Press, Cornwall 1929.

Godfrey, J., *The Church in Anglo-Saxon England*, Cambridge University Press 1962.

Grinsell, L. G., *Witchcraft at Barrows and Other Prehistoric Sites*, in *Ant* Vol 46 1972, p. 58.

Hibbert, S., *Memoir on the Tings of Orkney and Shetland*, in *Archaeologia Scotica* Vol 3 1831 (Ring of Brogar and Stennes folklore).

Hunter Blair, P., *An Introduction to Anglo-Saxon England*, Cambridge University Press paperback 1959.

Johnson, W., *Byways in British Archaeology*, Cambridge University Press 1912.

Rodger, I., *Megalithic Mathematics*, in *The Listener* Vol 27 Nov 1969, p. 731.

Swire, O. F., *The Outer Hebrides and Their Legends*, Oliver and Boyd 1966.

Watkins, A., *The Old Straight Track*, Garnstone Press reprint 1972.

## CHAPTER THIRTEEN

## The antiquaries

Aubrey, J., *Topographical Collections*, ed Jackson, J. E., Devizes 1862.
Cambry, *Monumens Celtiques*, Paris 1805.
Charleton, W., *Chorea Gigantum . . .*, London 1663.
Cooke, Rev. W., *An Enquiry into the Druidical and Patriarchal Religion . . .*, London 1754.
Grigson, G., *Stonehenge and the Imagination*, in *History Today* Vol 1 No 3, p. 22.
Higgins, G., *The Celtic Druids*, London 1829.
King, E., *Munimenta Antiqua*, London 1799–1805.
Meyrick, S. R., and Smith, C. H., *Costume of the Original Inhabitants of the British Isles*, London 1815.
Piggott, S., *William Stukeley*, Oxford 1950.
　　*Celts, Saxons, and the Early Antiquaries*, The O'Donnell Lecture 1966, Edinburgh University Press 1967.
　　*The Druids*, Thames and Hudson 1968.
Sammes, A., *Brittania Antiqua Illustrata*, London 1676.
Speed, J., *The Historie of Great Britain . . .*, London 1611.
Stukeley, W., *Itinerarium Curiosum*, 2 vols, London 1724.
　　*Stonehenge—a Temple restor'd to the British Druids . . .*, London 1740.
　　*Abury, a Temple of the British Druids . . .*, London 1743.
Webb, J., *The most notable Antiquity of Great Britain, vulgarly called Stone-heng, Restored*, London 1655.

## CHAPTER FOURTEEN

## Other interpretations of early Britain

Ivimy, J., *The Sphinx and the Megaliths*, Turnstone Press 1974.
Lethbridge, T. C., *Gogmagog, The Buried Gods*, Routledge and Kegan Paul 1957.
　　*The Legend of the Sons of God*, Routledge and Kegan Paul 1972.
Michell, J., *The View over Atlantis*, Garnstone Press 1969.
　　*City of Revelation*, Garnstone Press 1972.
　　*The Old Stones of Land's End*, Garnstone Press 1973.
Spence, L., *The Magic Arts in Celtic Britain*, Rider 1945.
Underwood, G., *The Pattern of the Past*, Abacus paperback 1972.
Williams, M. (ed), *Glastonbury, A Study in Patterns,* Research into Lost Knowledge Organisation 1969.
　　*Britain, A Study in Patterns*, Research into Lost Knowledge Organisation 1971.

# *Appendix Three*

## Exploring Early Britain

The casual visitor to prehistoric monuments will probably be content to see the well-known sites maintained and usually signposted by the Department of the Environment. For this purpose the list of historic monuments published by Her Majesty's Stationery Office is useful.

For the more adventurous, occasionally prepared to tramp across bog or moorland to find some of the less accessible sites, the first requirement is an Ordnance Survey map covering the area in question. Virtually all the monuments worth visiting in each region are listed and described in detail in the invaluable series of *Discovering Regional Archaeology* booklets published by Shire Publications, Tring, Herts. A fuller background discussion and a site-list can be found in each volume of the *Regional Archaeologies* series published by Heinemann Educational Books. Other useful guides are noted below.

These works cover much of the country in detail; only those sites mentioned elsewhere in the text are described here.

## ENGLAND

The best guides are Nicholas Thomas' *Guide to Prehistoric England* (Batsford 1960) and James Dyer's *Southern England* (Faber 1973).

## BEDFORDSHIRE

*Waulud's Bank* TL/062246
Late Neolithic enclosure
Flanked by modern flats. Reach by footpath opposite Three Horseshoes pub, Leagrave.

## BERKSHIRE

*Lambourn* SU/328828
Round barrow group
An imposing Bronze Age cemetery, including a double row of ten barrows easily accessible just off the B4001 between Lambourn and Kingston Lyle. Almost every type of barrow, including double-bowls and a chambered long barrow about $\frac{1}{2}$ mile to NW, is represented here.
*Wayland's Smithy* SU/281854
Chambered long barrow
Reach by B4000 1 mile S of Ashbury, then off east along Berkshire Ridgeway. The

walk to the site from the car park at Uffington Castle along the Ridgeway is recommended. The reconstructed megalithic chamber and its setting in a clump of trees on the crest of the Ridgeway are most impressive.

# CORNWALL

*The Hurlers* SX/258714
Stone circles
A group of three rings situated approximately on a line from Minions village to the Cheesewring, a natural rock formation. Approach along B3254.
*Merry Maidens* SW/432245
Stone circle with outliers
Reached by footpath S of B3315, and comprising 19 stones in a ring about 75 feet across. The stones in the ring are the petrified dancing Maidens, the two stones to the north are known as the Pipers, and the outlier to the west is the Fiddler.

# CUMBERLAND

*Castle Rigg* NY/292236
Stone circle
Perhaps the most impressive ring in northern England, with a rough diameter of 110 feet, and a rectangular stone setting on SE side. A Thom flattened 'A' type, with complex alignments. The site is 1½ miles E of Keswick.
*Long Meg and her Daughters* NY/571373
Stone circle and outlier
A ring over 300 feet across (Thom Type B) with 12 feet high menhir to SW with faint circular or spiral carvings. See also Little Meg cairn circle at NY/577375, including spiral carvings. Both sites off Little Salkeld to Gamblesby road.

# DERBYSHIRE

*Arbor Low* SK/160636
Stone circle within double-entrance enclosure
5 miles SW of Bakewell, signposted off A515, the site consists of an earth circle with a large cairn built over the bank to the S. Inside is a ring of stones now completely flattened and surrounding an apparent 'cove' at the centre.

# DEVON

See *Worth's Dartmoor*, by R. H. Worth, David and Charles 1967, for full discussion of megalithic sites and the possible interpretations of the stone rows.
*Hembury* ST/113030
Neolithic causewayed enclosure
Now almost invisible within Iron Age hill-fort, just N of A373, 3½ miles NW of

Honiton.

*Merrivale* SX/555744

Stone rows, cairns and stone circle

This is the most accessible group of Dartmoor monuments, a little to the S of A384 between Tavistock and Two Bridges. To the SW of the two double rows is a ring (Thom Type B) with tall menhir close by.

# DORSET

*Came Wood* SY/699855

Barrow group

With fine views over Portland Bill and the sea, this important linear cemetery lies just south of the minor Ridgeway road (E of A354 Dorchester to Weymouth). At W end of group, under trees, is Culliford Tree Barrow, once the local meeting place of a hundred. To the N is a pond barrow and further over to the E, a bank barrow with two round barrows at each end.

*Cursus* ST/971123 to SU/041188

The cursus runs S and very roughly parallel to the A354 from Salisbury to Blandford Forum. The most impressive section is now the W terminal in a field just off the minor road which joins A354 about $\frac{1}{2}$ mile W of Cashmoor Inn. The E terminal, now almost invisible, is just N of impressive long barrows on Bokerly Down and can be reached by footpath from Woodyates or path on top of and beside Bokerly Dyke (a huge 4th century AD defensive work, crossed by A354).

*Knowlton* SU/024100

Enclosures

Three circles lie along a line NNW-SSE, with central ring signposted and accessible off B3078. Inside is ruined Norman church with rectangular churchyard wall just visible. To the east is a massive round barrow, while many others have been ploughed out near by.

*Maumbury Rings* SY/690899

Neolithic enclosure and Roman amphitheatre

This celebrated earthwork now stands on E side of A354 in the suburbs of Dorchester. Only the NE entrance is original, and no trace of deep shafts around interior now visible. The inside was deepened and the sides of the banks modified when converted to an amphitheatre by the Romans.

*Mount Pleasant* SY/710899

Late Neolithic enclosure

The enclosure now occupies two large fields on a hill-top just N of junction between A352 from Dorchester and minor road to West Stafford. It is best seen from the minor road. The Conquer Barrow built over W bank of enclosure can be seen under trees near top of hill.

*Nine Stones* SY/611904
Stone circle
A small elliptical setting of stones immediately S of A35 beyond Winterbourne Abbas. Signposted.
*Oakley Down* SU/007154
Round barrow group
A splendid collection of disc, bowl and bell barrows immediately noticeable beside A354. Access most conveniently had by driving a short distance down minor road to W of the group, signposted to Cranborne, and walking down Ackling Dyke Roman road.
*Thickthorn Down* ST/972122
Long barrow
Just S of E terminal of Dorset cursus, clearly visible from minor road off A354 about ½ mile W of Cashmoor Inn.

# KENT

*Kits Coty* TQ/745608
*Lower Kits Coty* TQ/744604
Megalithic chamber tombs
These are the most accessible and striking examples of the Medway group of megalithic tombs. Both are signposted off the A229 near Aylesford.

# NORFOLK

*Arminghall* TG/240060
Neolithic enclosure
Now almost invisible, Arminghall lies beside an electricity pylon off the minor road from Trowse Newton to Caistor St Edmund.
*Grimes Graves* TL/817898
Flint mines
This famous site comprises the collapsed mouths of over 300 mining shafts. One or more excavated shafts, protected by a concrete cover, are open to the public, although the galleries are currently in a dangerous condition and are sealed off.

# NORTHUMBERLAND

*Roughting Linn* NT/984367
Cup-and-ring marks
A huge sheet of carvings near an Iron Age promontory fort.
*Old Bewick* NU/075216
Cup-and-ring marks
To the south-east of an Iron Age hill-fort, reached by path from Old Bewick, are a number of cup-and-ring stones.

# OXFORDSHIRE

*Rollright Stones* SP/296308
Stone circle
The ring known as The King's Men is situated beside a minor road off the A436 to Great Rollright. Across the road stands the stone called The King Stone, while to the east are the four remaining uprights and probable cover-stone of a chambered long barrow, The Whispering Knights. The names of the megaliths all derive from local legend about a king and his knights turned to stone by a witch.

# SOMERSET

*Stanton Drew* ST/603630
Stone circles and avenues
The village of Stanton Drew is about 6 miles S of Bristol. The cove, behind the Druid's Arms Inn, and the centres of two circles lie on a line running approximately NE-SW, and two convergent avenues run from the circles. There is a third circle to the S.

# SUSSEX

*Trundle* SU/877111
Causewayed enclosure
The ditches of the enclosure are still just visible within the impressive ramparts of the Iron Age fort crowning the Trundle, which is 4 miles N of Chichester and overlooks Goodwood racecourse.
*Whitehawk* TQ/330048
Causewayed enclosure
Traces of three out of at least four concentric rings of interrupted ditches are to be found on the racecourse in the E part of Brighton, just S of the grandstand. Details of the excavations in E. C. Curwen's *The Archaeology of Sussex*, Methuen 1937.

# WILTSHIRE

*Avebury* SU/103700
For a dramatic approach, turn N off A4 between the Sanctuary and Silbury Hill. The visitor is now provided with car-parking facilities, an excellent and recently renovated museum, and tea-rooms at the vicarage. Avebury Manor and zoo are also open to the public in season.
*Durrington Walls* SU/150437
Late Neolithic enclosure
The much-eroded bank and ditch of the huge enclosure are now cut by the A345

from Amesbury to Netheravon. One of the best views of the site is from the vicinity of Woodhenge to the S.

*Normanton Down* SU/115413

Round barrow group

One of the most impressive of the Stonehenge barrow cemeteries. It can be reached by driving or walking along a track running S from the A344 and A303, a little to the W of Stonehenge. The bowl barrow nearest to the track is Bush Barrow, and there is an extensive line of bells, bowls, saucers and discs beyond it.

*Marden* SU/091584

Late Neolithic enclosure

The village of Marden can be taken in on a drive from Stonehenge and Durrington up to Avebury. It lies on a minor road off the A342 which runs across the enclosure, best preserved under trees at the NW.

*Sanctuary* SU/118679

Late Neolithic timber setting

Post and stone-holes are now marked with concrete. The site is near barrows on the top of Overton Hill, just outside the transport café on S side of A4.

*Silbury Hill* SU/100685

Beside the A4 about 1 mile S of Avebury. Parking facilities are provided on the Beckhampton-Avebury road.

*Stonehenge* SU/123422

Stonehenge is about 2 miles W of Amesbury and on the S side of the A344, and now comes complete with sunken car-park, café, bookstall and souvenirs. The cursus is about a $\frac{1}{2}$-mile to the N, intersected by a track from the car-park, and past a line of barrows.

*West Kennet* SU/104677

Long barrow

The barrow was impressively restored by the Ministry after excavations in 1955–56, and can be reached by a signposted footpath running S from the A4, a few hundred yards E of Silbury. A torch is an advantage.

*Windmill Hill* SU/087714

Causewayed enclosure

A minor road runs to within $\frac{3}{4}$ mile of the classic site, situated $1\frac{1}{2}$ miles N of Beckhampton. The ditches are best preserved to the E. There are a number of prominent bowl barrows on the hill.

*Woodhenge* SU/150434

Late Neolithic enclosure and timber setting

The site stands a little to the S of Durrington, and the positions of the post-holes are marked with concrete posts. The regularly increasing proportions of the structure can be demonstrated with a ball of string stretched around the outside faces of each ring of posts in turn.

# YORKSHIRE

*Devil's Arrows* SE/391666
Alignment
The three large megaliths can be seen from the A1, but are best visited from Boroughbridge. They stand almost in a line N-S and are composed of millstone grit brought from over six miles away.
*Ilkley Moor*
Cup-and-ring marks
Groups of carvings can be found on dozens of the flat rock outcrops all round the edge of the moor. The articles cited under *Further Reading* provide several useful maps. The visitor should start with the Panorama stone (SE/115473) which is disappointing until rubbed; it is enclosed by railings opposite St Margaret's Church. Then see the Swastika Stone on Woodhouse Crag (094470). A short but steep climb from the upper road between the town and the Cow and Calf Hotel brings the visitor to the spectacular Hanging Stones group (128467). Other less accessible rocks are listed in the articles.
On Baildon Moor, see small stones grouped N and E of wall of Dobrudden Farm caravan park (SE/400138).
On Snowden Moor, find Tree of Life Stone (180511) off N road from minor crossroads on top of the moor. It is on the left-hand side of a steep path up from the road running beside an old field wall.
*Rudston* TA/097677
Standing stone
In the parish churchyard $5\frac{1}{4}$ miles W of Bridlington.
*Star Carr* TA/027810
Mesolithic settlement site
No traces visible.
*Thornborough* SE/285795
Enclosures
Three earth rings lie on a line NE-SW, with N one under trees beside minor road running S from B6267.

# WALES

The author has not visited Welsh sites, but to make up for this omission the reader is referred to the list of monuments by Grimes in *Culture and Environment*, ed I. Ll. Foster and L. A.cock, published by Routledge in 1963. See also *Wales: An Archaeological Guide* by Christopher Houlder, Faber 1974.

# SCOTLAND

The archaeological sightseer is well served by R. Feachem's *A Guide to Prehistoric Scotland* (Batsford, 1963) and additional background is provided by the Heinemann Regional Archaeologies (Scott, *SW Scotland*, 1966 and Ritchie, *SE*, 1972).

## ARGYLL

*Achnabreck* NR/856906
Cup-and-ring marks
The most extensive group of cup-and-ring markings in the country can be found on two rock outcrops behind a farm 1¾ miles from Lochgilpead, E off A816. A bucket of water to make the carvings show up is a useful accessory! Signposted.

*Ballochroy* NR/731524
Megalithic chamber and standing stones
The site is on the W coast of Kintyre 15 miles S of Tarbert, in a field to the E and above the A83.

*Ballymeanoch* NR/834964
Alignments
Two alignments, not quite parallel, run roughly NW-SE in a field beside the A816 about 1½ miles S of Kilmartin. Cup-and-ring marks are visible on the four-stone alignment, while 100 yards to SW is an earth circle about 130 feet across. Two cists were uncovered within the circle, one of which yielded Beaker pottery.

*Cairnbaan* NR/838910
Cup-and-ring marks
An important set of carvings reached by footpath running beside and behind Cairnbaan Hotel, next to B841 off A816. Be sure to see the smaller surface with its intricate designs beyond the larger and less interesting rock. Signposted.

*Kintraw* NM/830050
Cairns and standing stones
The main plateau at Kintraw lies conspicuously just to E of A816 as it winds steeply down the head of Loch Craignish about 6 miles N of Kilmartin. Access to the possible observation platform behind the site to the NE can be had with difficulty at the bottom of the bend, just beyond bridge over gorge.

*Nether Largie* NR/832985 to NR/828978
Linear cemetery
From low ground below Kilmartin Church there stretches a line of 7 cairns approximately 2¼ miles long to SSW. The oldest cairn, of Neolithic date, is Nether Largie South which is not far from the Temple Wood alignments. Most of the other cairns are well-signposted, and Nether Largie North is worth a special visit, since entry through trapdoor gives access to central cist and cover-stone with axe and cup carvings.

*Temple Wood* NR/826979
Stone circle and alignments
The circle and central cist, recently restored, can be seen just off the by-road from the A816. Note spiral carving near base of due north stone. About 300 yards to the SE is the X-shaped alignment of megaliths. Cup-marks are visible on the central stone, $9\frac{1}{2}$ feet high. The notch for lunar observations is directly behind stone circle when seen from the standing stones.

# ARRAN

*Tormore* NR/912324
Stone circle
An elliptical ring associated with other megalithic sites on Machrie Moor.

# CAITHNESS

*Mid Clyth* ND/294384
Stone rows
The site is 9 miles SSW of Wick and is reached along by-road from A9. Details of the other stone fans are in Feachem 1963 and Thom 1971.

# KIRKCUDBRIGHT

*Cairnholy* NX/517538
Chambered cairns
The spectacular remains of two excavated cairns of the Clyde-Solway group are on high ground above A75 from Gatehouse-of-Fleet to Creetown. Reach by farm road from Kirkdale Bridge.

*Cauldside Burn* NX/528572
Stone circle, cairns, cup-and-ring marks
Approach by minor roads and old military road from A75. In the Burn N of Cairnharrow Hill are the remains of a cairn cemetery and at least one stone ring about 70 feet across. On the other side of the Burn, just N of main cairn, is whinstone block featuring large spiral carving.

# LEWIS

*Callanish I* NB/213330
Cairn, stone circle and alignments
The village of Callanish is on the W coast of Lewis, about 15 miles from Stornoway. The main monument is well-signposted.

*Callanish III, Cnoc Fillibr* NB/225335
Stone circle
This monument consists of a double ring of megaliths (which Thom, 1967,

shows as a double ellipse). It is a short distance S of the A858 Stornoway to Callanish, about ¾ mile from the main monument.

*Callanish II, Cnoc Ceann* NB/222335
Stone circle and cairn
Five large slabs surrounding a small cairn, in a field visible from and SW of Callanish III. (Thom, 1967: an ellipse.)

*Callanish IV, Garynahine* NB/230303
Stone circle and cairn
Five slabs in an elliptical setting again surround a small cairn, with remains of cist. The site is on a hill about 150 yards W from minor road running S from A858 at Garynahine. Park about a mile from the main road.

*Callanish V* NB/234299
Alignment
This site is slightly more difficult to find, but is on a W-facing slope about ¼ mile E of minor road and Callanish IV, which is clearly visible from site.

*Clach an Trushal* NB/375537
Standing stone
Probably the tallest menhir in Scotland (about 19 feet high) can be found among farm lanes just W of A857 in township of Ballantrushal.

# NORTH UIST

*Pobull Fhinn* NF/844650
Stone circle
An intriguing monument by the shores of Loch Langass, less than a mile SE of A867 and about 6 miles from Lochmaddy. Walk there via Barpa Langass chambered cairn which is extremely well-preserved.

*Uneval, Leacach an Tigh Chloiche* NF/800669
Chambered cairn and standing stone
On the side of Uneval hill, facing SW, and about an hour's walk from the A865.

# ORKNEY

*Brogar* HY/294134
Enclosure and stone circle
The ring is 4 miles NE of Stromness and is beside the B9055 running NW from A965 Stromness to Kirkwall.

*Maes Howe* HY/317127
Chambered tomb
Most impressive of all the northern tombs, Maes Howe stands to the W of the A965 within sight of the Ring of Brogar.

*Mid Howe* HY/371306
Chambered tomb

The largest of five important stalled cairns lying close to the road along the SW coast of the Island of Rousay. It has been completely excavated and preserved inside a stone building near the shore. Mainland ferry runs from Tingwall to Brinyan.

*Skara Brae* HY/230187
Settlement site
The village is on the W coast of the Orkney mainland, about ½ mile from B9056 running from A967 Stromness to Birsay. The ruins are worth at least an hour's visit.

*Stennes* HY/306125
Enclosure and stone circle
Beside the B9055 a little to the SE of the Ring of Brogar. The earthwork has been almost entirely obliterated, and all that remains of the monument is four tall and impressive monoliths on the arc of a ring about 100 feet across. There is also a pseudo-dolmen dating from 1906. In the vicinity are several isolated stones, including the 19-foot Watch Stone by the Bridge of Brogar.

# WEST LOTHIAN

*Cairnpapple* NS/987717
Multi-period 'sacred' site
The site is protected by a concrete cover, and is situated on top of Cairnpapple Hill, 1¼ miles ESE of Torphichen.

# WIGTOWNSHIRE

*Drumtroddan* NX/362444
Cup-and-ring marks
An impressive set of carvings on private farmland (Drumtroddan Farm) off A714 about a mile E of Port William.

*Knock* NX/364402
Spiral carving
On a small ledge of rock near the top of a hillock overlooking the sea. Reach by minor road SW off A747 and gap in wall 75 yards beyond cattle grid. Hillock is same distance WSW.

*Torhouse* NX/383565
Stone circle
A well-preserved flattened ring of boulders beside the B733 Kirckcowan to Wigtown, about 3 miles from Wigtown. There is a rough alignment of three stones at the centre.

# IRELAND

A well-illustrated guide intended for the general public is Peter Harbison's *Guide to the National Monuments of Ireland*. It is published in paperback by Gill and MacMillan, Dublin 1970.

*Knocknarea, Co Sligo* G/627346
Chambered (?) cairn
An outstanding monument on a mountain-top visible from the town of Sligo, and about an hour's scramble from the road to the south. Remarkable views from the 35-feet high top of the cairn.

*Loughcrew, Co Meath* N/585775
Chambered tomb cemetery
A concentration of tombs on Slieve Na Calliagh, or Hill of the Witch, reached by minor roads running N from Oldcastle to Crossakeel road. Many of the cairns have decorated stones. Signposted.

*Lough Gur, Co Limerick* R/640410
Various sites
The map reproduced in Harbison 1970 and elsewhere is useful. The principal attraction is the great stone circle just N of the road from Limerick to Kilmallock. Enclosed in the field to the NW is the egg-shaped ring of stone blocks. The steep walk up to Knockadoon, reached by minor road to Bourchier's Castle, repays the visitor with fine views and a number of domestic and burial sites. Finally, see remarkable embanked circle a short distance E of road about $\frac{1}{2}$ mile N of Bourchier's Castle.

*Newgrange, Co Meath* O/007727
Chambered tomb
The famous sites in the bend of the Boyne lie off minor roads running from Drogheda to Slane road, about 5 miles from Slane. Guided tours of Newgrange operate in summer.

*Timoney Hills, Co Tipperary* S/193838
Standing stones
The Timoney Hills are about 5 miles SE of Roscrea. The stones can best be seen in two main groups of fields about $\frac{1}{4}$ mile apart, both reached by farm roads running SE of minor ridgeway road.

# BRITTANY

There is no comprehensive guidebook to the monuments around Carnac, but for a delightful account including almost everything the ordinary visitor will want to know, see Glyn Daniel's *The Hungry Archaeologist in France* (Faber, 1963). The sites are well-signposted and practically every monument marked on the map of the district is worth a visit. Boats for Gavrinis and Er-Lannic can be hired cheaply at Lamor-Baden.

# Index

Numbers in **bold** type refer to illustrations

Aberdeenshire, recumbent stone circles, 60, **61**, 98, 147
Achnabreck, cup-and-ring rock, 150, **150**, 230
Allen, G., 206–7
Arbor Low, stone circle, 224
Arminghall, earth circle, 38–9, **39**, 43, 226
Ashbee, P., 173
Atkinson, R. J. C., 40, 85, 87, 93, 96, 133, 186
Aubrey holes, *see* Stonehenge
Aubrey, J., 41, 129, 190, **190**, 192–5
Aulnay-aux-Planches, 171
Avebury, stone circle, 43, 45, 50–5, **51**, **52**, 57, 60–1, 70, 127, 130, 140, 186, 190–1, 194, 203, 207, 227

Baildon Moor, carvings, 141, **142**, **143**, 151, 229
Bailey, D. C., 147
Ballochroy, megalithic site, 107–9, **107**, **108**, 114–16, 119, 123, 135, 230
Ballymearoch, earth circle and megaliths, 76, 123, 230
Balquhain, stone circle, **61**
Barford, earth circle, 38–9
Barrows, long, 31–3, **32**, **34**
  round, 60, 69, 72–9, 160–1, **179**, **180**, 183
Bartram, W., 48
Bateman, **206**
Baudouin, M., 162
Beaker culture, 57–8, **57**, 77
Belle Tout, house sites, 68
Benie Hoose, house site, 69

Boian culture, 17
Borst, L., 188
Breuil, H., 138–9
Brigstock, temple, 171
Brittany, *see* Carnac
Brogar, Ring of, stone circle, 55, **56**, 57, 60, 65, 76, 130, 183, **183**
Broome Heath, early Neolithic site, 29
Browne, G. F., 147
Bush barrow, 77–8, 161

Caesar, 11, 169–70, 174
Cairnbaan, cup-and-ring rock, 141, 151, 230
Cairnholy, long cairn, 34, **34**, 231
Cairnpapple, multi-period site, 171, 233
Callanish, megalithic site, 65, 69, 101–6, **101**, **plan 103**, **102**, **104**, 118, 139, 182, 186, 188, 190, 197, 208, 231
Callanish II, 119, 232
Callanish V, 118, **118**, 232
Cambry, **153**, 202
Camden, W., 191, 193–4, **201**
Came Down, barrows, 139, **180**, 225
Campbeltown, megalith, 121, **122**
Camster, stone fan, **126**
Camster Long, long cairn, 33
Carnac, megalithic sites, 18, **18**, 152–67, **map 166**, 178, 202, 208, 234
Castle Rigg, stone circle, 127, 178, 224
Cauldside Burn, carving, 146, 151, 231
Causewayed camps, 35–7
Charleton, W., 192–4
Cherokees, 48
Chevalier de Fréminville, 152
Childe, V. G., 13

Clandon, barrow, 78
Clark, G., 207
Coilsfield, carving, 136
Coligny, calendar, 174, **175**
Colt-Hoare, R., 77–8
Cooke, W., 199–200
Creek Confederacy, 48, 68
Critchlow, K., 210
Crucuno, megalithic site, 162
Culliford, barrow, **180**
Cunnington, M. E., **131**, 132
Cup-and-ring carvings, 136–51, 180
Cursus monuments, 33–5, 37–8, 171, 225

Dalladies, long barrow, 139
Danby, W., **205**
Daniel, G. E., 162
Dartmoor, stone rows, 64
Darwin, C., 13, 204
Derrynablaha, carvings, **144**
Devil's Arrows, alignment, 187, 229
Diffusion theory, 13–28, **16**
Diodonus, 176
Dorchester, Oxfordshire, earth circles, 40–1, **40**, 91, 173
Druids, 80, 82, 168–77, 190–203
Drumtroddan, cup-and-ring rock, **138**, 233
Dryden, J., 192
Duke, E., **82**, 83
Durrington Walls, 42–7, **44**, **45**, 53, 68, 93–4, 132–3, 227

Earls Barton, barrow, 78
Eaton Heath, shafts site, 172
Eddowes, Dr, 83
Egypt, 11, 14–15, 17, 28, 78
Eightercua, **63**
Er Grah, *see* Grand Menhir Brisé
Er Lannic, megalithic site, 159–61, **159**, **161**

Flaubert, G., 156

Folklore, 178–83, 186
Four Stones, megalithic site, 178
Frilford, temple, 171

Garrywhin, stone fan, 126
Gavrinis, megalithic tomb, 19–20, **19**, 22, 24, 26, 28, 155
Geoffrey of Monmouth, 180–2, 191
Graig Lwyd, axe factory, 30
Grand Menhir Brisé, megalith, **134**, **158**, 162, 164–5, **164**, **166**, 167
Great Langdale, axe factory, 30
Greenwell, W., 136
Grimes Graves, flint mines, 30, 226
Grooved Ware, 41–3, **42**, 57, 66, 68
Gwithian, house site, 68

Hallam, B., 130, **130**
Hanging Stones, carvings, **140**, 141
Hawkins, G. S., 85, 87–92, 94–7, **96**, 105–6, 207–8
Hecateus, 176
Heggie, D. C., 127
Hembury, causewayed camp, 29, 35, 224
Herodotus, 11, 176
Heyerdahl, T., 13
Heyword, N., 145
Higgins, G., **153**
Holzhausen, shaft, 173
Hoyle, F., 87, 90, 96
Hurlers, stone circles, 178, 244
Hyperboreans, 176–7, 210
Hypogeum of Hal Saflieni, 21

Ilkley Moor, carvings, 141–3, **140**, **map 142**, **143**, 145, 229

Jones, I., 192

Keiller, A., 53
Kellythorpe, barrow, 72
Kercado, megalithic tomb, 18–19, **18**

Kerlescan, alignments, 155
Kermario, alignments, 154, **154**, 156, 158, 162
Kerran, megalith, 167
Kilmartin, cairns and megaliths, 74–6, **map 75**, 111, 144, **145**, 188, 230
Kilmichael Glassary, carvings, 141
Kintraw, megalithic site, 109–16, **111**, **112**, **113**, **114**, 230
Kits Coty, megalithic tomb, 178, 226
Knock, carving, 148, **148**, 233
Knockadoon, various sites, **68**, **100**
Knocknarea, cairn, **25**, 234
Knowlton, earth circle, 179, 185, 225
Knowth, passage graves, 24, 139

Lambourn, barrows, 73–4, 188, 223
Leacach, *see* Uneval
Le Menec, alignments, 152, **153**, 154, 158, 162–3, **179**
Le Moustoir, megalithic tomb, 167
Le Rouzic, Z., 155–6
Lethbridge, T. C., 208
Lhwyd, E., **112**
Libby, W., 15
Libenice, 171, 173
Llandegai, earth circles, 40
Lockyer, N., 83–4, **84**, 93, 98, **99**, 109, 132, 135
Long Meg, stone circle, 144, 178, 224
Loughcrew, passage graves, 24, 139, 234
Lough Gur, main stone circle, 61, **61**, 63, 76, **100**, 234
  house site, **68**
  other sites, 69, **100**, 127, **128**

Machrie Moor, stone circles, 133, **133**, 231
Mackie, E. W., 112–13
Maes Howe, megalithic tomb, 26, **27**, 33, 55, 232
Maiden Castle, temple at, **172**, 173
Malta, 14, 16–17, 21–2, 25, 28, 138

Mané-er-Hroech, megalithic tomb, 157
Mané hud, megalithic tomb, 157
Mann, L. M., 145, 147
Manton, barrow, 78
Marden, earth circle, 43, 45, 47, 53, 132, 228
Marshack, A., 207
Maumbury Rings, earth circle, 41, 73, 91, 173, 225
Maxey, earth circles, 40, 91
Megalithic sites, **map 58-9**
Megalithic tombs, 20–33, **map 24**
Merrivale, stone rows, **64**, 225
Merry Maidens, stone circle, 178, 208, 224
Michell, J., 208
Mid Clyth, stone fan, 64, 124, 126, **126**, 167
Mid Gleniron, long cairn, 33
Midhowe, megalithic tomb, 25, 232
Miln, J., 155–6
Montelius, O., 13
Montgomery, Col., 136
Morris, R. W. B., 144–5, 147, **148**
Mount Pleasant, earth circle, **42**, 43–5, **46**, **47**, 53, 68–72, **70**, 94, 132, 225
Musson, C. R., 132
Mycenae, connections with Europe, 11, 14, 16–17, 94, 207

Newgrange, passage grave, 22, **23**, 28, 33, 40, 42, 57, 106–7, **106**, 138–9, 234
Newham, C. A., 89–90, 93
Nilsson, S., 204
Nine Stones, stone circle, 127, 226
Normanton Down, barrows, 74, 228

Oakley Down, barrows, 74, 226
O'Kelly, M. J., 106
Old Bewick, carvings, 136, 226
Orkney, 24–5, **26**, 28, 55–7, 66–8

Parc-y-Meirw, alignment, 126

Panorama Stone, carving, 145, **149**, 151
Patrick, J., 129
Petit Menec, stone fan, 155, 167
Petit Mont, megalithic tomb, 167
Phobull Fhinn, stone circle, **60**, 232
Piggott, S., 144, 162, 169
Pliny, 170–1
Poltalloch, **79**
Posidonius, 168–9, 179
Prescelly, Mount, 55, 93
Proleek, megalithic tomb, **27**
Pythagorean philosophy, 173–5

Radiocarbon dating, vii, 15
Renfrew, C., 16–17
Richards, J., 198
Roberts, A., 210
Rollright, stone circle, 178, 227
Rothiemay, stone circle, 147
Roubien, Président de, 163
Roughting Lina, carvings, 136, 226
Roy, A. E., 133
Rudston cursus, 34
    megalith, **185**, 187, 229

St-Michel, tumulus, 152, 158
Ste Borbe, alignments, **163**
Sammes, A., **ix**, 193, **194**, 202
Sanctuary, timber buildings and stone
    circle, 45, 53–4, 228
Scone, stone circle, 57
Shapwick, barrow, **76**
Silbury Hill, 50, 54, **54**, 83, 187, 228
Skora Brae, settlement, 66–9, **67**, 233
Smith, Elliot, 13
Smith, John, 80–1
Smith, W. G., 206
Snowden Moor, carvings, 141, 151, 229
Somerville, B. T., 99, **100**, 102, 104–5
Speed, J., 197, **197**
Spencer, H., 204
Stall Moor, stone row, 64

Stanton Drew, stone circles and avenues,
    54, 70, 140, 178, 187, 227
Star Carr, Mesolithic settlement, 29, 226
Stone fans, 64, 125–6, **126**
Stonehenge, 14, 16, 28, 43, 57, 69, 73, 76,
    78, 80–97, **81**, **85**, **plan 86**, **89**, **94**,
    105–6, 140, 160, 175, 177–8, 186–7,
    191–2, 194–5, 200–2, **201**, 207, 210, 228
Stonehenge I, 41, 87–93, 173
Stonehenge II, 55, 60, 84, 93
Stonehenge III, 93–7
Stonehenge cursus, 33, **33**, 55
Suess, H., 15
Sunhoney, stone circle, 147
Swanwick, shaft, 173
Swastika Stone, carving, **140**, 141

Table des Marchands, megalithic tomb,
    163–4
Tate, G., 137–8
Taversoe Tuick, megalithic tomb, 25
Temple Wood, megalithic sites, 76, 123,
    **123**, 124, **124**, 135, 139, 144, 207, 231
Thickthorn Down, long barrow, **32**, 226
Thom, A., 104–5, 107–9, 112, 114–15,
    **134**, 162–3, 165, 167, 186, 207–8
    lunar theories, 116–27
    geometrical theories, 127–35
    cup-and-ring mark theories, 147–8
Thomsen, C., 13, 204
Thornborough, earth circles, 38, 229
Tievebulliagh, axe factory, 30
Timoney Hills, megaliths, **62**, 63, 234
Tippett, M., 203
Torhouse, stone circle, 127, 233
Tree of Life Stone, carving, 141, **142**
Trundle, causewayed camp, **35**, 227

Unĕtice culture, 16–17
Uneval, megalithic tomb, 119–20, **120**,
    **121**, 232
Upton Lovell, barrow, 78

Wainwright, G. J., 43–5, 48, **70**
Watkins, A., 187–8, 208
Waulud's Bank, 223
Wayland's Smithy, long barrow, 31, **32**, 33, 74, 223
Wessex culture, 72, 76–9
West Kennet Avenue, **51**, 53
West Kennet, long barrow, 33, 36–7, 60, 228

Whitehawk, causewayed camp, 37, 227
Wilsford shaft, 173
Windmill Hill, causewayed camp, 36–7, **36**, 228
Windypits, Beaker finds, 73
Woodhenge, timber building, 45, 127, 130–2, **131**, 162, 228
Wordsworth, W., ix–x, 202
Wren's Egg, alignment, **169**

## Acknowledgements

The author is grateful for the use of the following illustrations: Allen Collection, 36, 40, 81; British Museum, 112; Department of the Environment, 56; Edinburgh University Press, 17; Editions de Lys, 157; Educational Expeditions International, 125; Gandalf's Garden, 209; G. S. Hawkins, 96; D. C. Heggie, 51 (top), 54 (left); A. Keiller, Department of the Environment, 51 (bottom); E. W. Mackie, 114; R. W. B. Morris and A. Thom, 148; National Museum of Ireland, 77; J. Patrick, 23; Pictorial Colour Slides, 71; C. J. Ryder, 18, 153, 154, 159, 164; J. K. St Joseph, 73; Society of Antiquaries of Scotland, 27, 31, 61 (top); A. Thom, 134; G. J. Wainwright, courtesy of, 42 (bottom), 44, 46, 70 (top).

The following sources provided the basis for text figures: Anderson 1868, 126; Atkinson 1965, 32; Clark 1936, 39; Cowling 1940, 142; Cunnington 1929, 131; Curwen 1937, 35; Department of the Environment, 52, 86; Grimes 1963, 58–9; Hawkins 1970, 91, 95; Henshall 1963, 26; Kendrick 1966, 175; Le Rouzic 1909, 158 and 1930, 160, 161 (top); Ordnance Survey, 75; Piggott 1938, 161 (bottom) and 1968, 172; Roy 1963, 133; Scott 1947–8, 120; Simpson 1971, 68 (left); Society of Antiquaries of Scotland, 79; Somerville 1912, 103; Thom 1967, 88, 107 and 1971, 111, 117, 125; Trotter 1927, 84; Wainwright 1971, 42 (top); Windle 1912, 128.

The author also acknowledges the use of the following quotations: translation by courtesy of Ernest Black, 176–7; Clark 1962, Batsford, 207; Swire 1966, Oliver and Boyd, 182; Penguin Books, 180–1, 184; A. Roberts, 210; Lethbridge 1972, Routledge and Kegan Paul; Sir Michael Tippett's comments, 203, by courtesy of *The Listener*.

The Index is by courtesy of Paula Jennings and Sandhill Services.